Masked Atheism

Masked Atheism

*Catholicism
and the
Secular Victorian Home*

MARIA LAMONACA

THE OHIO STATE UNIVERSITY PRESS
Columbus

Cover Image: Lithograph depicting the appearance of Our Lady of Lady of La Salette, from *Rambler* 10 (December 1852). Image courtesy of Rare Books and Special Collections, The Catholic University of America.

Copyright © 2008 by The Ohio State University.
All rights reserved.

Library of Congress Cataloging-in-Publication Data
LaMonaca, Maria.
  Masked atheism : Catholicism and the secular Victorian home / Maria LaMonaca.
  p. cm.
  Includes bibliographical references and index.
  ISBN-13: 978-0-8142-1084-0 (alk. paper)
  ISBN-10: 0-8142-1084-8 (alk. paper)
  1. Catholic Church—In literature. 2. English literature—19th century—History and criticism. 3. English literature—Women authors—History and criticism. 4. English literature—Protestant authors—History and criticism. 5. English literature—Catholic authors—History and criticism. 6. Anti-Catholicism in literature. 7. Catholic Church and atheism—Great Britain—History—19th century. 8. Family—Religious life—Great Britain—History—19th century. 9. Secularism in literature. 10. Women and religion—Great Britain—History—19th century. I. Title.
  PR468.C3L36 2008
  820.9'38282—dc22
          2007039397

This book is available in the following editions:
Cloth (ISBN 978-0-8142-1084-0)
CD-ROM (ISBN 978-0-8142-9163-4)
Paper (ISBN: 978-0-8142-5659-6)
Cover design by Dan O'Dair
Text design by Jennifer Shoffey Forsythe
Type set in Adobe Minion Pro

*To my parents, Hugh and Jeanette LaMonaca,
with love and gratitude.*

The Pope He Leads a Happy Life
(1849; anonymous broadsheet ballad)

The Pope he leads a happy life,
He knows no care or marriage strife.
He drinks the best of Rhenish wine,
I would the Pope's gay lot were mine.
But yet all happy's not his lot,
He loves no maid, or wedded wife,
No child hath he to cheer his hope
I would not wish to be the Pope.

The Sultan better pleases me,
He lives a life of jollity;
Has wives as many as he will,
I would the Sultan's throne then fill.
But he is not a happy man,
He must obey the Alcoran,
And dares not taste a drop of wine,
I would not that his fate were mine.

So, here I take my lowly stand,
I'll drink "My own my native land,"
I'll kiss my maiden's lips divine,
And drink the best of Rhenish wine.
And when my maiden kisses me,
I'll fancy I the sultan be,
And when my cherry glass I tope,
I'll fancy that I am the Pope.

CONTENTS

ACKNOWLEDGMENTS / xi

INTRODUCTION
Masked Atheism / 1

CHAPTER ONE
Extravagant Creature Worship: Protestant and Catholic "Sermons" on Marriage / 33

CHAPTER TWO
"Sick Souls": Love, Guilt, and the Catholic Confessional in Victorian Women's Fiction / 68

CHAPTER THREE
Narratives of Female Celibacy / 95

CHAPTER FOUR
"Hoc est corpus meum": *Aurora Leigh*, *Goblin Market*, and Transubstantiation / 126

CHAPTER FIVE
The "Queen of Heaven" or a Very Confused Nun? Our Lady of La Salette, George Eliot, and Victorian Anxieties about God / 160

CHAPTER SIX
"Seven years a tiny Paradise a making": Michael Field's Domestic Piety / 190

CONCLUSION / 207

WORKS CITED / 213

INDEX / 225

ACKNOWLEDGMENTS

I GOT THE idea for this book on the day I defended my doctoral dissertation at Indiana University in 1999. As my committee members and I discussed my rather broad project on women and religion in the Victorian novel, Susan Gubar suggested that a book specifically on Victorians' attraction to Roman Catholicism would be "fascinating." So I want to thank Susan first, and also my dissertation director, James Eli Adams. This book is a completely separate project from my dissertation, but Jim's unflagging faith in the value of my research, his conviction of the centrality of religion in Victorian culture and society, and his tremendous excitement at my "discovery" of obscure figures such as Georgiana Fullerton and Elizabeth Missing Sewell, all sustained me in the eight years it took to envision, research, and write *Masked Atheism*.

To the Lilly Fellows Postdoctoral Program at Valparaiso University I owe a valuable two-year formation period, during which I was given considerable time and resources to write several journal articles that later became pieces of book chapters. Special thanks to Mark Schwehn, Project Director of the Fellows Program; Arlin Meyer, Program Director; and Paul Contino, my Lilly Program mentor. "Fellow Fellows," Kathleen Sprows Cummings and Michael Utzinger, provided me with encouragement, good cheer, and exceptional home cooked meals.

A collaborative scholarship grant from the Council for Christian Colleges and Universities (CCCU) provided several years' worth of funding for activities related to my work on this project. I wish especially to thank Pamela Corpron Parker, who spearheaded the application process for this grant, and my other co-recipients and scholarly collaborators, Alexis

Easley, Julie Straight, and Kathleen Vejvoda. I gained much from their feedback at our two CCCU-funded writers' retreats, and their delightful company (along with more good food!) was an additional perk.

Two grants from the National Endowment for the Humanities enabled me to research this book in British archives and university libraries. In 2002, I participated in an NEH summer seminar, "The Reform of Reason: Religion and Rhetoric in Nineteenth-Century Britain," which gave me access to archival materials at both St. Deniol's Library in Hawarden, Wales, and Cambridge University. All the members of this seminar were enormously supportive of my research, especially Carol Engelhardt Herringer, and seminar co-leaders Carol Poster and Jan Swearingen. A 2004 NEH summer stipend funded my second research trip.

Faculty development funds from Columbia College helped me to present portions of book chapters at annual national and regional conferences. I also received a one-time course release for work on chapter 2 of this book. My two department chairs, Sandra O'Neal and Michael Broome, tried to allow flexibility in my busy teaching schedule so I could keep writing during the school year. I am also grateful to work in what must be one of the most collegial English departments on the planet. My colleague Melissa Heidari, a fine scholar and teacher, was particularly encouraging of my research, and gave me much useful information on applying for NEH funding. Librarian Gina Dempsey filled out endless interlibrary loan requests for me, and administrative assistant Rosemary Broughton helped me with scanning images.

Nineteenth Century Studies, *Studies in the Novel*, and the *Victorians Institute Journal* all gave me permission to reprint articles or portions of articles for this book. David Hanson's meticulous editing of my *Nineteenth Century Studies* article helped me greatly in writing chapter 2. Richard Stein, as a reader for a journal that did *not* publish my work, gave me some wonderful suggestions for revising the *Jane Eyre* analysis that now appears in chapter 1.

I have also received permission from the John Henry Cardinal Newman Archive at Birmingham Oratory to cite Newman's unpublished letters and manuscripts. I thank the late Gerard Tracey, Newman archivist, for allowing me access to this collection. Excerpts from the correspondence of Bessie Rayner Parkes and Adelaide Procter appear with permission from the Mistress and Fellows, Girton College, Cambridge. Catherine Sinclair's letter to J. G. Lockhart (in introduction) is published by permission of the National Library of Scotland. I also wish to thank Paul Shaw, archivist for the Poor Servants of the Mother of God (St. Mary's Convent, Brentford, Middlesex), for providing me with one image of Georgiana Fullerton (reproduced in chapter 1), and telling me where to locate the other.

Sandy Crooms, acquisitions editor for The Ohio State University Press, helped to make the publication process for this book efficient, easy, and fun. I have also benefited from managing editor Eugene O'Connor's wonderful attention to detail. Sandy and Eugene have solicited my opinions and preferences throughout the whole process, which I greatly appreciate. I thank Maria Frawley and Frederick Roden, my OSUP readers, for their thoughtful, detailed, and generous feedback, which helped guide my final round of revisions.

I also wish to acknowledge a number of people who have contributed to this book in less formal, albeit very important, ways. I might never have completed this book, if it were not for the constant support, good humor, and advice of my friend and writing partner, Rebecca Stern. Rebecca's expertise was also invaluable to me as I pursued NEH funding for this project. My friend Carol Harrison also served as an excellent reader and critic, as did Ed Madden, fellow "Field-o-phile." Andrew Miller provided me with encouragement and a letter of recommendation at a moment when I especially needed both. Lori Branch has been a loving and loyal friend over many years, and her scholarship on religion, literature, and secularism has been an inspiration to me. My undergraduate honors thesis director, Deborah Morse, always cheers me on when we meet at Interdisciplinary Nineteenth-Century Studies conferences.

Finally, there is my family. My parents-in-law, Harold and Carmen Wisdom, are very, very excited about the publication of this book and I cherish their support. My loving parents, Hugh and Jeanette LaMonaca, to whom this book is dedicated, have inspired my research interests more than they realize. Aside from putting me through thirteen years of Catholic school, their deep personal commitment to Catholicism has shown me how much religion matters in many people's lives. Their example, more than anything else, has motivated me to respect religious belief and practice in all its forms, both in my scholarship and in other areas of my life. I thank my husband, John Wisdom, for his enormous patience with my all-consuming writing binges, my research clutter swamping our shared office space, and my weird fascination for nineteenth-century sermons and long-forgotten six-hundred-page novels. And were it not for his technical assistance, I might have lost my book manuscript to a computer virus or faulty hard drive several times over! But most of all, I thank John for the life we share when I'm *not* researching or writing: one richer and more rewarding than I ever dreamed possible.

Columbia, South Carolina December 2007

INTRODUCTION

Masked Atheism

> Popery is not a religion—it is only a crafty piece of masked atheism, pursuing secular objects with a sanctified face.
> –Charlotte Tonna, *Personal Recollections* (1854)

EVANGELICAL novelist Charlotte Elizabeth Tonna, who has been described as the "most prominent female anti-Catholic activist" in nineteenth-century England (Paz 271), expresses repeatedly in her writings the notion that Roman Catholicism was "masked atheism." It was, according to Tonna, the antithesis of Christianity and "civilized" religion; at worst, it was the tool of the devil himself: a "synagogue of Satan." Although Tonna's vehement anti-Catholicism would have been considered extreme even by many of her Victorian contemporaries, her assertion reflects a concept frequently articulated in Victorian literature and culture, that Roman Catholicism was a fake religion—a mask or "sanctified face" concealing the most profane excesses and tendencies of a fallen human nature. An anti-Catholic pamphlet of 1851, by a writer called "Paphnutius,"[1] also brims over with anxiety at the notion of profane concepts and deeds presented in the guise of Catholic doctrine and holy sacraments. Paphnutius describes the Catholic celebration of the Eucharist as "cannibalism," yet alternately suggests that priests fool gullible female believers into accepting a fake replica of the body and blood of Christ: "They may even so far impose on the rabid appetite of the multitude to substitute [. . .] something exceedingly like human flesh [. . .] and so nimbly insert it, with thumb and finger, into

---

1. "Paphnutius" explains that he has taken his name after the fourth-century Egyptian bishop who, at the Council of Nicea, strenuously opposed mandatory celibacy for the clergy.

the mouth of the believer, telling her to shut her eyes, and open her mouth wide, and then she will see what the god will send her" (8).

The Catholic Church, according to Paphnutius, not only distributes fake communion (in a transaction implicitly compared to a sex act), but also creates fake women and fake men. He marvels,

> That women should be more generally found to embrace this religion with peculiar ardour is extraordinary. We have generally been taught to believe that cannibalism is the vicious propensity of men rather than of women, but [...] [t]he sex, "for softness formed, and sweet attractive grace," displays a remarkable attachment to this revolting religion, the proportion of female [adherents] being ten to one of the other sex [...]. (10)

Not only are women debauched and literally turned into "man eaters" in a Catholic communion, but young boys are systematically unmanned; the smells and bells, argues Paphnutius, are "addressed to the feminine part of a boy's mind [...] the whole type and bearing of the [Mass] is eminently *feminine*" (22; emphasis in original). Finally, Paphnutius accuses this "gloomy and repulsive" religion of blood and death, of passing itself off as mere child's play, "made to appear charming even to infants, and impress[ing] them with the idea that the temple is only a *great baby-house*, with a *very large doll* [statue of the Virgin Mary] in it—an idea enchanting to the young female mind" (27; emphasis in original).

I begin this book with quotes by Tonna and "Paphnutius" because they emphasize two facets of popular Victorian perceptions of Catholicism crucial to this study: first, the notion that Catholicism, as a "feminized" religion, was particularly appealing to women, and second, that Catholicism appears to be one thing (a valid denomination of Christianity), but is always something else in disguise (profanity masquerading as sanctity; men masquerading as women; a "satanic synagogue" painted as a doll's house). Most anti-Catholic clergymen, novelists, and pamphleteers had little, if any, firsthand experience of Roman Catholicism, and their writings frequently present grotesque distortions of it. Nonetheless, their assertions about women's affinity for Catholicism had at least some basis in real life. Catholicism generated tremendous interest and fear among both men and women in nineteenth-century Britain, to the extent that, as D. G. Paz claims, anti-Catholicism "was an integral part of what it meant to be Victorian" (299). This was particularly the case in the 1840s, 1850s, and 1860s, a time when Roman Catholicism became increasingly visible in Victorian England. This study, focusing mostly on midcentury literary engagements with Catholicism, isolates a brief but intense period of popular fascination—shading at times into hysteria—toward Rome. It focuses further on women writers because Victorian women *were* uniquely intrigued by Catholicism. As numerous female-authored texts suggest, women related to, and engaged with, popular notions of a marginalized, feminized Catholicism in distinctive and powerful ways.

This study is not specifically about anti-Catholicism, but about how women writers of all Christian denominations (both Protestant *and* Catholic) appropriated popular Victorian notions of Roman Catholicism to articulate a shared set of anxieties about the increasing secularization of the Victorian domestic sphere. Their writings, examined here in the context of numerous, male-authored sermons, tracts, and pamphlets, point toward an even more pressing concern, one shared by Victorian men and women alike: the gradual waning of orthodox religious belief in society as a whole. The extent of these preoccupations is demonstrated by the variety of writers addressed in this study: Evangelical, Low-Church Protestants (Charlotte Elizabeth Tonna, Charlotte Brontë, Mary Martha Sherwood); High-Church or "Anglo-Catholics" (Christina Rossetti, Elizabeth Missing Sewell); Roman Catholic converts (Lady Georgiana Fullerton, Michael Field); a Congregationalist (Elizabeth Barrett Browning); and one agnostic (George Eliot). Many of these writers are deservedly entrenched in the literary canon; others, such as Fullerton and Sewell, have been long forgotten, and their work dismissed by twentieth-century critics. What ties the writers in this study together is not a shared attitude toward Catholicism, but the fact that all deploy representations of Catholicism, or "masked atheism," to pull the mask off ostensibly sacred cows in Victorian culture: popular constructions of domesticity, romantic love, matrimony, motherhood, and family. Throughout this study, even in women's texts that are ostensibly hostile to Catholicism, the most antireligious, "profane" menace that emerges is not Rome, but *home*. "Paphnutius" accuses the Catholic Church of disguising atheism beneath an alluring façade of domestic comfort—"a great baby-house . . . enchanting to the young female mind." Women writers, however, suggest repeatedly that Victorian domestic ideology itself, a secularized religion of hearth and home, masks other forms of atheism, and other, hidden threats to women's moral and spiritual integrity.

The notion that Catholic tropes can be usefully employed as a form of cultural critique has been well established by Jenny Franchot and other scholars; this study explores female-authored cultural criticism motivated specifically by anxieties about the disappearance of God in the modern world. Jenny Franchot, in her study of American antebellum writers, argues that "anti-Catholicism operated as an imaginative category of discourse through which antebellum American writers of popular elite fictional and historical texts indirectly voiced the tensions and limitations of mainstream Protestant culture" (xvii). Not only can images and representations of Catholicism provide a powerful vocabulary for social protest, but they can also, as Ellis Hanson, Ruth Vanita, Frederick Roden, Martha Vicinus, and Patrick O'Malley have all demonstrated, help marginalized groups, such as gays, lesbians, and "spinsters," create a sense of shared identity in contradiction to dominant cultural norms and repressive roles.[2] Catholic tropes could prove endlessly versatile: Vanita, for example, discusses how the Virgin Mary became "a site of free signification" for Protestant writers, who, unhampered by Catholic concerns about blasphemy, were "free to use the idea of Mary in transgressive ways" (19). Vanita's notion of "free signification" could usefully be applied to other elements of Catholicism besides the Virgin Mary. As texts in this study demonstrate, women writers adapted, revised, and even "reformed" multiple aspects of Catholicism, including auricular confession, the cult of the saints, and transubstantiation.

Although Catholicism, employed as a literary trope, was frequently antithetical to "real" Roman Catholic practices and doctrine, it would be a mistake, for the purposes of this study, to regard it entirely as free play or a set of alluring but empty signifiers. Some women writers who appropriated Catholic imagery, such as Charlotte Brontë and Elizabeth Barrett Browning, enacted "free signification" in sophisticated and deliberate ways; others, such as Charlotte Elizabeth Tonna and Mary Martha Sherwood, stumbled into "free signification" out of religious bigotry and a lack of substantial information about Catholicism. All of these women, however, with the single exception of George Eliot, identified themselves as Christians, and all professed a sincere belief in fundamental Christian tenets, chief among them the belief in God as the creator of the universe, the redemption of humanity through Christ's life and death, and the immortality of the soul. Writing about religious topics, for these women, was not merely "play." An acknowledgment of their religious identities and motivations is crucial to understanding how they perceived Catholicism, why they cared about it, and how they represented it in their writing. Although numerous studies have explored Victorian women's resistance to domestic ideology, most have emphasized secular rather than religious motivations for such critiques.

2. See Ellis Hanson, *Decadence and Catholicism* (1997); Ruth Vanita, *Sappho and the Virgin Mary: Same-Sex Love and the English Literary Imagination* (1996); Frederick Roden, *Same-Sex Desire in Victorian Religious Culture* (2002); Martha Vicinus, *Intimate Friends: Women Who Loved Women, 1778–1928* (2004); and Patrick O' Malley, *Catholicism, Sexual Deviance, and Victorian Gothic Culture* (2006).

Victorian women were, of course, vitally interested in temporal issues of money, property, legal rights, employment, and education; and religious experience is inextricably bound up with issues of gender, class, sexual orientation, and nationality. What often becomes obscured, however, is the fact that, in a culture that defined "good" women as predominantly moral and spiritual creatures, many women defined agency, first and foremost, as the ability to discern God's will and act upon it. As the writings in this study demonstrate, many women sought to practice their religions as their consciences dictated, and to maintain lives in conformity with the religious identities they constructed for themselves. My analysis of these texts attempts to capture some of the anxiety and frustration Victorian women of all denominations experienced, as the demands of an increasingly modern, industrialized, and secular culture proved incompatible with traditional Christian understandings of the "good life." The busy Victorian wife, mother of half a dozen children, and mistress of a comfortable middle-class household, would, by secular standards, have achieved the "good life." But where was the time for reflection, solitude, and prayer? Would the overwhelming devotion to husband and children enjoined by her society diminish or eclipse her love for God? How could she live a life of simplicity and charity while trying to keep up a respectable domestic establishment? Was her family life, as Evangelical tract writers promised, a foretaste of heaven on earth, or was it indeed "masked atheism"?

Just as Catholicism, in the Victorian imagination, was always something "other" than it purported to be, this project ultimately invites readers to look beyond preoccupations with Catholicism and gender to something much larger. This inquiry begins with a focus on women writers, in part because both the terms "Catholicism" and "home"—despite appearing mutually contradictory to many Victorians—would have summoned up images of the feminine. Morality (but not theology) and the home were deemed "respectable" subjects for women writers, and many female novelists, as Christine Kreuger has argued, found "in scripture calls to essentially literary vocations as preachers, prophets, and evangelists," authorizing them to "re-envision women's lives and represent them authoritatively" (9). But women writers, although keenly interested in the problems of their own sex (foremost among them, challenges to female authority and agency), were not content to stop there. They wanted, like men, to help reform the nation, and even the world. In her *Personal Recollections,* Charlotte Tonna describes her longing to help defend England against the snares of Rome, after the infuriating passage of the Catholic Emancipation Act in 1829:

But suppose a woman feels herself called on to take a personal interest in public affairs, what can she do, without stepping out of her proper sphere, and intruding into the province of the superior sex? I am going to tell you what a woman may do; for of us it may be surely said, "Where there's a will there's a way." When we set our hearts upon any thing, we are tolerably enterprising and persevering too, in its attainment; and this natural love of pleasing ourselves may be turned to a very good account. (292)[3]

For many women writers, that "way" was through fiction, and other works designed for women to consume (and read to their children) by the fireside. Historian William Lecky argued in 1869 that "[t]he family is the centre and archetype of the State, and the happiness and goodness of society are always in a very great degree dependent upon the purity of domestic life" (282). Lecky's view of the family was a popular one: why else would anti-Catholic writers point to Jesuit infiltrations of the home as their primary example of England's susceptibility to Romish corruption? And how else could Scottish domestic novelist Catherine Sinclair consider her *Popish Legends and Bible Truths* (1852) of such national importance that she begged her far more famous contemporary, writer and critic J. G. Lockhart, to review it favorably?[4] In a very deferential, apologetic letter of 1852, Sinclair explains to Lockhart her motivation for writing this volume: she is upset by the "clandestine means in daily action throughout the society of Edin[burgh]—at present to beguile the young over to Jesuitism." *Popish Legends* is intended to provide answers to "these controversial questions [about Roman Catholicism] by which very inexperienced young Protestants are now being misled without the knowledge of their own parents." She continues:

Much of my influence in this attempt must of course depend on the opinions of the press, & to you, whom I consider at the head of criticism in this country. [...] During the last twenty years, I have written fifteen volumes [...] and by subsequent editions there are now 57,000 volumes sold in England. [...] My works are all translated into German & French, & I have been honored with three letters from her Majesty, who reads them

---

3. For an in-depth discussion of Tonna's commitment "to secure a place for women's voices in social discourse," see chapter 7, "Preaching Fiction: The Contribution of Charlotte Elizabeth Tonna," in Christine Krueger's *The Reader's Repentance: Women Preachers, Women Writers, and Nineteenth-Century Social Discourse* (1992).

4. *Popish Legends and Bible Truths* is not itself a novel, but a long polemical work warning young people of the dangers of Roman Catholicism. However, one might consider Sinclair's later novel, *Beatrice* (1852) (half of which is set in polite drawing rooms, the other half in gloomy castles and dungeons), a novelistic version of *Popish Legends*.

regularly.—In the world of criticism my works have all remained unknown for except a few of the daily newspapers, no opinion either favourable or otherwise has ever yet been given of them. The sanguine hope of being favourably noticed is now nearly extinct,—& those are in the grave for whose sake, I should most deeply have valued a good word from the public [...] I have done for my new volume, what I never did for any of the others in asking whether you will second in my defence by your influence the earnest endeavor I have made in this volume to warn the young. . . excuse this intrusion from one who has long known you & yours [...].

In this letter, Sinclair, whose work undoubtedly attracted many female readers, including Queen Victoria, begs a figurehead of the male literary establishment for public recognition. Her request for Lockhart's approval is based not on the merits of her writing (or even her motherly concern for specific children of her acquaintance), but on a fact they would both (presumably) agree on: the future of the United Kingdom was in great jeopardy.

This awkward piece of communication from a relatively obscure woman writer to a lionized male writer might have been deemed audacious for several reasons, including the fact that it is *Sinclair* who invites Lockhart to assist *her* in a mission of national importance. More often, women writers longed for invitations from the male establishment; they craved the authority wielded by male preachers and orators, who thundered in pulpit and Parliament against England's enemies. In regard to Catholicism as a threat to national security, most women and men were on the same page. What sets women's writings on Catholicism apart is their construction of the home (often beset by Jesuit invaders) as a metonym for entities they were *not* authorized to write about: the nation and the world. Catholicism enabled women to present a far more pessimistic and critical view of the home than that embraced in popular culture, but to stop there would be to emphasize the differences between Victorian men and women much more than their similarities. What fascinates me most is how *unified* the majority of Victorians were, both in their terror of Roman Catholicism and in their anxieties about secularism. While this book ostensibly focuses on women writers, the voices of their male counterparts are far from silent. *Masked Atheism* places women's writings within a rich context of male-authored sermons, tracts, and pamphlets, and also emphasizes how often women's texts echo and mirror these documents.

This study also proclaims to be about Catholicism, but it is equally concerned with Protestant discourses and Protestant identities. This seems appropriate, given that Catholicism was often depicted as dangerously indistinguishable from virtuous Protestantism. What authorized most critics of Catholicism in the Victorian era was not gender identity but *Protestant* identity. As Jenny Franchot states of nineteenth-century American anti-Catholic rhetoric, "the Protestant invective against and fascination with Rome were clearly symptomatic of the modern West's withdrawal from a cohesive spirituality. [...] [T]he real enemy [...] was not Rome but a ghostly skepticism that would soon destroy even Rome's power" (xxvii). While this study supports Franchot's claim that Protestants utilized anti-Catholicism to condemn secularism, it also demonstrates that Catholics shared Protestants' concerns about secularism. Moreover, as some writers in this study demonstrate, pro-Catholic discourse could *also* serve as a powerful cultural critique both of Victorian domesticity and of secularism at large.

British Victorians' responses to Catholicism, still so compelling to modern-day scholars through their drama, their outrageousness, their prurience, and—in the best instances—their originality and creativity—functioned, in part, as an elaborate mask for social discourse. Under cover of the "masks" of anti-Catholicism, pro-Catholicism, or decided ambivalence, Victorian writers could articulate concerns about a phenomenon deeply disturbing to nineteenth-century believers: a secular world in which human identity itself—not merely religious identities or gender identities—would demand reassessment and reconfiguration, this time without the aid or comfort of Christian vocabularies, assumptions, or worldviews.

"Loving the creature"
The Protestant Evangelical Legacy

The majority of women writers in this study were Protestant, and inevitably their knowledge of Catholicism was more often gleaned from hearsay and propaganda than firsthand experience or observation. A study of this nature cannot attempt to provide an accurate picture of Victorian Catholicism; rather, its goal is to lead readers back to Protestant discourses, and ways in which they contributed to problems inherent within domesticity.[5] Scholars of the period are of course well acquainted with the cultural cliché of the Angel in the House; it was a powerful cultural symbol, but like

---

5. For more information on the history and practices of Victorian Roman Catholics, see Norman's *English Catholic Church in the Nineteenth Century* (1984) and Mary Heimann's *Catholic Devotion in Victorian England* (1995).

most gender-based ideologies, as Mary Poovey argues, "both contested and always under construction [...] always in the making, [...] always open to revision, dispute, and the emergence of oppositional formations" (*Uneven Developments* 3). The Protestant Evangelical revival contributed greatly to the popular notion of home and family as the locus of the sacred. Yet almost on the heels of Evangelicalism, Roman Catholicism became increasingly visible in British culture due to a combination of factors, including the Catholic Emancipation Act of 1829, the Oxford Movement within the Church of England, the "Papal Aggression" of 1851, and the rapid establishment of both Anglo- and Roman Catholic religious communities.[6,7] Evangelical Protestantism may have fostered Victorian notions of the domestic sphere in their infancy, but the discourses surrounding the Catholic revival, decades later, prompted writers to interrogate and critique Victorian Protestant domesticity as a mature and socially entrenched institution.

The fact that so many midcentury women writers employed images of "antidomestic" and "profane" Catholicism into their critiques of domesticity, attests to the extreme degree of frustration generated by the Evangelical Protestant legacy. As Victorian female-authored texts frequently attest, Evangelical Protestant constructions of both domesticity and femininity were fraught with contradictions. Victorian society called for devout wives

---

6. See Edward R. Norman, *Anti-Catholicism in Victorian England* (1968); D. G. Paz, *Popular Anti-Catholicism in Mid-Victorian England* (1992); and Michael Wheeler, *The Old Enemies: Catholic and Protestant in Nineteenth-Century Englilsh Culture* (2006) for comprehensive overviews of the Catholic/Protestant controversy at midcentury. Walter L. Arnstein, *Protestant versus Catholic in Mid-Victorian England: Mr. Newdegate and the Nuns* (1982), provides a more focused discussion of the convent issue. John Shelton Reed's *Glorious Battle: The Cultural Politics of Victorian Anglo-Catholicism* (1996) is a particularly readable study of the cultural issues underlying the Oxford Movement and Ritualism in the Church of England.

7. In *The Oxford Movement in Context,* Peter Nockles explains the origin of the term "Anglo-Catholic." Although "Anglo-Catholic" was originally interchangeable with the term "Anglican," Nockles notes that "the label increasingly was appropriated [in the nineteenth century] by the Tractarian party. [...] Later generations of the [Oxford] Movement's followers [...] would claim the term 'Anglo-Catholic' exclusively for themselves" (41–42). I use this term to describe women writers affiliated with the Oxford Movement, which sought, among other goals, "a revival of an ever-increasing number of beliefs and practices from the Church of England's pre-Reformation heritage" (Reed xxi). Aspects of this transformation included "the revivals of religious communities and the practice of confession," as well as "changes in worship, church furnishings, and extra-liturgical practices" (xxi); changes that appeared, to many Protestants, as a dangerous blurring of distinctions between Protestant and Catholic. While Anglo-Catholics, members of the Church of England, insisted on a clear distinction between themselves and Roman Catholics, they were frequently represented in the popular press as Papists in Protestant clothing. In this study I follow Michael Wheeler's lead in referring to all members of the Church of England (including Anglo-Catholics) and Dissenters as "Protestant," and Roman Catholics as "Catholic": This binary is admittedly somewhat crude, but I use it (as Wheeler does) for "convenience" (11).

and mothers to preside over morally pure homes, but the domestic realities of women's lives threatened to negate this moral power. Mary Poovey notes that Protestantism, by valuing the family and asserting the "priesthood of all believers," male and female, elevated women's status, but at the same time "rigidly emphasized the patriarchal family organization ratified by Scripture . . . [and] tended, in practice, to restrict women's activity to narrowly defined domestic duties" (7).[8] Monica Cohen highlights the renunciatory impulse of domesticity, noting, for example, that Dinah in Eliot's *Adam Bede* accepts domestic life as "a career whereby loving the creature [a phrase Cohen defines as "a life devoted to homecare"] entails an unparalleled sacrifice: the sacrifice of a religious self" (134).

Poovey and Cohen both remark upon the ways in which domesticity creates a defined, quasi-professional role for women yet limits them from complete agency. Yet the depth and complexity of the domestic woman's dilemma extends even further. As texts in this study repeatedly demonstrate, the issue for many women was not simply limited choices, diminished power, or even fewer opportunities for religious activity. More to the point, the Household Angel, so frequently depicted as an ethereal, spiritual, practically disembodied entity, was imprisoned within the realm of the material. By "material," I mean anything that Victorians might have considered antithetical to—or a distraction from—the cultivation and awareness of the sacred in everyday life. Of course, this category includes actual physical objects: In a culture experiencing economic prosperity and an unprecedented standard of living, middle-class domestic comforts no doubt worried devout Victorians who equated suffering and asceticism with moral heroism. As George Eliot notes of Dorothea Brooke in *Middlemarch*, "She could not reconcile the anxieties of a spiritual life involving eternal consequences, with a keen interest in guimp and artificial protrusions of drapery" (5–6).

A larger "material" obstacle for the writers in this study, however, was the body—especially the unruly female body and its many demands. Women's natural longings for sexual and emotional gratification were further stimulated in a culture that, as Robert Polhemus argues in *Erotic Faith* (1990), increasingly based its notion of transcendence on human erotic fulfillment rather than an apprehension of an otherworldly divinity (1). The writers in this study demonstrate no small amount of concern that even women's "vocation" of marriage and motherhood, ironically, could interfere with their spiritual agency.[9] Although the phrase "loving

---

8. Carol Christ makes a similar claim—that the ideal of husband as a woman's spiritual guide coexisted uneasily with notions of a morally superior "Angel in the House" (152).

9. As Leonore Davidoff and Catherine Hall point out, "Women who had encountered real religion were often worried about the effects which marriage would have on their spiritual lives,

the creature," as Cohen suggests, implies the love of home comforts, more frequently it was used to denote idolatry. As sermons, tracts, novels, and other writings reveal, nineteenth-century believers, both Protestant *and* Catholic, were preoccupied with the sin of idolatry, which they frequently describe as "creature-worship." Although idolatry could be the substitution of anything in the place of God (such as, most famously, the Israelites' golden calf), "creature-worship" was most frequently described as the act of loving another human being as (or instead of) God. Although men such as John Henry Newman expressed anxieties about idolatry, women seemed to have been especially concerned about it. Sermons against idolatry permeate Christina Rossetti's devotional prose; Charlotte Yonge worries about it in her correspondence; and, as this study demonstrates, women novelists and poets return almost obsessively to the violation of the first commandment in their creative work. If Victorian women were tempted toward idolatry, it is not difficult to see why. As "naturally" selfless beings, they were expected to attach themselves to parents, husbands, and children. While devotion to family might seem only admirable in our own time and culture, family as a potential obstacle to the life of the spirit seemed, to at least some Victorians, problematic indeed. And of course, the sexual dimension of romantic love could also unsettle those aspiring toward more transcendent goals.

This study concerns itself not only with the notion of domesticity, but also with constructs of female identity, as the two were so closely intertwined. The secularism of the domestic sphere had both temporal and spiritual implications for women. From a more immediate perspective, material domesticity threatened women's identity because Protestant ideology posited female piety as an essential component of femininity.[10] John Angell James, in *Sermons to Young Women* (1852), states that "[i]t is in the female bosom [...] that piety finds a home on earth. The door of women's heart is often thrown open to receive this divine guest, when man refuses it an entrance" (16). Yet just as women are privileged by their susceptibility to religious feeling, they are all the more degraded if they deny it: "An infidel of either sex is a foe to our species," continues James, "[...] but a female infidel is the most dangerous and destructive of the furies" (16). Similarly, Harvey Marriot, in *Sermons on the Character and Duties of Women* (1832), states that "[a] professed infidel among men is

whether they would become too concerned with worldly matters [...] to allow enough space for spiritual life" (90).

10. Patrick O'Malley emphasizes the intricate links between gender and religion in the nineteenth century; he argues that "the production of nineteenth century genders and sexualities so persistently both shapes and is shaped by that of religious identities and practices that cultural studies must consider them in relation to each other" (7).

nothing regarded, whilst the woman who manifested herself ashamed of her religion would, by the public voice, be named a monster in society [...]. Hence women have much influence, from the very circumstance of its being *expected* that they should not be professedly irreligious" (7; emphasis in original).

While male preachers admonished women not to lose their religious faith, it never seems to have occurred to them—as it did to a number of women writers—that the demands of family and home could stand in the way of it. Florence Nightingale (who at one time nearly joined a Catholic sisterhood) complained bitterly of "the degree to which [the Evangelicals] have raised the claims upon women of 'Family'—the idol they have made of it. [...] They acknowledge no God, for all they have said to the contrary, but this Fetich" (qtd. in Allchin 115).[11] Aside from questions of female identity, this is where the stakes, for some women, became even higher. For if the demands of the everyday, domestic world obscured women's view of God in this life, then it seemed unlikely that they would see Him in the next. And to a woman who believed, as did so many Victorians, in the reality of hell and eternal damnation, this would have been a most terrifying thought indeed.

Women Writers' Appropriation of Pro- and Anti-Catholic Discourse

Evangelical Protestantism was a religion of the Word, and appropriately it proselytized through the printed word: sermons, tracts, and pamphlets that inevitably colored women's representations of the domestic sphere. By the middle decades of the nineteenth century, a second wave of religious discourse influenced women writers. Victorian women and men of all classes and denominations would have been saturated with texts about Catholicism. In an 1853 issue of the *Rambler*, England's foremost Catholic periodical, an anonymous British Catholic complains of the ubiquity of anti-Catholic sentiment in popular literature of the day:

---

11. For further information on the centrality of the home and family in Protestant Evangelicalism, see Ian Bradley's *Call to Seriousness: The Evangelical Impact on the Victorians* (1976) and Elisabeth Jay's *Religion of the Heart: Anglican Evangelicalism and the Nineteenth-Century Novel* (1979). As for Florence Nightingale, Roman Catholic beliefs and organizations (especially orders of nursing sisters) had a large impact on her, and tensions between Catholic and Protestant sisters, nurses, and patients (in addition to anti-Catholic sentiment back home) proved a sizable challenge for her nursing work in the Crimea. For further information, see Gillian Gill's *Nightingales: The Extraordinary Upbringing and Curious Life of Miss Florence Nightingale* (2005).

[T]he miscellaneous literature of the country is so infected with this anti-Popish mania, that a Catholic is never safe from some offensive or insulting insinuation or accusation, whatever kind of book he takes up. Go into a railway carriage, and ensconcing yourself snugly in a well-cushioned corner, prepare to wile away an hour or two with a cheap edition of a novel: before you have passed the next station, the author is flinging a handful of mud in your face, and suggesting crimes against the clergy and laity, *as a body*, which revolt the commonest sense of decency. [. . .] For what we have said of fiction and travels applies to every species of literary work. In the strictest sense, it is not safe to put any book into the hands of the young without first examining its contents. ("Protestant Authors," 94; emphasis in original)

One cannot help but suspect that the "young person" in question here is—like Podsnap's blushing daughter in *Our Mutual Friend* (1864–65)— female. While women's understanding of Catholic teaching and doctrine may have been incomplete or even at times misinformed, what *was* readily available to them, as this *Rambler* essay attests, was Protestant constructions of the Church of Rome (and, by implication, reading material that was often prurient and sexually suggestive). Women were not, moreover, passive consumers of anti-Catholic messages, but actively participated, alongside of men, in generating them. Despite D. G. Paz's assertion that anti-Catholicism in Victorian England was "more exclusively a male activity" (274), a huge number of women contributed to the controversy with their pens.[12] "Miscellaneous literature" was the only avenue through which a woman, barred from the pulpit, could publicly disseminate her theological views. Very often, those "cheap novels" which so affronted the Catholic railway passenger were authored—and consumed—by women.[13] Women writers attacked the Catholic Church just as aggressively as their male counterparts, with a vehemence that probably would have been deemed unladylike in reference to any other topic. Charlotte Elizabeth

12. Paz suggests that women were, at best, passive participants in anti-Catholic activities, explaining that "women could best combat popery by being nurturers: by keeping alive the issues of the day in their households, by teaching Protestantism to their children, and by encouraging their husbands and their brothers to be active in the Protestant cause" (273).

13. In the Garland Reprint Series of Victorian "Novels of Faith and Doubt" selected by Robert Lee Wolff, eleven of the twenty-one "Catholic and Anti-Catholic" novels are authored by women, and eleven of the twenty-five "Tractarian and Anti-Tractarian Novels" (that is, novels relating to the Anglo-Catholic movement) are by women as well. Wolff's survey, although broad, is far from comprehensive: considering the hundreds of long-forgotten titles he omits (such as the anticonvent novels I discuss in chapter 3), women's novels of Catholic religious controversy may well represent more than half of the total. See Wolff's *Gains and Losses: Novels of Faith and Doubt in Victorian England* (1977) for the specific authors and titles Wolff selected for the Garland series.

Tonna, for example, was particularly harsh; in her autobiography she describes the Catholic Church (alongside her many other colorful epithets for it) as "an apple of Sodom, beneath the painted rind which is a mass of ashes and corruption" (*Personal Recollections* 150).

Tonna and other women writers, in declaring their aversion to Catholicism, repeated many of the arguments made by clergymen and other male authors. Mid-Victorian opponents to Catholicism, both men and women, were responding to a series of political and religious events, beginning with Catholic Emancipation in 1829. The notion of Catholic landowners attending university, participating in elections, and sitting in Parliament aroused fears that Rome was slowly invading England with the aid of a vast network of sinister Jesuit spies. Thus Catholicism was constantly depicted as dangerously foreign and un-English. As Kevin Morris notes, "[T]he worse Catholicism was pictured, the better Britain and its rulers seemed. It was useful as a demonstration of what Christianity and Englishry were not, and so had a rôle in the process of national redefinition" (214). Other common accusations against Catholicism, as outlined by Morris and D. G. Paz, include the following: it was superstitious and irrational; Catholic priests were "bloodthirsty and scheming" (Paz 60–61); Catholicism was, in the popular press, "an effective vehicle for [tales of] sex and death" (Paz 62). It was, furthermore, a religion marred by "idolatry, saints . . . miracles and fanaticism [. . .] celibacy, monasticism [. . .] confession [. . .] asceticism," and thus proved its "irrelevance to British needs in the modern, scientific, democratic, freedom-loving, progressing age" (Morris 214).

What made Catholicism particularly relevant to women and to women writers, however, was its perceived threat to hearth and home. The most frequent accusation against Roman Catholicism was that, as a religion which elevated celibacy and monastic life over matrimony, it schemed to undermine the primacy and integrity of the English family. Anti-Catholic novels such as *Father Clement* (1823), *Beatrice* (1852), and *Under Which Lord?* (1879) present Jesuit priests infiltrating the family primarily through its women, romantic and weak-minded souls whose religious conversion is described in terms of sexual seduction. In Elizabeth Lynn Linton's *Under Which Lord?* the heroine goes on to divulge her husband's secrets in the confessional, ship her daughter off to the convent, and transfer the family fortunes to the pope's coffers.

Poisoning the home in its pursuit of Mammon, the Church of Rome was frequently depicted as a commercial, "public" religion in contrast to the domestic, private creed of Evangelical Protestantism. Taking advantage, no doubt, of growing cultural anxieties about industrialism, utilitarianism, and consumerism, other writers depicted Catholicism as a growing, rapacious, multinational corporation. Benjamin Scott, for example, explains that Catholicism is successful because it can best market itself: "It is unhappily the case in this world of ours, both in commerce and in religion, that the corrupted debased, adulterated article passes too frequently for the genuine and the pure, upon the word of the loudest and boldest asservator" (209). The language of the marketplace also emerges in anticonvent novels. Such books depict the convent not as home, but factory, which transforms living, breathing women into faceless automatons: "That system [the convent] is antagonistic to the laws of nature and the instincts of humanity," insists Eliza Smith Richardson in *The Veil Lifted* (1865); "and, when they [the nuns] became its devotees, they entered upon a life-long warfare with these blessed laws and instincts" (151). Richardson and her contemporaries present nuns as less than human, stripped of both their individuality and their womanly feelings, mere mechanical cogs in the great Romish system.

Many women writers, such as Charlotte Brontë (chapters 1 and 2) and Mary Martha Sherwood (chapter 3), made materialistic, idolatrous Catholicism a signifier for the home stripped of its Protestant sanctity through the modern forces of capitalism and secularism. However, Roman and Anglo-Catholic writers, such as Lady Georgiana Fullerton (chapters 1 and 2) and Elizabeth Missing Sewell (chapter 3), drew upon Catholicism to develop the idea that female sanctity might flourish best *outside* an increasingly materialistic, worldly home.[14] Fullerton, for example, upheld women's spiritual prerogative to confess their sins directly to God (albeit through the intercession of a male priest) rather than to their husbands. Sewell, in the *Experience of Life* (1852), incorporates Anglo-Catholic veneration for the virgin martyrs to construct the ideal of a heroic vocation to chastity, one superior to the call of marriage and motherhood. For these writers, Catholicism presented an alternative set of values through which to view and critique the Protestant domestic sphere. This juxtaposition of positive and negative representations of Catholicism in women's texts reveals a fascinating commonality: the same anxieties about secular and

---

14. By addressing the varied spectrum of attitudes toward Catholicism as demonstrated by Victorian writers, I hope to shed light on some relatively unexamined facets of midcentury Victorian literary appropriations of "Romanism." Recent studies, including Susan Griffin's *Anti-Catholicism and Nineteenth-Century Fiction* (2004) and Diana Peschier's *Nineteenth-Century Anti-Catholic Discourses: The Case of Charlotte Brontë* (2005), while compelling, focus almost exclusively on negative literary depictions of Roman Catholicism.

material domesticity that led some women to condemn Catholicism in their writing compelled others to celebrate it.

Given that Catholicism, in the Victorian imagination, was emblematic of the clash between sacred and secular, it was a promising medium through which women writers could express anxieties about the secularization of the ostensibly sacred home. For many women writers, as well as for male writers, Catholicism served as metonym for a godless world. It was common to compare Catholicism directly with paganism; Benjamin Scott's *Contents and Teachings of the Catacombs at Rome* (1853), an address to working men which drew heavily upon Charles Maitland's *Church in the Catacombs* (1846), employs architectural evidence to argue that the church of Rome has become, since ancient times, corrupted by pagan beliefs and practices. In *The Image-Worship of the Church of Rome Proved to be Contrary to Holy Scripture* (1847), Tyler J. Endell, the rector of St. Giles in the Fields, London, describes the Catholic veneration of saints as a pagan practice, exclaiming, "How any distinction can be maintained between the miraculous images of the heathen world of which we read in ancient mythology, and in the fabulous histories of pagan Rome, on the one hand, and, on the other, those miraculous images of the Virgin Mary . . . we cannot see" (264). An anonymous sermon entitled *Popery like Paganism* (1840?) states that "the resemblance between Popery and Paganism in Italy strikes every impartial observer. The names of things only are changed" (1).

Catholicism's presumed emphasis on idolatry and superstitious religious practices also aligned it with the most menacing aspects of Empire—another threat to the civilized domesticity of home. Mary Martha Sherwood, in her autobiography, describes how pagan idolatry followed her family on board a voyage home from India:

> I have little worth recording of our long sea voyage, saving that we had one awful storm, which had scarcely passed away before a black Ayah, who had charge of two English children, passengers on board, made an attempt to mislead our two little ones, by drawing the figure of some Hindoo god on the deck, and making poojah (worship) to it, and getting my children to do the same with hers. I found them bowing and bending before the grim figure, though I think they had no idea what they were really doing, yet I was very much shocked, and very angry with the elder ones especially, for not hindering it. (507)

As terrifying as the "black Ayah" was to Sherwood, she seems to have made no distinction between her foreign shipmate and the Catholic idolaters at home, whom she attacked vigorously over the course of an extremely prolific literary career. Indeed, Catholics were repeatedly compared to Muslims and "Hindoos."[15] Protestant missionary W. Keane, in *Romanism and Hinduism*, states that "[i]n places where the Romanists are at all numerous in India, it were not easy to distinguish between the illuminated altars, and the gay and noisy processions of them and the Heathens (10); [...] [W]here, is the difference between the oft-reiterated Sanskrit 'Mantras,' counted by strings of beads, and the Latin Rosary of 'ten Aves and a Pater' again and again repeated? Are they not both alike 'the sacrifice of fools?'" (11). In *Beatrice*, Catherine Sinclair's heroine makes a similar comparison between "the dignified purity of a [Protestant] spiritual worship [...] which needs no visible object of adoration" and the Catholic practice of venerating statues and crosses. "We pity the Egyptians for worshipping bulls, cats, and leeks, and the South Sea Islanders for adoring pigs," exclaims Beatrice, "but prayers to a wooden image are equally incomprehensible!" (II:76). This dimension of anti-Catholic language is especially significant, for it suggests one way in which anxieties about the imperial Other informed fears of the domestic, Catholic Other. Ultimately, such comparisons between Catholics and Hindoos portray the insidious influence of Catholicism in England as representative of further-flung, even more mysterious, beliefs and practices threatening the British Empire. As Susan Griffin argues of Sinclair's novel, for example, *Beatrice* exposes fears that "the growing heterogeneity of the British Empire threatens its very identity" and "focuses on the weaknesses of modern British bodies, depicting their vulnerability as emblematic of that of the British Empire" (115).

Aside from its foreign associations, Catholicism was also useful to women writers in addressing anxieties about a rising middle-class standard of living and a domestic culture increasingly devoted to the pursuit of physical comfort. Anti-Catholic writers charged Rome with pampering the body at the expense of the spirit; Hugh M'Neile argues that eventually Rome "began to draw down ... the very shape of God himself, into an exterior and bodily form [...]. They hallowed it, they fumed it, they sprinkled it, they bedecked it [...] till the soul by this means of over-bodying herself [...] forgot her heavenly flight, and left the dull and droiling carcase to plod on in the old road [...] of outward conformity" (23). This equation

---

15. According to Miriam Burstein, another popular tactic was to compare Catholicism and Judaism; "most Protestant denominations represented Roman Catholicism and Judaism as structurally and temperamentally identical, a claim stretching back at least to Martin Luther. [...] Victorian Protestants accused both religions of substituting man-made laws for biblical truths; of elevating priestly authority above private judgment; and of forbidding laity access to the Bible" (133).

between Catholicism and gross corporeality led some women writers, such as Charlotte Brontë in *Jane Eyre* (chapter 1), to appropriate Catholicism to represent the flame of female spiritual agency virtually quenched in a tide of sensual pleasures: Jane committing "Catholic" idolatry in her sexual passion for Rochester. Christina Rossetti, on the other hand, did not represent Catholicism so negatively; rather, her Anglo-Catholicism informed her deep suspicion of the physical comforts of domestic life. In "Triad," the one woman who makes a conventional marriage "grew gross in soulless love, a sluggish wife" (l.10), her existence, like that of the bitter spinster and the prostitute, "All on the threshold, yet all short of life" (l.14). Elizabeth Barrett Browning, in contrast to Brontë and Rossetti, achieved less conflicted representations of matrimony and female sexuality, suggesting in *Aurora Leigh* (chapter 4) that a woman cannot truly fulfill her spiritual and artistic vocation without feeding her physical and emotional cravings for marriage and motherhood. Yet even this positive representation of married, corporeal bliss is enabled by Catholicism—in particular, Barrett Browning's reliance on Catholic sacramental imagery and the doctrine of transubstantiation (the affirmation of Christ's actual physical presence in the Eucharist).

To What Extent Were Victorian Women Uniquely Attracted to Catholicism?

The previous section demonstrates some ways in which women writers' responses to Catholicism paralleled those of male clergymen and tract writers. But did women simply shift the discourse of Catholicism from male-dominated literary genres to the female world of domestic fiction? Where do we see innovations on the part of women writers, and to what extent can one craft an argument for women's unique attraction to Roman Catholicism? Catholicism inspired similarly ambivalent attitudes for both men and women in Britain, but women's texts (both pro-and anti-Catholic) do suggest that Catholicism offered possibilities for women that Victorian Protestant culture did not. Although, as John Shelton Reed observes, it would be a mistake to equate Victorian Catholicism with twentieth-century concepts of feminism, Catholicism presented a model of female sanctity more ideologically consistent than the fractured domestic sphere informed by Protestantism. It offered women a broader scope of opportunities for benevolent agency, especially through organized sisterhoods and lay volunteer work. Catholicism also elevated celibacy over marriage, providing a challenge to the hegemony of matrimony in Victorian culture and an incentive to those increasing numbers of women for whom marriage was not an option.

Moreover, Catholicism was a marginalized religion traditionally depicted as feminine, in contrast to "masculine" Protestantism. This mode of representation was hardly new to the Victorians; Frances Dolan, in *Whores of Babylon*, notes the frequency with which seventeenth-century Protestant texts associated Catholicism with "disorderly women." "[A]nti-Catholic polemic," she explains, "often represents its object as feminine, despite the fact that men dominated the institutional church" (8). Dolan interprets this phenomenon as a response "to the perceived importance of women in Catholic theology [and] iconography" and popular anxiety that Catholicism would endow women with a dangerous degree of both spiritual and temporal power (8). This anxiety is reflected in anti-Catholic pamphlets and tracts that represent weak-minded women as especially susceptible to the allure of Rome. An 1835 tract entitled *An Address to Every Lady in Britain by a Protestant* (with a dainty pink cover, no less) cautioned women to stay away from theological controversy and theological writings—especially those by Roman Catholic theologians. The writer argues:

> [I]f all women devoted their lives to the study of controversy, what would become the duties of their station? What would become of the charities of life? Who would perform the social part allotted to them? And which, if properly performed, is enough to occupy the time of every one?
>
> You must perceive at once this would be an *impossible* and *unnatural* state of things; it cannot therefore be *right*.
>
> Neither is Controversy on subjects with which she is conversant becoming in a woman. Her reasoning powers are generally weaker than those of men: whether it is so by *nature* or *education*, signifies little to the present purpose. It is evidently the will of God. . . . (9–10; emphasis in original)

The writer concludes by sending her female readers to the Bible to find for themselves proof that Roman Catholic practices and doctrines are not necessary to salvation. "[S]tudy the word of God, and not the doctrines of men. Again, I say, *do not study the doctrines of men*. It is these which every day lead aside silly women, and make such inroads on the peace of our families" (12; emphasis in original).

In Victorian culture, Catholicism was associated with destructive—and virtually irresistible—female sexuality. For example, in a sermon of 1855 attacking the new Roman Catholic doctrine of the Immaculate

Conception, Bishop Samuel Wilberforce compared the Catholic Church to a sorceress and a siren:

> There are her spells; and mighty hearts—on that the Spirit of the Lord might set them free!—have sunk entranced beneath them. Let no man undervalue their potency or trifle with their might. It is the very character of the cup of the sorceress, that its lightest taste so besots the subtlest intellect and subdues the strongest will, that her victim follows her bidding, lead him whithersoever it may. The only safeguard, therefore, is in the earliest and most instant refusal to drink the wine of her fornication. (27)

When the dark side of female nature is unleashed, the result is power over men. Perhaps partly for this reason, some women writers made Catholicism a signifier for female human nature, which must either constrain itself within, or free itself from, the shackles of social convention. Jane Eyre's cravings for love, her idolatrous tendencies, and her longing for domestic comforts are coded Catholic; significantly, her dark double, Bertha, really *is* Catholic, with her Spanish Creole ancestry, her crucifix, and her images of saints. Barrett Browning's Anglo-Italian Aurora Leigh also has an "inner Catholic," but in this case Romanism signifies positive qualities (ones nonetheless discouraged by Aurora's society) such as artistic and sexual expression. Despite the differences in their representations of Catholicism, both Brontë and Barrett Browning use it to construct a "secret" female self that threatens to disrupt the social status quo.

Although Brontë's and Barrett Browning's use of Catholicism as a signifier for the disorderly female self is highly innovative, we can nonetheless discern the influence of anti-Catholic sermons on both narratives, as clergymen frequently portrayed Catholicism as "substantially the spirit of Human nature" (Whateley 9). In an 1848 sermon, for example, Hugh M'Neile argues that, in contrast to Protestantism, which expresses "*antagonism to human nature as it is*, with the high and determined aim to renew it in conformity with God" (14; emphasis in original), Romanism, by alternately indulging both the passions of the body and the qualms of the conscience, "is congenial to human nature as it is: and therefore Romanism, with her black Lent and red Carnival, can prosper with the unconverted multitude. She gives or takes, smiles or frowns, according to circumstances" (14). Rev. C. S. Hawtrey also expounds this view, explaining to his congregation in 1826 that "the materials of Popery are within us" (14):

Do we wish thoroughly to understand in what Popery consists? [...] [L]et us look into our own hearts, let us search deeply the "chambers of imagery" within us. [...] In our self-righteous pride, in our love of ostentatious display, in our carnal policy, in our contempt of God's word, in our attachment to blind traditions, in our indolence and want of spirituality, in our voluptuousness, in our uncharitableness, in our formality, superstition, and hypocrisy, in our light thoughts of sin, in our love of cruelty,—*in all these things (and the seeds of all these evils are in us) we see the materials of which Popery is constructed. Let us, then, learn to regard it as a mirror, in which we may behold a full length picture of ourselves; and having seen it let us be humbled, and smite upon our breasts, and say, God be merciful to us, sinners.* (Hawtrey 12; emphasis added)

Undoubtedly, the notion that even the staunchest of Protestants was "naturally" Catholic made Romanism seem especially terrifying—as well as intriguing. Protestants' repeated warnings of the deadly attractions of Catholicism surely increased its allure; as I suggest in chapter 4, one might easily associate Rossetti's luscious Goblin Fruits with the fruits of Romanism. Although the impulse to associate Catholicism with the "secret self" might not have been new to women writers, their use of Catholicism as a "full length mirror" enabled them to represent highly complex and original female subjects.

Women Who "Went Over" to Rome

Only three of the authors in this study, Lady Georgiana Fullerton, Katherine Bradley, and Elizabeth Cooper (Bradley and Cooper are collectively known as Michael Field), converted to Rome. While this is not a book about Catholic converts, their letters and manuscripts, which I discuss briefly in this section, provide a useful context for the preoccupations of the novelists and poets I examine in the following chapters. Just as Protestant women writers' responses to Catholicism overlapped with those of their male counterparts, so also did male and female converts articulate similar perceptions of Rome. Catholicism, in the eyes of Protestant women writers, may have suggested expanded agency for women, but they did not equate it with feminism. Neither, it seems, did Catholic converts.[16] Female

---

16. Joyce Sugg, in her edited collection of women's letters to John Henry Newman, states that "not one of the Catholic women converts known to Newman espoused the cause of women's

converts appear to have embraced Catholicism for the same reasons men did, and foremost among them was a terror of religious doubt and a desire to save their immortal souls. In contrast to conflicted and divided Protestantism, Catholic converts presented their church as a bulwark of moral certainty. "Except in communion with the Holy See," states Robert Belaney, "[...] where shall we see anything but one tide of opinions after another flowing in ceaseless succession, stunning the world each with its own momentary noise?" (52). Similarly, John Gordon states that those who remain outside the Catholic Church "must for ever go on doubting and disputing, demanding intellectual demonstrations for spiritual truths, which it is impossible to convey to them [...]."

This construction of the Catholic Church as infallible moral guide is echoed by poet Adelaide Procter, who converted to Rome in 1851. In an undated letter to Bessie Rayner Parkes, she explains what she perceives as a moral imperative to settle questions of religious doubt: "I do not think there is any neutral ground in belief. It seems to me one cannot climb a mountain top and watch the stream of events out of it oneself. [...] [D]epend upon it if God made any truth from mankind—he made every mind capable of receiving it." Not long after Procter's death, Parkes herself converted to Catholicism, to the horror of her friend Barbara Bodichon. In a letter of 1861, before her conversion, Parkes explains to Bodichon that "at 32, with neither a strong body nor a strong brain I feel I require a settled belief in religious matters to keep me sane, healthy, happy." Catholic nun Margaret Frances Cusack, in her autobiography, says doubt about the nature of the Eucharist helped steer her toward the Catholic Church: "I now saw plainly," she notes, "that there could be no shades of opinion about this matter—either our Divine Lord was really [in the sacrament], or He was not there [...]." Frustrated with Protestant clergyman, who "worshipped something [in the sacrament], they knew not what, nor could they clearly define their own views" (177), she eventually went over to Rome. "Here," she states, "there were no questions, no difficulties, no doubts. Christ speaks through Peter, and we, the sheep and the lambs committed to his care, have but to hear and obey" (202).

Another parallel between Catholic converts, male and female, and writ-

---

emancipation." These women did not, as Suggs notes, seem to have been actively discouraged from supporting social progess; rather, "they simply did not see this as a cause to be supported" (159). John Shelton Reed, who describes Anglo-Catholicism as a movement particularly attractive to women for the range of opportunities it offered them, resists equating it with Victorian feminism. "It embodied some of the same values," he notes, "but in such a limited and tentative way, and incorporating so many patriarchal assumptions of the time, that it might be better to regard it as an alternative to feminism" (209).

ers such as Brontë, Rossetti, Barrett Browning, and Eliot, is their intense desire to locate and preserve a sense of the sacred in an increasingly secular world. For some Victorians, conversion to Catholicism implied a return to the sacred. It seems ironic that while Protestants accused Catholics of promoting secularism beneath a veneer of sham spirituality, Catholic converts, in turn, decried the worldliness of Protestantism, its religious authority eroded by doctrinal squabbles. Frederick Lucas, a lawyer who left the Society of Friends for the Catholic Church, explains that spiritual worship requires "the feeling of the close connection between the supernatural world and human daily life." Unfortunately, however, "The spirit of Protestantism which produced, and has been in its turn influenced by the skeptical, worldly tendencies of modern times, has endeavoured as much as possible, to refine away every thing supernatural out of the domain of modern life" (12). Lucas's 1839 apologia, addressed to the Society of Friends, is simultaneously a manifesto against secular modernity: "We have studiously brought every thing down to the same vulgar level [...] we have done our best, and in sooth with unmatched success, to Paganize every thing that the eye can look upon, or the ear can hear, or the hand can touch, and we wonder at the result" (94). Converts' quest for the sacred in the midst of secular modern life simultaneously functioned as powerful cultural critique.

Both fiction and nonfiction writings, upon close analysis, caution the scholar and historian against claiming for Victorian women an experience with Catholicism too distinctive from that of men.[17] Yet women, charged with the task of keeping religious faith alive through their vocations as housekeepers, wives, and mothers, were threatened by secularism in a way that men were not. Questions of the hereafter aside, secularism threatened to rob women of a broad path of agency open to them in mid-Victorian culture: the power to discern God's will and act upon it for the good of themselves and others. Catholicism, with its highly controversial figures of female spiritual agency (whether nuns or the Virgin Mary), must have appeared an especially seductive alternative for many women. Not only did Catholicism suggest an alternate role for women, but its locus of sanctity was situated well outside the walls of the problematic Victorian home. In

---

17. In *Catholic Devotion in Victorian England* (1995), Mary Heimann notes that "women seem to have been disproportionately prominent in every aspect of Catholic practice, from attendance at church services to participation in extra-liturgical devotions and enrolment in devotional societies." She steers away, however, from any claim of women's greater affinity for Catholicism: "Since men, albeit in smaller numbers, were also involved in all of these activities, it seems to me that one can justifiably speak of Catholic rather than of gender-linked piety" (127).

contrast to the empty, crumbling Protestant church buildings that permeate Dickens's fiction, writings by Anglo- and Roman Catholics testify to the existence of vibrant church sanctuaries and sublime rituals enacted therein. Female converts' descriptions of Catholic Mass and other devotions portray *nondomestic* enclosures which seem to lift them beyond their secular lives and worldly cares. In 1844, Mary Holmes, a Catholic convert, describes to her former spiritual director (John Henry Newman, who at the time was still an Anglican priest) her impressions of a Catholic church in Birmingham:

> [Early in the morning, there arrived] young men and women of the lower class, dirty mechanics, shopmen, dress-making girls; number of these persons [...] with clasped hands and focus wrapt in devotions, kneeling before the pictures against the pillars, or bowing down before the Chapel of the Blessed Sacrament. And this in a town so notoriously wicked as Birmingham. [...] Many kneel for hours. [...] Children kneeling about the Church, so still. Oh it was a beautiful sight. I could have fancied myself abroad, or in the middle ages. (Qtd. in Newman, "History of a Conversion")

This fascination for Catholic spaces also permeates *Margaret Percival*, an 1847 novel by Anglo-Catholic Elizabeth Missing Sewell, which was *supposed* to be an attack on Rome. Nonetheless, one of the most striking contrasts in the novel is the tension between the peaceful Roman Catholic churches that so fascinate the novel's Anglican heroine and the clamorous, contentious, and distracting environment of her own family home. Margaret's impressions of a French Catholic cathedral are remarkably similar to Mary Holmes's account:

> [B]efore her [...] [were] altars and chapels, some dark and scarcely to be distinguished, others touched by the light of the dying day, as its mellowed rays shone mistily through the deep yet gorgeous colours of the windows. A few figures were scattered about the building, but none were moving. Kneeling before the shrine of the Virgin or the image of a favourite saint, they were apparently absorbed in devotion; and, except the distant murmur of the world's cares, which reached even to that temple of God, no sound fell upon their ear, save from the farthest end of the south transept, where, before an illuminated altar which shed a flickering light upon the bases of the pillars near, a priest was chanting a mass for the repose of the dead. Margaret stood motionless: she thought of nothing—observed nothing—her whole soul was absorbed in a feeling of intense awe. (129)

In the midst of her transcendent encounter, Margaret still discerns "a distant murmur of the world's cares," and such descriptions often simultaneously betray an awareness of the fragility and precariousness of this sacred world. In some of these accounts, the marked tension between an ideal of the sacred and the prosaic reality of everyday life is poignant and sometimes even humorous. Bessie Rayner Parkes, in a fragment of an 1865 letter, exclaims over the otherworldly appearance of Cardinal Manning at Mass: "The Consecration has been a wonderful Sight. The thin, spare, ascetic looking man looking ready to faint under the weight of his Mitre; the spiritual weight I mean; but his features are almost too unearthly to be in the juxtaposition of jewels and gold." Mary Holmes, in another letter written to John Henry Newman while both were still Anglicans, reports her initial disappointment with a too-corpulent bishop at Catholic Mass. "His appearance is sadly against him; and in his mitre and pontificals he looked just like a fat jolly Abbot, such as Protestant stories abound with; but, as soon as he began to speak, one forgot his appearance. The language, voice, manner, all was perfect. At Mass I felt much affected. When the Saving Victim was raised, I felt as if I dare not refuse to go to my Saviour" (20 April 1844; qtd. in Newman, "History").

Perhaps the most striking tension between the sacred and the profane, however, comes from a description of Newman himself. Emily Bowles, Newman's longtime friend and also a Catholic convert, records in her unpublished memorial to Newman her first impressions of the great Tractarian, at Littlemore in 1840:

> The little Church at Littlemore (then as first built by him) was overflowing to the very brim. [...] But there was the figure, ascetic in its spareness, one head, wonderful in its intellectual moulding, one face, grand, reticent, powerful both in speaking and at rest, and slightly forbidding, that detached itself from all the others, and thenceforth always stamped upon my mind. He glided from the body of surpliced clergy and acolytes, noiselessly appeared in the pulpit [...] and began at once to preach [...] [like] a messenger sent direct from God. As the exquisite voice, so full, so thrilling, so silvery yet so trumpet-like, poured itself out, absolutely stripped of self, of all human fear, and as it seemed, of all human feeling because the humanity was [abrogated?] in the visible sense of God, a wave of such emotion swept through me as I had never felt before in my life.

Immediately after the service, at lunch, the great man spoke to Bowles for the first time: "'*Will you have some cold chicken?*' And the sound of the same voice uttering those words [...] so bewildered me," she recalls, "that

I think my dear mother was obliged to answer for me [. . .]" (emphasis in original). Although the image of the messenger of God descending from on high to offer young Bowles some light refreshment (and a sobering reminder of things domestic) is an amusing one, Bowles's gentle self-parody perhaps best encapsulates the central issue facing all the writers in this study. Although with the exception of Georgiana Fullerton and Michael Field, these writers were *not* Catholic converts, all of their texts demonstrate a sense of existing in two worlds increasingly at odds with each other.

Overview of *Masked Atheism*

In the opinion of Protestant polemicists, Catholicism challenged a multitude of cherished Victorian values and ideals. This book focuses on a series of issues that were not only among the most visible and contentious in Protestant-Catholic controversy, but also ones that signaled for Protestants perversions of various facets of Victorian domesticity. The texts I discuss in chapters 1 and 2, with their emphases on idolatry and Catholic confession, disclose the possibility of marriage as a type of spiritual enslavement. Chapter 3 suggests that Victorian condemnations of celibate women (whether nuns or spinsters) mask concerns about the banality and materialism of middle-class homes. Chapter 4's focus on transubstantiation evokes a sinister dimension of the ordinary, domestic activities of eating and drinking. Chapter 5, on "Mariolatry," is as much about a collective fear of abandonment—that is, bad mothering—as it is about the longing for signs of transcendence. Chapter 6 also discusses abandonment, as the death of Michael Fields's dog, Whym Chow, symbolizes for Bradley and Cooper the profanation of their once transcendent domestic idyll. Taken together, these chapters and these domestic perversions trace the outlines of a much larger issue—a preoccupation with the disappearance of the sacred in modern culture.

The study incorporates both canonical and minor women writers, in part because I wish to recreate a sense of the literary world as Victorian readers experienced it. I also hope to invite reflection upon how a work's religious content can shape—or doom—its literary posterity. While novels by Lady Georgiana Fullerton and Elizabeth Missing Sewell may, in some ways, lack the sophistication of those by Charlotte Brontë and George Eliot, their almost complete erasure from literary history in the twentieth century—given the popularity and impact of their works in the nineteenth century—is a glaring oversight. For example, despite the fact that the early novels of Lady Georgiana Fullerton (a High Anglican who converted to Catholicism in the 1840s) were reviewed favorably in tandem with those of Charlotte Brontë and Charles Dickens in major periodicals in the 1840s and 1850s, today she is remembered (or more accurately, forgotten) only as a minor novelist who promulgated the views of Oxford Movement. The other interesting points of Fullerton's work become obscured by her religious views.[18]

Conversely, early feminist scholarship on *Jane Eyre* either overlooked the novel's profoundly religious dimension entirely, or presented Jane as a rebel against Christian patriarchy.[19] When works by Brontë, now the best-known Victorian anti-Catholic female novelist (however inaccurate the designation), is placed alongside those of the era's most popular Catholic novelist, the comparison facilitates new understandings of each author. No one, for example, would think to pigeonhole *Jane Eyre* as a "religious novel," yet like Fullerton's *Lady-Bird* (1853) it is centrally preoccupied with issues of spiritual integrity, moral and ethical agency, and divine salvation. And *Lady-Bird,* despite its religious emphases, engages with very earthbound issues of gender and power, its plot culminating in a stinging critique of popular ideals of romance and marriage. So powerful is this juxtaposition that I have elected—rather than write a separate chapter for each author—to discuss them in tandem in the first two chapters.

The first chapter examines concerns that marriage itself—as defined by Evangelical Protestantism—could be a stumbling block for devout Victorian women. Whereas Protestant clergymen frequently upheld Milton's Adam and Eve as a template for the ideal Christian marriage, Charlotte Brontë in *Jane Eyre* and Lady Georgiana Fullerton in *Lady-Bird* both suggest that the dynamic of such a marriage—"he, for God alone, and she, for God in him"—robbed women of the spiritual agency and autonomy necessary for their salvation. If a woman viewed her husband as an intermediary for God, these novels suggest, how easily might she come to view her husband *as* God? This, of course, was the sin of idolatry. Since this transgres-

---

18. Georgiana Fullerton (1812–1888) was born Georgiana Charlotte Leveson-Gower, the daughter of Lord Granville Leveson-Gower and Lady Harriet Cavendish. For more information on her life and works, see chapters 1 and 2.

19. Two examples of such approaches are Sandra Gilbert and Susan Gubar's reading of *Jane Eyre* in *The Madwoman in the Attic: The Woman Writer and the Nineteenth-Century Imagination* (1979) and Adrienne Rich's "Jane Eyre, the Temptations of a Motherless Woman" (1973).

sion was most frequently associated with Catholics and their adoration of spurious saints and the Virgin Mary, it hardly seems surprising that both Brontë and Fullerton drew upon Catholicism to expose the idolatrous potential of Victorian matrimony. Here, however, the differences cease: whereas Brontë condemns Jane's tendency toward creature worship by associating it with Catholic symbols and practices, Fullerton draws upon the Catholic tradition of celibacy to free her heroine from an idolatrous marriage at her novel's conclusion. Both authors, writing from different ends of a doctrinal spectrum, employ Catholic imagery to articulate very similar concerns about Victorian matrimony. This testifies not only to the power and pervasiveness of Catholic discourses at midcentury, but also the extent to which women's anxieties about marriage transcended religious denominations.

A similar phenomenon can be observed in chapter 2, which juxtaposes Brontë's representation of confession in *Villette* with Fullerton's defense of it in her 1844 novel, *Ellen Middleton*. Both novels, despite contrasting doctrinal positions, suggest that women require a space set apart from the rigid constraints of the domestic sphere to acknowledge, despite their outwardly feminine roles, the existence of less "angelic" qualities, such as sexual desire and rage. Catholic confession, as a "nondomestic" space removed from the prying eyes of fathers and husbands, allows women to confess sin and reconcile with God (in the case of Ellen Middleton) or, like Lucy Snowe, to embrace an essential part of themselves that society refuses to recognize. These representations of confession as attractive, and even necessary, for women contradict a prevailing public attitude of suspicion and outrage over Catholic confession in the 1840s and 1850s. Protestant fears of the priest's authority in confession centered around women and the family; opponents of confession argued that the rite, by compelling women to confess their sins to clerical outsiders, would effectively drive a wedge between husbands and wives, violate the sanctity of the home, and perhaps even end in sexual seduction and ruin of female penitents. Yet this very "nondomestic," potentially scandalous, element of the rite is what renders it so attractive to the heroines of Brontë's and Fullerton's novels; only within the confessional can each woman begin to reconcile conflicting aspects of her identity.

Chapter 3 demonstrates the ways in which Catholic discourse helped structure women's literary representations of alternatives to traditional domesticity: the celibate paths of spinsterhood and religious sisterhood. In the first section, an analysis of Elizabeth Missing Sewell's *The Experience of Life* (1852) explores how Sewell's Anglo-Catholic spinster *bildungsroman* appropriates elements of Roman Catholic hagiography to present the lay single life as a domestic vocation that simultaneously calls into question the entire concept of domesticity. This novel presents spinsterhood as a sacred calling, drawing its authority from tales of the virgin martyrs. It works so hard to present spinsterhood as a rigorous, "muscular," and heroic path for women that marriage and maternity, in contrast, appear to diminish, rather than enlarge, women's potential for spiritual and moral agency. The second half of this chapter, focusing on Mary Martha Sherwood's *The Nun* (1833) and other anticonvent literature, reveals how anti-Catholic attacks on female religious orders also, ironically, betray subliminal anxieties about marriage, motherhood, and domesticity in Victorian culture. Sherwood and other Protestant writers attempt to portray convent life (a topic about which they knew little, at best) as the antithesis of the Protestant English home—self-indulgent, materialistic, trivial, and spiritually deadening for women. These laboriously constructed binaries, however, collapse upon closer analysis: what emerges instead are moments of genuine anxiety about apparent *similarities* between domestic life and Protestant fantasies of convent life.

Whereas the first three chapters examine women's representations of the domestic sphere as potentially antithetical to the sacred, chapter 4 addresses how women poets employ Catholic Eucharistic imagery in an attempt to reconcile women's lofty spiritual vocations with their more earthbound callings as wives and mothers. In Elizabeth Barrett Browning's *Aurora Leigh* (1856) and Christina Rossetti's *Goblin Market* (1862), Catholicism's emphasis upon the physical body—in particular, its doctrine of the Eucharist—becomes a framework through which women poets can construct the notion of a female body that is at once sexualized *and* sacred. In *Aurora Leigh*, Barrett Browning repeatedly employs the image of Roman Catholic transubstantiation (the doctrine of the literal transformation of bread and wine into Christ's body and blood) to signify the merging of Aurora's identity as artist and spiritual muse with her calling to marriage and the building of God's kingdom on earth. In *Goblin Market*, Rossetti represents an intensely corporeal Eucharistic moment between Lizzie and her fallen sister Laura, thereby elevating the "base" female body as an agent of human redemption. Such redemption can only occur, moreover, once Lizzie ventures beyond the safe confines of the domestic sphere and risks physical seduction by Goblin men. Although Rossetti and Barrett Browning achieve a more satisfactory reconciliation between women's competing identities than other authors in this study, figures of fallen women (Jeanie, "who should have been a bride," and Marian Earle) linger uneasily in the background of each text, testifying to the endurance of the culture's strict binary between angelic and embodied women.

Chapter 5 addresses some of the culture's more overt anxieties about secularism and atheism as they emerged in controversies over Roman Catholic veneration for the Virgin Mary and specifically in the British responses to a purported apparition of the Virgin Mary in La Salette, France, in 1846. To many Protestants, Catholic veneration for the Virgin, along with their credulity in such "sham" miracles as the apparition at La Salette, threatened to eclipse or deny God altogether. At the very least, the ludicrous nature of Catholic apparition claims might, as Protestants argued, provide the perfect motivation for reasonable, critical-minded individuals to reject Christianity and theism. George Eliot's *Romola* (1862–1863), a novel obsessed with the demise of religious authority and the absence of God, appropriates elements of Marian apparition stories at first to critique Catholic veneration for the saints and the Virgin Mary. Such practices, Eliot suggests, simply reinforce humans' egoistic tendencies and do nothing to promote personal virtue or altruism. In the course of the novel, however, Eliot revises traditional understandings of the Madonna and of the cult of the saints to envision the possibility of human moral evolution *made possible* by the absence or "death" of God. Eliot's heroine, at the end of *Romola*, becomes a morally powerful agent (and a secular Madonna) only through the loss of all paternal sources of guidance and authority.

Some of the most interesting work to date on Catholicism and nineteenth-century literature focuses on the fin de siècle; the book's final chapter, therefore, attempts to draw connections between women writing at midcentury and those a few decades later, when popular antagonism toward Catholicism was presumably on the wane. At first glance, lesbian poets and lovers Michael Field may seem a complete departure from the other writers in this study (the thought of Lady Georgiana Fullerton and Elizabeth Sewell mingling at the same dinner party with Katherine Bradley and Edith Cooper has, I confess, been an amusing diversion for me as I finished this book). On closer examination, however, Bradley and Cooper, self-proclaimed "pagans" who converted to Roman Catholicism after a domestic calamity (the death of their pet dog, Whym Chow), form a perfect ending point for this study. Focusing exclusively on the 1906 volume of the Fields' vast diary, *Works and Days*, I explore the Fields' construction of a unique domestic piety—one that accommodated Bradley and Cooper's unconventional religious and sexual identities before their conversion, weathered Whym Chow's sudden death in 1906, and adapted to the paradigm shift of their successive conversions in 1907. For the Fields, Catholicism was not so much a radical departure from their secular, "pagan" past, but a means of bridging the "pagan," Dionysian aspects of their identities with their newfound desire to create meaning out of suffering and loss. Although the Fields undoubtedly demonstrate the most daring and creative appropriations of Catholicism, texts by all the writers in this study highlight Catholicism's usefulness in the nineteenth century as an inspiration for artists, an instrument for cultural critique, and a palliative for the growing pains of a rapidly changing society.

CHAPTER ONE

Extravagant Creature Worship

Protestant and Catholic "Sermons" on Marriage

> Let me caution you against permitting your affections to be placed on any one who is not a partaker of the grace of God. Suffer no attachment to take possession of your breast, upon which you cannot conscientiously ask your heavenly Father's blessing. How is it possible for you to enjoy happiness with one who is still in a state of nature? For one, professing religion, to unite himself to an irreligious person, is like a man uniting himself to a dead corpse.
>
> —Thomas Jackson, *Marriage and Adultery Considered*, 1810

THE extent to which the Evangelical Revival insisted on the sanctity of the family is evident in the wealth of early nineteenth-century Protestant sermons and tracts on marriage. Repeatedly, texts such as Jackson's present marriage as a sacred institution and its primary function to foster the spiritual salvation of husband, wife, and children. The very vehemence of preachers' warnings against "ungodly" marriage—conveying images resonant, in this case, of Mary Shelley's *Frankenstein* (1816)—attest both to the growing secularization of marriage and the enormous cultural anxieties generated by it. We cannot fully understand Victorian novelistic depictions of marriage—complete with all their inconsistencies and ambivalence—unless we familiarize ourselves with Protestant religious discourses on the same. Sermons were enormously popular as leisure reading in the nineteenth century, and the older genre of the sermon cross-pollinated the newer, if more worldly, genre of the novel.[1] Nowhere is this more clearly

---

1. The relationship between nineteenth-century preaching and women's domestic fiction is discussed in depth by Christine Kreuger in *The Reader's Repentance: Women Preachers, Women Writers, and Nineteenth-Century Social Discourse* (1992).

FIGURE 1.1 *Portrait of Lady Georgiana Fullerton. Image reproduced by permission of the Generalate of the Poor Servants of the Mother of God*

the case than in intersections between sermons on marriage and the courtship plot in Victorian novels. This chapter explores the ways in which both Charlotte Brontë and her Catholic contemporary, Lady Georgiana Fullerton, appropriate elements of Catholicism to critique Protestant constructions of marriage.² Although each author's text represents Catholicism very differently, ultimately each makes a similar argument: the Protestant construction of "sanctified" marriage could prove just as much an obstacle to women's spiritual integrity as any profane or worldly distraction. Brontë

---

2. Fullerton was born Georgiana Charlotte Leveson-Gower, the daughter of Lord Granville Leveson-Gower and Lady Harriet Cavendish. She married Alexander Fullerton, heir to landed estates in England and Ireland, and a member of the Guards, in 1833. Upon Alexander's appointment as attaché to the English embassy in Paris, the Fullertons traveled extensively, taking up residence in both France and Italy. Alexander converted to Roman Catholicism in 1843, and Georgiana joined the church three years later. Fullerton claimed to write in order to raise money for her many charities, and her works deal with explicitly religious themes. In addition to *Ellen Middleton* and *Lady-Bird,* Fullerton published six other novels, assorted short stories, biographies, poems, and a play. Although her first three novels (including *Grantley Manor* [1847]) received considerable public attention, her later works appear to have been popular predominantly among Catholic circles in England and France. More biographical information about Lady Fullerton is available in Henry James Coleridge, *Life of Lady Georgiana Fullerton,* from the French of Mrs. Augustus Craven, 2nd ed. (1888); Fanny M. Taylor's *The Inner Life of Lady Georgiana Fullerton* (1899); and the *Oxford Dictionary of National Biography* (entry by Solveig Robinson).

FIGURE 1.2 *Lady Georgina Fullerton with her son, William Granville.* Image reproduced from Susan Oldfield, Some Records of the Later Life of Harriet, Countess Granville (1901)

and Fullerton were, as women, of course barred from the pulpit. But both their novels can be read as revisionary sermons on marriage. *Jane Eyre*, like the sermons that influence it, persists in constructing the ideal marriage as an emphatically Protestant one. Fullerton's *Lady-Bird*, almost certainly a deliberate "Catholic rewriting" of *Jane Eyre*, proposes Catholic sanctity as an antidote to the spiritual pitfalls inherent in Protestant and secular ideas of marriage. Although each novel asserts the power of religious faith to help women balance the competing demands of sanctity and domesticity, the conclusion of each text betrays a lingering apprehension of the overwhelming secularism of Victorian marriage.

Despite the great disparities between Charlotte Brontë and the aristocratic, Catholic Lady Fullerton, their work exhibits some striking parallels indeed. Most critics who reviewed the works of these women together did not remark upon this. However, in 1853, when each novelist published her third novel (*Villette* and *Lady-Bird*), a reviewer in the *Christian Remembrancer* explained his rationale for reviewing these two best-selling authors in tandem:

> There is enough of a resemblance in the two authoresses [. . .] to justify placing them in contrast and juxtaposition. [. . .] Both excited a very unusual interest and attention by a work of fiction [*Jane Eyre* and *Ellen Middleton* (1844)] . . . both chose female autobiography as the form in which to express, with much energy and power, [their views] [. . .] both, while professing a zeal for religion and a reverence for morality, allowed a heated imagination to betray them into scenes opposed to the interest and dictates of either. (401)

Although we are accustomed to thinking of Brontë as a rebel and a freethinker (however overstated that assessment may be), what surprises here is the critic's accusation of *Fullerton's* seeming disdain for religion and morality. Fullerton, in fact, led so pious a life that her friends and associates attempted, after her death, to build a case for her beatification in the Catholic Church.[3] What really seems to have provoked the reviewer is not Fullerton's piety (or lack thereof), but her unconventional representation of women and female passion. According to this same reviewer, both Brontë and Fullerton endorsed "extravagant creature worship" (402): that is, they "opposed" themselves to religion and morality in making human, romantic love (rather than religious devotion) the highest aspirations of their heroines. Moreover, because Brontë and Fullerton similarly depicted women displaying unsolicited love and passion toward male characters, their female characters were, in the reviewer's estimation, "without the

---

3. In their efforts to build a case for her beatification, Fullerton's friends and biographers downplayed her literary output and emphasized instead her extensive work in philanthropy (see *The Inner Life of Lady Georgiana Fullerton* [1899]). Fullerton gave a great deal of time and money to charitable causes; most notably, she cofounded, with Fanny Margaret Taylor, a Catholic sisterhood, the Poor Servants of the Mother of God. Fullerton would have been pleased that her reputation as a philanthropist soon eclipsed her role as a novelist. Literary accomplishments generated a considerable amount of anxiety for Lady Fullerton's scrupulous conscience. In the later years of Fullerton's life, she took to burning her favorable literary reviews as an exercise in spiritual mortification (*Inner Life* 248). Fullerton's piety was never officially recognized by the Church, but its outward manifestations seem to have been exceptional even among Catholic converts. After the death of their only son, William Granville, in 1855, Georgiana and her husband, Alexander Fullerton, joined a Catholic lay order, The Third Order of St. Francis. From 1857 until her death in 1885, Fullerton devoted herself to ascetic practices, religious contemplation, and care of the poor—all the while continuing her literary work to raise money for charity.

feminine element, infringers of modest restraints, despisers of bashful fears, self-reliant, contemptuous of prescriptive decorum" (442). "A restless heart and a vagrant imagination, though owned by a woman," concluded the review sadly, "can have no sympathy or *true insight* into the really feminine nature" (443; emphasis added).

This critic unwittingly observes what twentieth-century scholars have overlooked—Fullerton's novels, although hardly radical at first glance, *do* exhibit a contempt of prevailing social values—in particular, the Victorian fetish for romantic love and matrimony. Ironically, however, this critic also accuses both Brontë and Fullerton of *promoting* "extravagant creature worship," seemingly unaware that each author's depiction of it was a cautionary example in their respective "sermons" against the sin of erotic idolatry. The fact that both authors, despite their widely diverging religious beliefs, were so fascinated with idolatry attests to a much larger cultural preoccupation with it. In an 1845 sermon, *Beware of Idolatry*, Joseph Irons defines idolatry as a "departure from the simplicity of the worship of God." Irons explains that any obstacle between the worshiper and God can constitute idolatry: "I do not ask whether it is Baal [. . .] or whether it is Dagon, whether it is literature, attainments, personal parts and talents, applause of creatures [. . .], any thing that hath thy heart rather than God, thou art an idolater, and God abhors thee" (156). Many Victorians who articulated their anxieties about idolatry seem to have been concerned primarily about substituting human beings for God. And women were deemed particularly susceptible to this sin. In a letter of 1853, Charlotte Yonge describes the spiritual pitfalls of idolizing others, remarking that "I know women have a tendency that way [toward hero-worship], and it frightens me, because the most sensible and strong-minded are liable to be led astray [. . .]. I am very much afraid of live Bilds [heroes]" (qtd. in Christabel Coleridge 190).

Perhaps most often, however, Victorians equated idolatry with Roman Catholicism—a religious system that appeared to clutter the worshiper's relation with God not only with priestly intermediaries, but also with innumerable saints, liturgical formalities, "sacred" relics, and other material fetishes. Evangelical novelist Charlotte Tonna, in her memoirs, describes how she inculcated a young deaf boy with a thorough hatred of Catholic idolatry, so that one day he "worshiped" a hairbrush in mockery of Catholics and then scolded it: "Bad god, Bad god!" (201). Tonna reports being at once startled and gratified by the "sudden and violent turn his feelings took against Popery" (201). "How guilty I felt!" she exclaims. "However, I distinctly intimated my detestation of idolatry, and confirmed his strong repudiation of it" (*Personal Recollections* 203). Tonna's anti-

Catholicism seems to have been extreme even for her time, but she was far from alone in calling Catholics idolaters. Walter Farquhar Hook, in an 1842 sermon entitled *Peril of Idolatry,* argues that despite "much to admire in the Romish church" and "many similarities" between Catholicism and Anglicanism, Catholic idolatry (which he identifies primarily as Catholics' devotion for the Virgin Mary) will forever stand in the way of ecumenical reconciliation. Indeed, the frequent interchange of "idolater" for "Catholic" in much popular literature constructed the two words as synonyms in the Victorian imagination.[4]

Considering the extent to which *both* romantic love and Catholicism were troped as idolatry in Victorian culture, it should be no surprise that women, in representing and critiquing Victorian marriage as potentially idolatrous, should appropriate aspects of Catholicism as well. Brontë and Fullerton both suggest, however, that Catholics did not have the corner on idolatry; Evangelical Protestantism, in its zeal to reclaim marriage as a holy vocation, could in turn thwart women's *ultimate* vocation to serve God. To understand how Protestantism could be deemed implicit in idolatrous practices, we must examine more thoroughly Protestant discourses on marriage, and, in particular, the figure of Milton's Eve. Eve figured prominently in early nineteenth-century sermons and tracts on marriage, and both Brontë's and Fullerton's novels attempt to come to terms with Eve's implications for Victorian women of faith.

Searching for Miss Righteous

The Protestant Evangelical Context

A survey of eighteenth- and early nineteenth-century conduct books and sermons on the topic of marriage reveals two points in common: first, a pressing concern over the growing secularization of marriage, and second, the extent to which the model of Milton's Eve enchanted clergymen across religious denominations. Repeatedly, conduct books and sermons urged readers to choose marriage partners who were earnest and upstanding Christians. Sermons such as Thomas Jackson's represented religious compatibility not merely as preferential, but *essential* to happiness both in this world and the next. After likening the unbelieving wife to a corpse, Jackson explains: "In a word, she is dead in trespasses and sins. Go, and be happy

---

4. Kathleen M. Vejvoda emphasizes this connection in her dissertation "The Dialectic of Idolatry: Roman Catholicism and the Victorian Heroine" (2000). Vejvoda's work is an excellent resource for further study of Victorians' obsession with idolatry, which they considered "a serious and compelling moral problem" (Vejvoda, "Idolatry in *Jane Eyre*," 241).

in such a partner if you can! Think what gloomy evenings you must pass in such society; there can be no spiritual conversation [. . .]." Even more serious, however, than "gloomy" nights at home and awkward mixings in society, is the risk posed to the believer's immortal soul. "Even Ahab would not have been half so wicked," cautions Jackson, "if he had not married a Jezebel" (31). In his popular treatise, *The Golden Wedding Ring* (1813), Anglican preacher John Clowes, in an attempt "to restore marriage to its primitive sanctity, purity, and bliss, by pointing out its connection with religion" (Foreword), describes "pure conjugal love" as "a representative image or picture, of the union of all divine and heavenly principles, from their SUPREME SOURCE to their lowest state of descent and operation" (13). Not surprisingly, such comparisons of marriage to the divine hierarchy inevitably relied upon gender hierarchy and essentialist claims. Clowes casts husbands in the role of Supreme Being, while wives represent the "lowest state." "For contemplation he and valour form'd," declares Clowes of the husband, quoting Milton's description of Adam; "For softness she, and sweet attractive grace; / He for GOD only, and she for God in him."

The perfect wife, like Milton's Eve, was to rely upon her husband's judgment in matters of religious opinion and even morality. Clowes states that "every sensible and well-disposed woman attaches herself to a man of *understanding*, and that every sensible and well-disposed man attaches himself most to the woman who *most loves his understanding*. Here then is the true ground of the *union of minds* between two persons of different sexes" (9; emphasis in original). Because women's salvation relied so heavily on men's "understanding" of religion and God's will, conduct books and sermons urged women to be especially careful in their choice of a spouse. In his often-reprinted sermon, *The Mutual Duties of Husbands and Wives* (1801), Dissenting minister William Jay (who also quotes Milton) allows that "[i]f the demands of a husband oppose the will of GOD, you are pre-engaged by a law of universal operation, and 'ought' [sic] obey GOD rather than man'" (10). Yet Jay never provides any examples or explanations of such "exceptional" cases. He then goes on to say that although man "is often absurd in his designs, capricious in his temper, tyrannical in his claims, and degrading in his authority," women, by consequence of Eve's original sin, "cannot dispense with this subjection [to husbands] without opposing the express will of GOD, and violating the marriage laws to which you have acceded" (13).[5]

By invoking Milton's Adam and Eve as a model for the perfect mar-

---

5. Similarly, the Presbyterian minister James Fordyce, in *Sermons to Young Women* (a text that ran through at least fourteen editions between 1765 and 1809), lauds "that obsequious majesty ascribed [by Milton] to innocent Eve" (130). He urges his female readers to "command by obeying, and by yielding to conquer" (131).

riage, preachers drew upon a literary tradition that was unmistakably Protestant. Only Protestant Christianity, these sermons implied, restored to marriage the dignity that God originally intended it to have. Robert Sandeman, in *The Honour of Marriage Opposed to All Impurities* (1800), describes the destructiveness of Catholic monasticism: "By extravagant commendations of virginity and single life [. . .] the honour of marriage in general was greatly sunk, and marriage forbidden to numerous classes of men altogether, by which means uncleanness reigned through the nations called Christian, attended by the most inhuman cruelty, now necessary, to conceal its effects" (20). Luke Barlow, in *Marriage Commended, and Adultery Condemned* (1816), piously affirms that "in opposition to the doctrine and practice of that 'Mother of Harlots,' we have the testimony of God, and of the most pious men in the purest state of the church in [marriage's] favor" (15). And Jackson, quoting Hebrews 13:4 ("Marriage is honourable in all"), explains that "it is highly probable that the *Holy Spirit* intended, in this scripture, to anticipate and expose the sentiments and the practice of the *church of Rome;* who denies marriage to her clergy, under the idea that persons set apart to sacred offices are too holy to enter into it" (21; emphasis in original). Jackson, calling this idea an "antichristian sentiment," also establishes it as an anti-Protestant one as well.

By presenting the marriage bond as primarily an instrument of divine salvation, preachers sought to achieve a fundamental goal of Evangelicalism—to infuse the sacred into everyday life. But the transference of this doctrine into the genre of domestic fiction reveals the slipperiness of boundaries between sacred and secular. Hannah More, in her phenomenally popular novel *Coelebs in Search of a Wife* (1808), delivers a fictionalized sermon on holy marriage consistent with Evangelical preaching. The novel's hero, young Charles ("Coelebs" means "bachelor"), sets out upon the death of his beloved father to find a wife worthy of his high religious and moral principles. Charles embarks on a Protestant quest; a clergyman in the book, describing the right to marry as "emancipation from the old [Catholic] restrictions," advises Charles that "we ourselves ought, by improving the character of our wives, repay the debt we owe to the ecclesiastical laws of Protestantism for the privilege of possessing them" (70). Charles does due honor to the Protestant reformers. After meeting a great many silly, frivolous women in the course of his travels, Charles arrives at the home of his father's friend, Mr. Stanley, and finds his perfect Christian mate in Stanley's daughter Lucilla, a woman whose upbringing has been deliberately patterned on Milton's Eve. Lucilla is virtuous, quiet, and possesses no opinions independent of what she has been taught. She will, the novel assures us, be ideally suited for a Miltonic marriage, in which Charles lives "for God alone, and [Lucilla] for God in him." When Charles seeks Lucilla's hand in marriage, Mr. Stanley reveals that he had conspired with Charles's late father in "educating our children for each other; in inspiring them with corresponding tastes, similar inclinations, and especially [. . .] *an exact conformity in their religious views*" (223; emphasis added).

The fathers' successful scheme, and the novel as a whole, presents religious compatibility as a crucial foundation to a happy marriage. Yet the novel's emphasis on what Mr. Stanley describes as "the great arts of *home enjoyment*" (112) exposes the material underpinnings of this idyll. Evangelicals sought to enter God's heavenly home, but in the meantime they would enjoy domestic bliss on earth. While much of "home enjoyment" seems to depend on what Stanley calls the "*morality* of being agreeable and even entertaining in one's own family circle" (112; emphasis in original), certainly Stanley's wealth does not diminish the pleasantness of his domestic life. Charles notes that Stanley's mansion is "commodious and elegant" (59) and that his table is well supplied for guests. Aside from material resources, this home comfort also depends upon the considerable exertions of Lucilla Stanley. Having taken over the household duties from her mother at age sixteen, Lucilla oversees the accounts, supervises the servants, teaches her younger siblings, cares for the poor, acts as her father's secretary and nurse, and tends the lush gardens on the estate, all the while keeping up a course of improving reading (62). No wonder that Florence Nightingale criticized the Evangelical family as being all-consuming for women.

More's novel also has mixed success in counteracting what Mrs. Stanley describes as "the omnipotence of love" (82) promoted by so many foolish popular novels. More's novel—like the sermons surrounding its production—insist that men choose women for spiritual and other interior qualities rather than mere surface attraction. Not surprisingly, however, this heightened dimension of compatibility also serves to render romantic love more irresistible than ever. And despite the novel's insistence on *religious* partnership, the notion of literally creating two people *for* each other (as Charles and Lucilla's fathers do) resonates uncannily well with secular notions of finding a "soul mate" and "the one," ideals disseminated in twenty-first-century romantic comedies and Internet articles on dating.

These tensions between spiritual and worldly marriage, barely perceptible in More's novel, are confronted head-on in Brontë's *Jane Eyre*. Charlotte Brontë, as the daughter of an Anglican clergyman with pronounced Evangelical views, undoubtedly was familiar both with More's novel and with Evangelical tracts and sermons on marriage. *Jane Eyre*, in which the heroine narrates *her* travels and *her* quest for the perfect mate, could be considered a rewriting of *Coelebs in Search of a Wife*. Jane's search for a husband levels a stinging critique of Evangelical models of marriage patterned on Milton's Adam and Eve. At the same time, Jane longs for a marriage of true spiritual and emotional compatibility, and the narrative struggles to frame Jane's marriage as a sanctified vocation, one in which she and Rochester, like Lucilla and Charles, can enjoy domestic bliss while also ensuring the joys of the world to come. *Jane Eyre's* resemblance to a Protestant sermon on marriage is intensified by the subtle but pervasive references to Catholicism throughout the narrative. Just as Protestant clergymen presented Catholicism as the enemy of godly marriage, Catholicism in *Jane Eyre* is almost always aligned with behaviors and interpersonal dynamics antithetical to Jane's ideal of true love. Unlike the sermons, however, *Jane Eyre* suggests a dangerous slippage between the seemingly polar opposites of Protestant and Catholic. While Jane's ideal marriage is still a Protestant one, the novel suggests that Protestant constructions of marriage—in particular, the model of Milton's Adam and Eve—could contain within them the seeds of Catholic idolatry.

Jane in Search of a Husband

In *Coelebs in Search of a Wife*, Charles's challenge is to find a woman and a home compatible with his Christian worldview. Jane Eyre's journey is significantly more complicated by the fact that at the beginning of the book she could not even be considered a Christian. Although Brocklehurst's examination of Jane reveals that she is familiar with some parts of the Bible (mostly the Hebrew Scriptures), her subsequent conversation with Helen betrays an ignorance of the basic tenets of Christianity. Until meeting Helen Burns, "an eye for an eye"—a tenet Helen labels as "heathen" and "savage" (68)—is Jane's governing creed. Clearly, young, "heathen" Jane is the product of Mrs. Reed's neglect and a domestic sphere that is cold, comfortless, and most important, thoroughly secular. Jane's journey exposes her to a succession of domestic spaces, few, if any, of which provide Jane with the proper balance of spiritual nourishment and temporal comfort. Jane's search for a comfortable yet sanctified domestic space parallels the development of a spiritual self that struggles to love God above any human creature.

Protestant discourses on marriage seem to influence Jane's longing for a spiritually and emotionally compatible soul mate, yet she emphatically resists the role of Milton's Eve. In contrast to Milton's account, which, like Genesis itself, renders Eve an agent in Adam's fall, *Jane Eyre* implies that Adam could be as much a stumbling block for Eve. A revisionary Protestant "sermon" on marriage, *Jane Eyre* explores the theological dangers inherent in both Milton's and More's marital ideal through the novel's insistent concern with idolatry. Jane's idolatry for Rochester, which temporarily "eclipses" God (307), and St. John's arrogant certainty of God's will suggest a dangerous conflation between male spiritual mediators and the divine itself. Rather than regard her husband as the mouthpiece of God, the novel suggests, a woman might come to mistake her husband *for* God. And while Jane identifies herself as a Protestant Christian, the novel's critique of Protestant models of marriage and of human idolatry relies heavily on images and popular stereotypes of Catholicism.

While I have argued elsewhere that idolatry in *Jane Eyre* is a *leitmotif* centrally bound up with the heroine's spiritual progress, I am indebted to Kathleen Vejvoda's 2003 essay, "Idolatry in Jane Eyre," for drawing my attention to the prominence of Catholic imagery in the novel and its relation to Jane's struggles with idolatry.[6] Vejvoda regards Rochester as the figure in the novel most closely associated with Catholicism; his Continental wanderings and his "customary reliance on the rhetoric of Roman Catholicism" (245) in his conversation mark him as a figure especially susceptible to "creature worship" who also encourages it in others, namely Jane. Rochester's Thornfield, as Vejvoda notes, is described more like a church than a home, and Bertha's attic "is a repository of symbols linked to medieval Catholicism" (246). Vejvoda's insightful essay has inspired me to identify further appropriations of Catholicism in the novel. Catholic associations, in fact, saturate nearly every domestic space Jane inhabits on the course of her spiritual progress. Furthermore, while the novel appropriates Catholic imagery to code certain characters, behaviors, and attitudes as idolatrous, "Catholicized" spaces throughout *Jane Eyre* also demonstrate the narrative's preoccupation with the dangers of a wholly secular, material domesticity that pampers the body at the expense of the spirit. Throughout the novel, Jane seeks not only a way to love erotically without affronting God, but a domestic space in which she can be at once physically comfortable *and* spiritually vital.

Jane's obsession with physical comfort is evident from the first lines of the novel: "We saw no possibility of taking a walk that day," she notes,

---

6. I have already discussed *Jane Eyre*'s representation of Victorian marriage as potentially idolatrous in my article "Jane's Crown of Thorns: Feminism and Christianity in *Jane Eyre*" (2002). My later reading of Vejvoda's article, "Idolatry in *Jane Eyre*" (2003), helped me to see the "Catholic" resonances of idolatrous marriage in Brontë's novel.

as the "cold winter wind" and "rain so penetrating" had driven all the children inside. "I never liked long walks [. . .] dreadful to me was the coming home in the raw twilight, with nipped fingers and toes [. . .]" (13). At splendid Gateshead, Jane experiences a paradoxical life of asceticism in the midst of luxury; while her cousins Eliza and Georgiana revel in their splendid holiday clothes and John "gorged himself habitually at table" (16), Jane, in contrast, is beaten up, tied up, and locked up in the book's opening chapters. So traumatized is she by this experience that she considers "never eating or drinking more, and letting myself die" (22). Jane's early experiences of physical mortification seem to contribute to her constant cravings for material comfort throughout the novel. While still at Gateshead, Jane rejects the idea of living with poor relatives, dwelling on the thoughts of "ragged clothes, scanty food, [and] fireless grates" (32). Jane's forced asceticism, combined with her longing for creature comforts, is aptly represented through Gateshead's Catholic associations. In Victorian anti-Catholic propaganda, Catholicism is condemned *both* for pampering the bodily senses *and* unnaturally repressing and mortifying them. Brontë, like many anti-Catholic writers of her era, seems strangely unconcerned with this obvious contradiction in popular perceptions of Catholicism.[7] But this paradox serves Brontë well, since her novel appropriates Catholic elements to represent any domestic space that is "unbalanced" in its orientation toward either the material or the spiritual. And just about every space Jane inhabits fits this definition, as she seeks a truly Protestant domestic space like that of Hannah More's novel, in which an interest in flowerbeds is not incompatible with larger spiritual strivings.

Gateshead's Catholic associations are all the more significant because they are concentrated in the Red Room, the "womb" of Jane's self, and the real starting point of her *bildungsroman*. As Gilbert and Gubar note, Jane's traumatic experience in the Red Room "forces her deeply into herself" (340); it is a place where she becomes cognizant of the extent of her entrapment: psychological, physical, and social. Gilbert and Gubar describe it as a paradigmatic scene in the novel, since later, crucial moments in Jane's life are "variations on the central, red-room motif of enclosure and escape" (341). Indeed, the red room is a clear and highly effective symbol for Jane's rage at the circumstances in which she finds herself. But what do we make

---

7. In *Villette*, Lucy Snowe observes that in the Catholic school in which she teaches, "great pains were taken to hide chains with flowers: a subtle essence of Romanism pervaded every arrangement: large sensual indulgence (so to speak) was permitted by way of counterpoise to jealous spiritual restraint. [. . .] There, as elsewhere, the CHURCH strove to bring up her children robust in body, feeble in soul, fat, ruddy, hale, joyous, unthinking, unquestioning. 'Eat, drink, and live!' she says. 'Look after your bodies; leave your souls to me.'"

of the fact that the Red Room is also a parodic description of a Roman Catholic sanctuary?

> [. . .] [I]t was one of the largest and stateliest chambers in the mansion. A bed supported on massive pillars of mahogany, hung with curtains of deep-red damask, stood out like a tabernacle in the centre, the two large windows, with their blinds always drawn down, were half shrouded in festoons and falls of similar drapery; the carpet was red; the table at the foot of the bed was covered with a crimson cloth [. . .]. Out of these deep surrounding shades rose high, and glared white, the piled-up mattresses and pillows of the bed, spread with a snowy Marseilles counterpane. Scarcely less prominent was an ample, cushioned easy-chair near the head of the bed, also white, with a footstool before it; and looking, as I thought, like a pale throne. (21)

In the anti-Catholic Protestant Victorian imagination, red would immediately have conjured up images of the Scarlet Woman and the Whore of Babylon. The four "massive pillars" sheltering a tabernacle calls to mind the sanctuary of St. Peter's Basilica at the Vatican, complete with a crimson-covered "altar" and a bishop's throne. This association of the "womb" of Jane's self with a Catholic church is highly significant. Clearly, young Jane harbors tendencies toward Catholic excesses such as idolatry, materialism, and unnatural asceticism; all these tendencies, along with Jane's antisocial rage, must be contained and properly channeled for her to become a mature, moral, and productive member of society. While still at Gateshead, however, Jane's rampant, unacceptable impulses are also coded Catholic through her half-humorous reference to herself as "a sort of infantine Guy Fawkes" and the fact that she is expected to confess her sins to Aunt Reed. When Jane, as a grown woman, returns to the bedside of her dying aunt, she recalls the footstool "at which I had a hundred times been sentenced to kneel, to ask pardon for offences, by me, uncommitted" (258).

When Jane leaves Gateshead for Lowood, she encounters the first of three male characters (two of whom are Protestant clergymen) who are convinced that they know God's plans for Jane. The Reverend Brocklehurst tells Jane's fellow pupils that she is not "one of God's own lambs" but "a little castaway: not a member of the true flock, but evidently an interloper and an alien." He tells her teachers to monitor her every act and to "punish her body to save her soul; if, indeed, such salvation be possible" (78). Brocklehurst, by attempting to condemn Jane in God's name, sets himself up as the voice of God, or an idol. This dynamic between Brocklehurst and his students is emphasized by Rochester's later, ironic comment, "[Y]ou girls probably worshiped him, as a convent full of religieuses worshiped their director" (140). Although Jane emphatically denies that she or her schoolmates "worshiped" Brocklehurst, the description of Lowood and its inhabitants indeed suggests a Catholic convent. The house, which had a "church-like aspect," was surrounded by a fenced-in, "convent like" garden (59). Brocklehurst, in his attempt "to mortify in these girls the lusts of the flesh" (76), dresses them alike, subjects them to a harsh ascetic regimen, and, most significant, cuts their hair—an act traditionally required of nuns upon taking the veil. Despite Brocklehurst's militant Evangelicalism, which would have distanced him doctrinally from Catholicism, his status as an "idol" renders him a Catholic figure, and Lowood another Romish landscape. Jane, in moving from one "Catholic" setting to another (from the church to the convent), is still far from finding a true, Protestant home.[8]

Fortunately, Reverend Brocklehurst's power is limited. Helen Burns quickly exposes him as a sham: "Mr Brocklehurst is not a god," she tells Jane, "nor is he even a great and admired man" (81). At the same time, Helen warns Jane of her sinful tendency to privilege human over divine love: "Hush, Jane! You think too much of the love of human beings [...] God waits only the separation of spirit and flesh to crown us with a full reward" (81–82). The extent to which Helen's teaching takes root is not clear at first; however, from the first moments of her love for Rochester, Jane is aware of the perils of human idolatry. Jane's passion, as much as Rochester's arguments, distorts her judgment, so that "while he spoke my very Conscience and Reason turned traitors against me, and charged me with crime in resisting him" (356). Jane is particularly susceptible to Rochester's seduction because he makes his appeal on religious and moral grounds. Rochester puts upon Jane's shoulders the responsibility for his moral rebirth: "Is the wandering and sinful, but now rest-seeking and repentant man," he queries, "justified in daring the world's opinion, in order to attach to him for ever, this gentle, gracious, genial stranger; thereby securing his own peace of mind and regeneration of life?" (246). Rochester, rake that he is, attempts to manipulate Jane through the same Miltonic notion of male moral superiority so celebrated by nineteenth-century Protestant clergymen. Rochester insistently describes his romantic desire as a product of God's will when he proposes to Jane, explicitly an Eve-figure in his "Eden-like" orchard (278), contending that "my Maker sanctions what I do" (287).

---

8. Although of course she gets glimpses of one, as the motherly Miss Temple treats Jane and Helen to tea and seed cake in her room, which "contained a good fire, and looked cheerful" (86)

While Jane recognizes the presumptiveness of Rochester's position, she nonetheless cannot resist the role Rochester has assigned her. In response to his religious arguments, Jane retorts: "Sir [. . .] a Wanderer's repose or a Sinner's reformation should never depend on a fellow-creature. Men and women die; philosophers falter in wisdom, and Christians in goodness: if any one you know has suffered and erred, let him look higher than his equals for strength to amend, and solace to heal" (246). Jane's insistence that an individual's salvation "should never depend on a fellow-creature" is consistent with Evangelicalism's emphasis on a "religion of the heart"—that is, an intimate, direct, and unmediated relationship between the soul and its Creator. But Jane cannot live up to her spoken convictions.[9] Shortly afterwards she reveals the extent of her spiritual dependence upon Rochester, who has become "almost my hope of heaven." More frequently, however, the text emphasizes Rochester's spiritual dependence upon Jane. Victorian readers, familiar with Christian typology, undoubtedly would have noticed the strong religious resonances of Jane's account of the first Thornfield fire: "I [. . .] deluged the bed and its occupant, flew back to my own room, brought my own water-jug, baptized the couch afresh, and by God's aid, succeeded in extinguishing the flames which were devouring it" (168). While the flames enveloping Rochester prefigure the second, devastating fire at Thornfield, allegorically the text depicts Jane throwing the waters of baptism—spiritual rebirth—upon Rochester, ostensibly quenching the fires of Hell which threaten to devour him.

Not surprisingly, Thornfield, as the site of Rochester and Jane's mutual idolatry, is no more of a proper home for Jane than Lowood, despite its luxurious contrasts. Jane, upon first meeting Mrs. Fairfax, knitting by the fire, marvels over "the beau-ideal of domestic comfort" she encounters. But Thornfield is *too* comfortable. Jane, rather like Goldilocks trying out beds, surveys her new existence at Thornfield and declares it a "too easy chair" (133). Jane's life there—at least before she is confronted with the challenge of reforming Rochester—is "an existence whose very privileges of security and ease I was becoming incapable of appreciating" (132). But even Rochester's arrival at Thornfield cannot transform it into a proper home for Jane. Rochester understands the moral contagion housed in Thornfield; when Jane refers to it as "a splendid mansion," Rochester retorts, "[Y]ou cannot discern that the gilding is slime and the silk draperies cobwebs; that the marble is sordid slate, and the polished woods mere refuse chips and scaly bark" (242). Because there is no spiritual element to Rochester's life at Thornfield, his home is nothing but a pile of material dross.

9. Charlotte Brontë, along with many of her contemporaries, "did not look with favor upon the 'serious conversation' in which many Evangelicals delighted, preferring to keep their religion a matter for private contemplation" (Elisabeth Jay 255).

To further emphasize the antidomestic character of Thornfield, it, like Lowood, is implicitly compared to a convent. Anti-Catholic Protestant tales of convents—a popular nineteenth-century genre that I discuss in chapter 3—presented them as dark, corrupt, gothic interiors: the antithesis of happy Victorian homes. Vejvoda has argued, persuasively, that Eliza Reed is "a nun shadow-self whom [Jane] must disavow" (249). Bertha Mason is another, more sinister nun "shadow" for Jane. When Jane sees Bertha for the first time, she stands before the mirror wearing Jane's wedding veil, which she then rends apart. If Bertha is Jane's "truest and darkest double," as Gilbert and Gubar argue, is her headdress a bride's veil or a nun's veil? Victorian anti-Catholic literature commonly represented the newly professed nun as radically opposite—and at once perilously similar—to the radiant Victorian bride.[10] Moreover, insane nuns (their brains addled from their "unnatural" existence) were stock characters in Victorian anti-Catholic novels, and they were usually kept locked away in some remote part of the convent. Bertha's nun-status is also reinforced by the fact that, as a Spanish Creole, she is most likely Catholic as well. Her third-story quarters, after all, contain a massive cabinet bearing "an ebon crucifix and a dying Christ" (237). Considering Jane's own repressed Catholic sympathies and leanings, Bertha's Catholicism and nunlike existence add an additional, sinister dimension to her role of "externalizing the free, uninhibited, often criminal self" (Rosenfeld qtd. in Gilbert and Gubar 360).

Of course Jane flees the "convent" of Thornfield, as well as the temptation to make Rochester her god: "Not a human being that ever lived could wish to be loved better than I was loved; and him who thus loved me I absolutely worshipped: and I must renounce love and idol. One drear word comprised by intolerable duty—'Depart!'" (354). While this temptation is difficult to resist, Jane nonetheless remains firm in her resolution to leave Thornfield and expresses little genuine doubt about her decision. Surprisingly, it is St. John Rivers—that ostensibly unattractive, even repulsive character—who poses to Jane the greater temptation, the one she clearly has the more difficulty resisting. The difficulty of Jane's position at this point of the novel only becomes evident once we accept that Jane truly and sincerely regards her cousin as a saintly, devoted Christian. In light of Evangelical tracts and sermons counseling women to think more of religion than love as a foundation for marriage, St. John would have

---

10. See chapter 3 for explicit comparisons of nuns' profession ceremonies to Victorian weddings.

been viewed in many circles as a most eligible bachelor indeed.[11] Thus while Jane has no trouble resisting the sophistry of the religious hypocrite Brocklehurst, and can, with difficulty, see through the machinations of the all-too-human Rochester, how can she repudiate a "good man, pure as the deep sunless source," in possession of a "crystal conscience" (458)?

Critics have filled pages detailing the reasons why St. John repulses Jane, but although he is clearly self-aggrandizing, manipulative, inflexible, and legalistic, these traits are presented to the reader less as inconsistencies or blemishes within his otherwise sterling character,than as the inevitable result of it. In short, St. John buckles under the weight of his own perfection. His countenance—so perfect and regular it suggests the hard lineaments of Greek statuary—accurately reflects a soul made rigid by its own moral strengths. Despite Jane's recognition of St. John's personal shortcomings, she does not let her awareness of "the corrupt man within him" (457) diminish her veneration for the "pure Christian" (457) side of his nature. Jane even suggests that St. John's faults are part and parcel of a truly great and active nature: "[H]e was," she observes, "of the material from which nature hews her heroes—Christian and Pagan—her law-givers, her statesmen, her conquerors: a steadfast bulwark for great interests to rest upon; but, at the fireside, too often a cold cumbrous column, gloomy and out of place" (438).

Considering Jane's "veneration" of St. John, then, his attractiveness to her—and the difficulty with which she turns down his proposal—is more complex than any Freudian inclination for abjection or self-punishment. As Jane considers St. John's offer, Brontë does not ironize her reflection: "[I]s not the occupation he now offers me truly the most glorious man can adopt or God assign?" (450). That Jane believes in St. John's cause is perhaps best demonstrated by her complete willingness to help spread the Gospel in India, despite all its attendant privations, on the condition that she be allowed to remain single. To complicate matters further, Jane must once again deal with a domineering male character who is firmly convinced of God's will for them both. Because God is all-knowing, St. John seems to believe that he himself, as God's servant, is likewise omniscient. "I am the servant of an infallible master," he exults, "I am not going out under human guidance [. . .] my lawgiver, my captain, is the All-perfect" (447). Just as Rochester perceives in Jane "an instrument" of God and tries

---

11. *Considerations on Marriage, Addressed to Christian Professors* (1840) urges women to think of love "as little as possible" (11) and "never to give their hearts to an object, whose heart was not, as far as they could judge, on scriptural grounds, given to God [. . .] never to arrange, by their own choice an act, to spend a life of unsanctified enjoyment on earth, with one with whom they cannot hope to spend an eternity of hallowed happiness in heaven" (13).

to convince her that to abandon him would be an act of wickedness, St. John warns Jane, "[I]f you reject [my offer], it is not me that you deny, but God" (455).

All these elements—Jane's veneration of St. John as a stalwart Christian, her support of his missionary cause, and St. John's unwavering certainty of God's will for them both—appear to cloud and obscure her judgment even more than her passionate love for Rochester had. At this crucial juncture of the narrative, Jane—just moments away from being "chained for life to a man who regarded one but as a useful tool" (463)—cannot bring herself to rely solely on St. John's judgment: "I could decide if I were but certain," she tells him, "were I but convinced that it is God's will I should marry you, I could vow to marry you here and now—come afterwards what would!" (466). At this point in the novel the reader arrives at that notorious "thumping piece of Gothic claptrap" (Prescott 90) which depicts Jane, in response to her frantic prayer, suddenly able to hear Rochester's voice summoning her. Her reaction:

> I broke from St. John; who had followed, and would have detained me. It was my time to assume ascendancy. My powers were in play, and in force. I told him to forebear question or remark; I desired him to leave me: I must, and would be alone. [. . .] I mounted to my chamber; locked myself in; fell on my knees; and prayed in my way—a different way to St. John's, but effective in its own fashion. I seemed to penetrate very near a Mighty Spirit; and my soul rushed out in gratitude at His feet. I rose from the thanksgiving—took a resolve—and lay down, unscared, enlightened [. . .]. (467; emphasis in original)

When read as a Protestant "sermon," this scene is indisputably the climax of the narrative. Jane, placed in the position of Milton's Eve by St. John, a man she regards as a Christian hero, nonetheless finds the strength to resist his influence and instead turn to God directly in prayer. Her way of praying is different than St. John's but "effective in its own fashion," and Jane, who retires feeling "unscared" and "enlightened," has demonstrated that she needs no male spiritual intermediaries, no matter how noble their intentions or saintly their characters.

While there are fewer Catholic allusions in the Moor House section of the novel than elsewhere, some hints nonetheless point both to St. John's idolatry and the fact that residence at Moor House, although pleasant for Jane, is still not her true calling. Although St. John wants to marry Jane, his renunciation of his family and of his true romantic desires for his vocation liken him to a Catholic priest. As St. John contemplates the lovely

Rosamond Oliver, he crushes a tuft of daisies with his foot (406), representing the "unnatural" repression of his feelings. Clerical celibacy was presented as similarly "unnatural" in Victorian anti-Catholic literature. St. John's training of Jane is also telling; he teaches her Hindustanee to prepare her for the mission field. By doing so, however, St. John figuratively transforms Jane into one of the same "idolaters" that she is meant to help convert in India. Finally, although Moor House is decidedly not a convent, Rochester's earlier comment about Lowood—that the girls all must have "worshiped" their director—echoes uneasily through this part of the novel. Clearly, Diana and Mary have minds of their own, and they are far less susceptible to their brothers' influence than Jane is. Yet curiously, almost every domestic scene in the novel (with the exception of Gateshead) contains a community of women looking up to, or directed by, an authoritative male figure. Jane and Rochester may seem alone much of the time at Thornfield, but Mrs. Fairfax, Adele, Grace Poole, and Bertha are also indisputably part of their household. And despite the rich possibilities of the female community Jane so enjoys at Moor House, Brontë chooses to disrupt it (much as she does in *Shirley*) for a romantic dyad at the end. Rochester becomes Jane's only community—the Rivers sisters each marry, and even poor Adele gets packed off to boarding school. This ambivalence about female community is a disturbing element of all Brontë's novels, and leads us to wonder whether Brontë, like so many outspoken critics of female convents, considered permanent female communities as "unnatural."

But convent or no convent, Moor House, like Thornfield, is simply too comfortable for Jane. When Jane comes into her inheritance, her first act is to transform Moor House into her ideal of domestic bliss. She says to St. John:

> My first aim will be to clean down [. . .] Moor House from chamber to cellar; my next to rub it up with bees-wax, oil, and indefinite number of cloths, till it glitters again; my third, to arrange every chair, table, bed, carpet, with mathematical precision; afterwards I shall go near to ruin you in coals and peat to keep up good fires in every room; and lastly, the two days preceding that on which your sisters are expected, will be devoted by Hannah and me to such a beating of eggs, sorting of currants, grating of spices, compounding of Christmas cakes, chopping up of materials for mince-pies, and solemnizing of other culinary rites, as words can convey but an inadequate notion of the uninitiated like you. (435)

When we recall that the last Christmas Jane described was at Gateshead, when she was excluded from all festivities, we can well understand the importance of this Christmas feast (and the variety of sensual comforts it promises) for Jane. St. John, in response, admonishes her not to turn "slothful" and advises her to "look beyond Moor House and Morton, and sisterly society, and the selfish calm and sensual comfort of civilized affluence. [. . .] And try to restrain the disproportionate fervour with which you throw yourself into common-place home pleasures" (436). Jane immediately dismisses St. John's response, and, like her, we may see little else in it beyond St. John's usual overzealous and curmudgeonly nature. But taken within the context of Jane's anxious search for a comfortable *and* spiritually uplifting domestic space, St. John's condemnation of "common-place home pleasures" assumes greater weight and significance.

When Jane arrives at the site of her final home, Ferndean, her description of its uncomfortable accommodations might please even an ascetic such as St. John. Because of Ferndean's "ineligible and insalubrious site" (478) Rochester had left it untenanted; the rooms were mostly unfurnished, and when Jane arrives, she notes its "dank and green [. . .] decaying walls" (479). Jane, with her longings for comfort and domesticity, truly has her work cut out for her; Rochester himself, like his house, is a wreck. Jane immediately sets out to "clean down" both. "Summoning Mary, I soon had the room in more cheerful order: I prepared him, likewise, a comfortable repast" (485). After supper, Jane combs Rochester's hair and resolves on the morrow "not to rise on your hearth with only a glass of water, [. . .] I must bring an egg at the least, to say nothing of fried ham" (487). Jane and Rochester's domestic situation is a peculiar one, indeed, but it seems appropriate that Jane's residence at Ferndean—and, more important, her marriage to the maimed, blind, and demanding Rochester—require a certain degree of self-denial, especially after St. John's warnings about "sensual comfort." Jane's final domestic situation is not comfortable, but it does satisfy her deepest hungers for love. Jane's marriage, therefore, is framed as self-gratification rather than self-renunciation. When Rochester suggests that Jane "delight[s] in sacrifice," Jane replies, "To be privileged to put my arms round what I value—to press my lips to what I love [. . .] is that to make a sacrifice? If so, then certainly I delight in sacrifice" (494).

Ultimately, both extremes, self-indulgence and self-restraint, must be purged from the text before Jane and Rochester's domestic paradise can be realized. Just as Bertha, the lascivious madwoman, conveniently falls to her death, St. John, Jane's *other* double, must remove himself to the deadly privations of missionary life in India. St. John's prominent position at the book's conclusion also helps Jane to frame her own marriage to Rochester as a kind of religious vocation. St. John and Jane, each in their "own fashion," have discerned God's will for themselves and are living out their respective callings. But several elements of the conclusion threaten to undermine this neat binary and, consequently, the spiritual integrity of Jane's happy home. Jane and St. John's callings are certainly different, but they are not equal. As Jane herself notes, St. John "aims to fill a place in the *first rank* of those who are redeemed from the earth [. . .] who are called, and chosen, and faithful" (502; emphasis added). Certainly, St. John's vocation, at the novel's conclusion, is presented as more selfless, heroic, and spiritual than Jane's. This inequality is further reinforced when Jane notes that St. John continues to warn her about the perils of secular domesticity: "[H]e hopes I am happy, and trusts I am not of those who live without God in the world, and mind earthly things" (499). Despite Barry Qualls's assertion, then, that Jane in her marriage to Rochester opts for a more secularized earthly paradise "and alliance [of nature and religion] which does not oppose [. . .] a genuinely human and creative life lived in this world" (46), the conclusion's ambivalence about this secular paradise cannot be overlooked. By the novel's conclusion, Jane and her narrative seem awkwardly straddled between this world and the next. Jane, unwilling to sacrifice herself for heaven, betrays genuine anxiety and guilt about living on earth.

A similar kind of ambivalence also lingers around the issue of idolatry in the novel. Has Jane purged her inner Catholic and overcome her idolatrous tendencies? The book's conclusion offers one, final, explicit Catholic image—Jane figured as the Virgin Mary. This comparison could suggest Jane's acquisition of an autonomous spiritual power. Aside from "keeping and pondering," like Mary, miraculous events in her heart, Jane, when the chastened Rochester first glimpses her, is garbed in a light blue dress, the traditional color of the Virgin. In the very next paragraph, Jane describes Rochester receiving his infant son into his arms. As Rochester holds the infant and "acknowledged that God had tempered judgment with mercy" (501), the reader is reminded once again of Christ's birth and of the infant who came to redeem humankind from sin and death. Jane, initially faced with the dilemma of Milton's Eve, has been transformed from a woman relying on her fallen husband as an intermediary between herself and God, to a woman who is figured in Scripture as favored daughter of the Father and the Holy Spirit. Christian theologians have traditionally figured Mary as a Second or New Eve, one who would, by bringing Christ into the world, participate in the atonement of Eve's Original Sin. Mary's obedience to God's will ("be it unto me according to thy word" [Luke 1:38])[12]

---

12. All scripture passages are taken from the Revised Standard Version of the New Testament.

atones for Eve's original disobedience; Jane, accordingly, through accepting what *she* perceives as Divine Will, has mastered the temptation to be led astray by others. Although faithfully reflecting scriptural precedent in this regard, Jane's retelling of Eve's story is nonetheless a radical departure from Milton's account: Milton (in common, no doubt, with the original writer[s] of Genesis) had not considered that Adam and the Snake might, for Eve, be one and the same.

However, the Marian allusions also raise questions as to what extent Jane has truly liberated her spiritual self from dependency upon fallible human beings and human relationships. Jane's association with Mary may signify a special, unmediated relationship between herself and the Father; it also suggests, however, that Jane now acts as a Mediatrix for Rochester, or even an idol, considering that Victorian anti-Catholic propaganda depicted Catholics "worshiping" Mary. Keeping in mind the fire-quenching scene earlier in the novel, the reader is left with the impression that Jane has simply reverted to her earlier role as her master's Savior. While Jane is still pondering St. John's marriage offer, she tells him, "[B]efore I definitely resolve in quitting England, I will know for certain, whether I cannot be of greater use by remaining in it than by leaving it" (461). Recalling St. John's dedication to potential Indian converts, Jane invests her relationship to Rochester with redemptive, Evangelical overtones. Although Jane's marriage, framed as an alternative missionary endeavor, could be perceived as "balancing the book," ultimately Jane—having taken upon herself the redemption of her husband—rejects Eve in favor of another conventional female role: that of the Victorian household angel. Rochester, who is unable fully to recognize God's love and mercy until Jane returns to him, becomes spiritually as well as physically dependent upon her. Jane, by taking on the role of divine intermediary for Rochester, ironically renounces spiritual autonomy for a reciprocal dependence. Just as St. John cannot follow the will of God and carry out his vocation unless he goes to India, it is only through Rochester, we are led to infer, that Jane can fulfill *her* religious and spiritual destiny.

Jane Eyre's ambivalent conclusion leaves open the possibility that Jane may not have fully resolved her struggles against human idolatry or her desire to reconcile domestic comforts with religious and spiritual integrity. While this compromises the successful outcome of Jane's *bildungsroman,* it does not blunt the force of the novel's critique of Protestant ideals of marriage that mandate women's subordination to husbands in matters of religion and morality. However, Jane's inability to fully reconcile spirit and matter, heaven and home, in her quest points to a problem much larger and more pervasive than traditional Protestant doctrine. Although the novel implies that Protestant teachings on marriage contribute to idolatry, Jane's inability to relinquish fully her idolatrous tendencies or to find a domestic situation that truly measures up to St. John's spiritually heroic vocation is troubling. Jane's problems persist even *after* she has rejected her culture's tradition of female religious subordination (as represented by St. John Rivers); Jane's tendencies toward idolatry are sanctioned not just by human nature, but by an increasingly secular culture that—like Catholicism—celebrates and gratifies innate human desires. This culture is exemplified by the structure and conventions of the relatively new courtship novel, which, for Victorian women, proved a particularly challenging medium through which to articulate doubts about matrimony and domesticity. While Brontë's reservations about marriage and domesticity arguably clash with narrative convention and readerly expectation in all her novels, Fullerton's *Lady-Bird* explicitly targets the romance novel in its condemnation of human idolatry, in part through creating a self-consciously "Catholic" commentary on Brontë's *Jane Eyre*.

Fullerton's *Lady-Bird*: A Catholic Response to *Jane Eyre*

There are numerous likenesses between *Jane Eyre* and *Lady-Bird* in matters of plot, character, and theme.[13] Most significant, each novel's heroine must conquer her tendency to value human love over moral duty in the course of her spiritual progress. Each novel's engagement with the issue of idolatry forms part of a larger, implicit critique of Victorian gender and domestic ideals. These similarities notwithstanding, Fullerton's condemnation of idolatry is no mere shadow of Brontë's. By defining its heroine's spiritual agency and integrity in terms of a Catholic notion of vocation, *Lady-Bird* subverts the expected marriage plot. And while Jane Eyre seeks just the right balance of ease and asceticism in her domestic life, Fullerton's domestic economy allows little room for comfort. Jane's painful sacrifices are temporary and ultimately reap her a greater domestic bliss, but Fullerton does not allow her heroine (or her readers) such consolation. For Fullerton, true love *is* suffering, and that love justifies an intensity of pain that would otherwise seem masochistic. Many of *Lady-Bird*'s critics, unconvinced by this implicit logic, labeled its representation of extreme suffering as "morbid" (Jaeger 302); Emily Dickinson's brother Austen, for example,

---

13. I could not find evidence that Fullerton had read *Jane Eyre*, but it is reasonable to assume that she did, given the novel's popularity and its apparent influence on *Lady-Bird*.

described *Lady-Bird* as "an unhealthy book [. . .] a story of deeper suffering than many ever know—that it's not best *any* should *know* till they are obliged to" (qtd. in Jaeger 302; emphasis in original). The discomfort, even indignation, that the novel sparked in its readers attests to the strength of Fullerton's "sermon." For all its resemblance to Brontë's novel, *Lady-Bird* offers in some ways a stronger, more daring interrogation of Victorian cultural *and* literary conventions.

Lady-Bird's heroine, Gertrude Lifford, is an imaginative, passionate, and impulsive girl whose loveless childhood renders her both rebellious and starved for affection. The sin of idolatry overshadows Lifford Grange, just as it taints so many domestic spaces in *Jane Eyre*. Gertrude's father, a cold, proud, authoritarian man, has no love for Gertrude's mother, an aristocratic Spaniard. An early, failed love affair had "burned out of [Lifford's] heart every trace of gentle feeling and affection," and Gertrude's mother soon realizes that "the little affection his nature was susceptible of had been previously expended on another" (I:214). Angustia herself, however, has also committed idolatry. "[H]alf in weakness, half under a transient impression wrought on her fancy" (I:213) for Henry Lifford, she had renounced her vocation to the religious life. Broken down by her loveless marriage, Angustia has become a paralytic. This family dysfunction is represented in the novel's description of Lifford Grange. Like Gateshead, it possesses "a certain kind of grandeur [. . .] but there was a total absence of comfort in its arrangements, and of charm in its aspect both within and without" (I:4). It is surrounded by "sepulchral-looking" yew trees (I:2), and a nearby stream flows "deeply and sullenly" (I:3) past the dismal garden. Despite the fact that Gertrude's wealthy, distinguished family stems from a long line of Catholic recusants, the book does not employ Catholic stereotypes or imagery in describing her home. Here, the contagion of idolatry is not coded Catholic; rather, the practice of idolatry is linked to Henry's *lack* of Catholic faith. Henry demonstrates merely "an hereditary attachment to a religion, the precepts of which he did not observe, the spirit of which he certainly did not exhibit" (I:5).

The loveless, deathlike atmosphere of Lifford Grange oppresses Gertrude, and she attempts to escape through daydreams and books. In a scene which closely parallels one of Jane Eyre's experiences at Gateshead, the novel describes how Gertrude finds refuge in the window seat of the family library:

> It was a dull desolate-looking room, but yet Gertrude liked it, and had spent in it some of the pleasantest hours of her life. [. . .] She could take down a volume from the aforesaid bookcase, and sit for hours on one

of the window-seats, alternately reading and gazing on the sky and the careening clouds; or watching with interest the struggles of a fly in some spider's web, or the resuscitation of a paralysed moth, on which a ray of sunshine might have accidentally fallen. (I:193)

In *Jane Eyre*, we see Jane, through her reading and daydreaming, developing a rich inner life that will sustain her throughout the narrative. *Lady-Bird*, however, implies that Gertrude's reading habits are excessive, as well as dangerous. Gertrude's favorite reading material—the romance novel—inclines her to mistake fiction for reality. In a conversation with her saintly friend Mary (the Helen Burns of the novel), Gertrude reveals that her idea of love has been exclusively shaped through novel reading. "[A] quiet calm feeling I do not think [love] can be. I have read that it stirs up the heart and moves the inmost soul, as a storm does the sea, or a hurricane the forest." Mary gently responds that this passionate, tumultuous, idealized emotion "is not the right sort of love [. . .]. What is right should be calm" (I:43). When Gertrude's uncle, a Catholic priest, finds his niece reading an Italian version of *Romeo and Juliet*, he condemns the book for expressing "[n]othing but praise of that poor creature for killing herself on the body of her lover." "I had not thought of that," replies Gertrude. "But do you think Juliet could have helped being in love with Romeo?" "Of course she could," [responds Father Lifford]. "Why, if Romeo had been a married man—and so he might have been for aught she knew at first—what would she have done? Put him out of her head, of course, or been a great sinner" (I:275).

Although here the novel seems to poke a little fun at the gruff, unimaginative priest, his warning foreshadows the central conflict of Gertrude's spiritual life. Gertrude, in short, is easy prey to the temptations of human idolatry. While in *Jane Eyre*, Jane's control of her idolatrous impulses is equated with renouncing "Catholic" tendencies and behaviors, Gertrude, in contrast, can conquer idolatry only by becoming a better Catholic. Specifically, she must renounce all temporal values through cultivating self-discipline and otherworldly focus.

A tendency to ennui, joined to a craving for excitement even of the most trivial description, is the disease of certain minds, and there is but one cure for it. Call it what you will; self-education, not for this world but for the next; [. . .] the dream of human happiness resigned, and in the same hour its substance regained; the capital paid into the next world, and the daily unlooked-for interest received in this;—such is the strange alchymy [*sic*] in which God deals, and the secret of so many destinies which the world wonders over, and never learns to understand. (I:56-57)

Although Fullerton's economy of renunciation—that is, renouncing this world's "capital" in the expectation of heavenly dividends—is never explicitly labeled as Catholic, the only characters who model this orientation for Gertrude are devout Catholics such as Mary Grey, Father Lifford, and, especially, Adrien d'Arberg.

Gertrude's greatest temptation to human idolatry is all the more insidious as it comes in the person of Adrien d'Arberg, who is an overt masculine double of Gertrude's saintly friend Mary. Gertrude cannot imagine how her love for the pious d'Arberg, a Catholic writer and theologian, could bring her anything but closer to God. Gertrude imagines that marriage with Adrien will bring her pleasure *both* for this world and the next. "While she knelt at church by his side, she once thought if ever she became his wife, how easy a thing it would be to be good,—how every duty would be a pleasure, *and life a foretaste of Heaven*" (II:176; emphasis added). As Gertrude gazes adoringly at Adrien during Mass, his sanctity takes on a near-erotic dimension:

> There is something more touching in a man's devotion than in a woman's; when it is earnest it is so real, so humble, and so deep. It seemed to her as if the light of heaven played round that noble head bowed down in intense adoration. Though she was looking at him, she knew he would not look at her. His spirit was soaring far above earthly thoughts, and she was glad of it [. . .] a glance from him at that moment would have disappointed her. (II:157; emphasis in original)

Aside from conveying some ominous signs of the extent of Gertrude's infatuation—in Fullerton's novels, there is no true foretaste of heaven on earth—this passage locates d'Arberg's sexual appeal in his wholly masculinized, direct communion with God, as opposed to the feminine, subordinate, and idolatrous position occupied by Gertrude. While Adrien's gentleness toward others, his "adoration" of God, and his "tendency to mysticism" seem feminine, this passage emphatically stresses the masculine character of his piety. Adrien's devotion seems more "real," "humble," and "deep" than Gertrude's not from any essential quality, but because of his relative position to Gertrude. In the role of Gertrude's spiritual superior, Adrien, a former army commander, now takes on the status of a heroic leader in God's own army, much as Jane compares St. John Rivers to "the warrior Greatheart." Although subordinate to his God, Adrien retains his masculinity (and his erotic appeal) because Gertrude knows that "Adrien [. . .] would never love her in that way, he never would adore her" (II:207). As Gertrude's idol, however, Adrien easily assumes power over her heart, mind, and soul: "His unconscious power over her was unbounded. She did not conceive the possibility of differing with him in opinion, of ever acting again in any way that she might have heard him casually condemn. His slightest word was law, his books [were] her daily meditation" (II:124).

In *Lady-Bird* and *Jane Eyre*, each heroine's spiritual dilemma—and the dangers it poses to her religious, spiritual, and moral integrity—is practically identical. Gertrude, like Jane, is placed in the position of Milton's Eve—Fullerton's novel, in fact, makes this association even more explicit in its description of the happy couple, "both so handsome and so highly-gifted, and looking formed—"He for God only; she for God in him" (II:194). Once again, the novel reminds us of the dangers of playing Eve. Gertrude's love for Adrien seems to bring her closer to God, but it is only a superficial devotion. "She had not gone with [Adrien] to the source whence he drank, she had only caught the drops as they fell from his cup: he did not see this and, in his admiration of the fruit, he saw not or could not see that the roots had not struck deep into the soil" (II:194).

The novel's many warnings of the illusion of earthly happiness include another Eve-figure, Lady Clara Audley, a wealthy friend of Gertrude's. Lady Clara does not idolize her husband—fortunately, she "loved him enough [. . .] [but] not too much to give her any of the heartaches which are almost invariably attached to an absorbing affection" (II:55). However, the pleasant tenor of Lady Clara's life is unbroken by any ennobling struggle. Audley Hall, in contrast to Lifford Grange, is a bastion of domestic comfort—indeed, it is described as one large flower garden. Even inside the house, "Flowers, birds, children's laughing faces, ivy wreaths and clustering grapes, sunny landscapes and graceful figures, appeared at every turn [. . .] Gertrude closed her eyes for a moment [. . .] [and imagined herself] transported to one of those fairy abodes which she had so often pictured to herself in her childhood" (II:44). Gertrude is enchanted by her friend's domestic paradise, but d'Arberg voices a gentle criticism. "[W]as she," he queries, "sent into the world to live the life of a rose, or to bear her part in the great battle-field of life? Her existence always seems to me too much like Eve's in Paradise—Eve *before* not *after* the Fall" (II:140; emphasis in original). Although the book portrays Lady Clara in a positive manner, it nonetheless conveys through her character a sense of wasted potential, as there was "in her nature a power of loving which had not been called into full exercise" (II:56).

Fortunately for the salvation of Gertrude's soul, a series of plot complications arise to bar her from any chance of domestic bliss. Gertrude and Adrien pledge to marry, but Gertrude's father forbids the union. Adrien leaves England, and some time later Gertrude hears a rumor that he has joined the priesthood. Gertrude takes rumor for fact; at the same time her father tries to force on her a suitor of his own choosing. Instead, Gertrude desperately marries Maurice, a poor composer who breaks off his engagement with Mary Gray to marry the woman whom *he* has idolized from childhood. But Gertrude, "looking more like a corpse than a bride" (III:35), cannot forget Adrien and cannot love Maurice. Counseled by Father Lifford to "devote yourself to your husband as if you loved him" (II:85), Gertrude settles into an even more harshly uncomfortable domestic space than her first home:

> She worked at her needle for several hours in the day; she went into the kitchen, and [. . .] mastered all the details of domestic economy, and spent less money, and made her husband as comfortable as the most experienced housewife could have done. She never had spoken harshly, or unkindly to him. Her submission was implicit. [. . .] With him she went wherever he asked her [. . .]. Some have walked on hot ploughshares and not winced as they did so, weak women as they were, when their honour was at stake. Perhaps they did not suffer more than she did during these summer walks by the cool river [. . .]. She toiled all day long. She copied out music for him till her head throbbed, and he snatched the pen from her aching fingers; but she never asked him to play. (III:94–95)

Given the novel's emphasis on the spiritual value of suffering, we might expect Gertrude's arduous domesticity to transform her into a saint. But what Gertrude lacks is love—not the pleasant, comfortable love she learned about in romance novels, but true Christian love. "She never tried to love or prayed for the power of loving her husband" (III:97). Had Gertrude only prayed, the reader is urged to believe, God might have worked a transformation on her mind and heart, and her suffering, motivated by love, would then reap spiritual benefits. This lesson seems inspired by Paul's epistle to the Corinthians, in which he explains that the Christian value of self-renunciation is rooted in love for others: "If I give away all I have, and if I deliver my body to be burned, but have not love, I gain nothing" (1 Corinthians 13:3).

Gertrude persists in her empty gestures of self-sacrifice until, to save Maurice from debtor's prison, she relinquishes her inheritance and devises a plan for them to emigrate to America. Gertrude's progression from one dismal domestic space to another is as striking here as it is in *Jane Eyre;* Gertrude has exchanged a humble, loveless domestic existence for cramped, third-class steerage in "[o]ne of those vast receptacles of human beings, one of those floating worlds, those temporary homes [. . .]

one of those ocean caravans that bear away so many youthful energies, and so much life, and spirit, and hope, and sorrow from our shores to the New World [...]" (III:144–45). On this voyage, Gertrude's spiritual crisis comes to a head: Adrien—who has not joined the priesthood after all—takes passage on the same ship. As Adrien and Gertrude still love one another, it is obviously a painful and frustrating situation for both. It is, moreover, an increasingly dangerous one, for by this point, Gertrude and Adrien are not merely susceptible to idolatry, but adultery as well. It is a situation that leads even the near-perfect Adrien into error. Taking random circumstances for evidence of God's will, Adrien suggests to Gertrude that they have been thrown together again because God "deigns to use me as His instrument to reawaken in you [...] the deep enthusiasm of a real vocation" (III:193). Although well intentioned, Adrien's self-construction as God's "instrument" ominously echoes Rochester's declaration that he considers Jane a divinely ordained "instrument for my cure." Gertrude, however, unquestionably accepts Adrien as "God's instrument": "Teach me, then, to submit," she cries, "[...] show me the way" (III:189–90).

Jane Eyre and Gertrude Lifford thus face a similar temptation, in which the lure of adultery is mingled with the temptation of idolatry. Both heroines ultimately resolve their dilemmas through the same course of action: active self-denial and prayer. Jane and Gertrude both perform sacrificial gestures that resemble what James Eli Adams calls a "virtuoso ascetic regimen" (7)—that is, a strenuous, active, heroic form of self-renunciation most at odds with Victorian ideals of passive feminine endurance. In Jane's case, we see this active embrace of suffering most clearly in her resolution to leave Rochester, when she invokes Scripture's command to pluck out any eye, or tear off any hand, that causes one to sin. Jane also hears a seemingly miraculous call from Rochester right at the moment of St. John's proposal, but not before she has cried out to heaven to show her the way. Once Jane physically tears herself away from St. John, she rushes to her room and prays. Of course Jane's insistence on praying her "own way" is crucial here—St. John Rivers may be convinced of God's will for himself, but he cannot dictate God's will for Jane.

Similarly, Gertrude prays her way to redemption. Although both Fr. Lifford and d'Arberg urge Gertrude at various times to pray, prayer brings Gertrude to her own understanding of God and God's will. The turning point in Gertrude's progress occurs when Gertrude, nursing her sick husband on board ship, accidentally administers to him a draught of poison. Although the text carefully points out that Gertrude does not intentionally poison her husband, she had caught herself the day before wishing for freedom through Maurice's death: "If *he* were to die, I should be free"

(III:206). Obviously, Maurice's poisoning is classic subconscious wish fulfillment; Gertrude's guilty, adulterous thoughts have literally turned to poison. As Adrien d'Arberg (who claims more medical skill than the ship's doctor) works through the night to save Maurice, Gertrude fervently prays for her husband's life. Gertrude's prayers—her *direct* appeals to God—are answered and then some: not only does Maurice survive the night, but another, wondrous transformation occurs. Gertrude's adulterous, idolatrous longing for Adrien is supplanted by her overpowering love for her husband:

> She vowed to love her husband. O, she loved him already. A single hair of his head had grown precious to her heart, and her burning lips were pressed to his cold hands with feelings that hope and joy could never give. Truly, as Adrien was striving and watching by her side that livelong night, [. . .] she felt that an angel had come to her aid; but earthly passion passed away, even then, from her soul, and never from that day forth did she think of him but as one of those ministering spirits who lead the way to Heaven, but are not destined to walk the common paths of life by our side. (III:226–27)

In the course of a single tortuous evening, all is resolved. Maurice commences a rapid recovery. Gertrude herself is a changed woman, her love for Maurice subduing the violent passions with the "unspeakable peace [. . .] reigning in her soul, and hovering over her every moment." Here the narrative most explicitly points to the moral of Gertrude's suffering:

> She remembered [Fr. Lifford's] words—"If light sufferings are not enough to bring you to His feet, God will in His mercy send you some of those strange trials which break what would not bend, and crush what would not yield." But He had not crushed her—no; He had bowed her down under His Almighty hand, and showed her in one horrible hour what His wrath can do; and then His saving hand was stretched out, and she stood on the shore, strong and erect with the strength He had given her, with the energy He had implanted in her. (III:230–31)

The brief sermon on God's loving punishment echoes a speech made by another character similarly purged of adulterous inclinations, Edward Rochester: "Divine justice pursued its course; disasters came thick on me: I was forced to pass through the valley of the shadow of death. His chastisements are mighty; and one smote me which has humbled me for ever. [. . .] I thank my Maker that in the midst of judgment he remembered Mercy" (495). Although God's divine justice forces Rochester to repent and recognize his wrongdoing, it does not, as we have seen, seem to cure him entirely of creature-worship. Gertrude's reconcilement with her Maker, however, also erases from her heart any human passion which would be an obstacle to her religious and spiritual growth. At the end of the twenty-fourth chapter, on the eve of disembarking in New York, Adrien takes a last farewell of Gertrude and Maurice. Although Gertrude weeps at this moment, "There was no passion in that grief, no bitterness in that parting" (III: 233). Adrien delivers parting words befitting the closing scene of a novel, "God bless you both for ever!" (III:234). And as he moves away, the novel gives us what would seem to be a last glimpse of Gertrude and Maurice: "[. . .] [B]oth for a few minutes wept together. She was the first to dry her tears, and when he raised his eyes to hers there was not a cloud on her brow" (III:234).

Having delivered Gertrude from near-fatal "creature-worship," demonstrated the importance of direct, unmediated prayer for women as well as men, and preached a lesson on the virtue of religious suffering, the novel would seem to have arrived at a satisfactory closure. And if the reader can believe that Gertrude really no longer loves Adrien, she might breathe a sigh of relief at the prospect of the long-suffering Gertrude finally enjoying a quiet, loving, even comfortable domestic life with Maurice. But inexplicably, Fullerton unsettles both her heroine *and* her readers. In a final chapter that looks suspiciously like an afterthought, the ship catches on fire. While this plot development brings to mind the devastating, yet purging, fire at Thornfield, there seems little left to purge in the wake of Gertrude's spiritual reformation. But the fire does, indirectly, kill Maurice, who is also guilty of idolatry in his selfish and overpowering love for Gertrude.[14] This plot development leads readers to believe that Gertrude, newly widowed, will end up with Adrien after all. And this makes sense: didn't Jane Eyre get Rochester as a reward for renouncing him? Maurice, in his dying speech, only reinforces these readerly expectations. Declaring that he has stood between Gertrude and d'Arberg for too long, Maurice joins their hands at his bedside: "Promise me that you will marry," he says. "For my peace, my sake" (III:246).

According to the old and revered tradition of the death-bed scene (a literary device dating back at least to the late medieval period, but particularly favored by Evangelical tract writers and other Victorian

14. Gertrude flees to Maurice's home (and away from a father trying to force her into an arranged marriage) under the mistaken impression that d'Arberg has abandoned her for the priesthood. Maurice knows this assumption is false, but conceals the information from Gertrude because he wishes to marry her himself.

authors [Jay 154]), Gertrude and Adrien would of course honor Maurice's dying request not only out of respect for the dead, but out of some vague acknowledgment that Maurice, as a man with one foot already in Paradise, possesses privileged knowledge of the mind and will of God. After encouraging all readerly hopes that the pair, destined for one another, will finally marry, however, the novel frustrates these expectations. While Gertrude and Adrien do not give an outright and direct refusal to a dying man's last wish—perhaps an integrity too harsh for Victorian readers—neither do they give a definite assent. Immediately after Maurice's funeral, Adrien and Gertrude go their separate ways, never to meet again on earth.

Why this rebuke to novelistic conventions, an act that one reviewer criticized as "unreasonable self-sacrifice" (*Christian Remembrancer* 402)? The resistance to conventional narrative closure is perhaps intended to remind readers that the will of God may often be radically opposed even to a course of behavior that society—and institutionalized religion—might fully approve. Although no obvious legal, social, moral, or religious encumbrances now exist to prevent Gertrude and Adrien's marriage, each has bypassed social and religious intermediaries to determine God's will directly through prayer. And if prayer has truly transformed Gertrude's heart and mind, marriage to Adrien would simply be a relapse into the disease of creature worship. Gertrude's ultimate fate is more consistent with a narrative that—in the interests of her spiritual health—continually denies her domestic stability or comfort. After parting with Adrien, Gertrude bears Maurice's son and passes several years serving the Irish poor in New York. Finally, Gertrude returns to England and Lifford Grange and spends the rest of her life caring for her son and elderly father (with whom she has reconciled) and doing charitable works. In the closing paragraph of the novel, she assures her brother Edgar that she is happy, but clearly it is a happiness built on spiritual rather than temporal rewards: "[She possessed] a heart full of the peace and joy which the world cannot give nor the world take away" (III:271).

As a novel warning readers against the dangers of human idolatry, *Lady-Bird* is not without its problems. The novel so romanticizes—even as it condemns—Gertrude and Adrien's idolatrous passion that female spiritual autonomy triumphs only at the novel's end, with Gertrude and Adrien safely residing at opposite ends of the earth. Moreover, Gertrude would never have arrived at this spiritual maturity, the novel suggests, without Adrien's help and guidance. *Lady-Bird* upholds a relationship between women and God that is distinctly separate from men's encounters with the divine, yet the ensuing models of female religious agency, while separate, are not exactly equal. In *Lady-Bird* (as in *Jane Eyre*), women continue to exercise religious agency by quietly, passively serving others in domestic settings, whereas men's agency resides in active, spiritual leadership and ostensibly heroic missionary work overseas. The novel's final pages also include a laudatory newspaper account of Adrien, now indeed a priest "braving the danger of martyrdom in the remote countries where his zeal has led him [. . .] preaching the Gospel to the children of Asia" (III:262). At the novel's end, Adrien's career as a Christian warrior is as much lauded and magnified as St. John's otherworldly heroism at the conclusion of *Jane Eyre*.

Lady-Bird's conclusion obviously chooses a radically different strategy in its attempt to uphold female spiritual integrity and autonomy than does the final chapter of *Jane Eyre*. Neither choice is, in the end, completely satisfactory for readers. In *Jane Eyre*, not only does Jane's vocation—and her hope of salvation—still revolve around Rochester, but her spiritual gains are rather difficult to represent. In the course of the novel, Jane continually chooses the straight and narrow path—rejecting Rochester, and later even St. John, presumably in the interests of preserving her immortal soul. Yet the only way the novel can convincingly represent the rewards of Jane's spiritual sacrifice is through temporal goods—matrimony, money, and status. Brontë was well aware that her audience would find the words "Reader, I married him" more compelling than "come Lord Jesus." And for this reason *Lady-Bird* is both a more daring and a more "painful" novel than *Jane Eyre*. Although Gertrude's sufferings are not necessarily more pronounced than Jane's, they are not visibly rewarded in the end. How *can* one represent "the peace and joy which the world cannot give nor the world take away" in a narrative form that is preoccupied with representing the material world?

Jane Eyre's ambivalence between the worlds of flesh and spirit is surely part of the novel's enduring appeal as a rich and challenging literary work. But as a social critique, *Lady-Bird* issues a stronger, more challenging "sermon." In *Lady-Bird*, Gertrude must fight the temptation of idolatry from without—that is, idolatry as promoted by popular romance novels, Protestant models of marriage, and her secular culture's mistaken ideas about love. By rejecting the world and its values, Gertrude simultaneously triumphs over the problem of idolatry. *Jane Eyre*, however, by equating idolatry with Catholicism, implies that idolatry is a natural human tendency—in particular, a symptom of Jane's "Catholic" shadow-self. Not only does Jane have to distinguish between her Catholic and Protestant selves, repressing the one and affirming the other, but she must also sift through her Protestant culture's teachings on marriage, rejecting those that encourage Catholic idolatry. In short, idolatry in *Jane Eyre* is figured in the same way many Victorian Protestants represented Catholicism: deep-rooted, easily hidden, and extremely difficult to eradicate. It is rather hard to fault society for Jane's idolatry, when she sees it so deeply embedded within herself.

Finally, Jane Eyre's most enthusiastic affirmation of Victorian social values is of course her choice of marriage and motherhood. The strongest facet of Fullerton's social critique, on the other hand, is her radical suggestion that Victorian women might find their true vocation outside of marriage and traditional domesticity. In contrast to Evangelical Protestantism, which based its understanding of vocation on constructs of home and family, Catholicism presented to women other valid alternatives, such as lay ministry and organized religious life. Authorized by the Catholic tradition, Fullerton seems to have been less constrained than Brontë in stretching the envelope of novelistic convention in crafting her heroine's unique "happy ending." Fullerton's *Lady-Bird*, with its daring, albeit unpopular conclusion, presents a Catholic challenge not merely to the social status quo, but to the form and genre of the novel itself.

We may be tempted to think that Brontë and Fullerton, with their daring critiques of Protestant domesticity and matrimony, were distinctly at odds with the male-authored values and institutions of their era. This is to some extent true, but as Victorian sermons on marriage, both *Jane Eyre* and *Lady-Bird* share the same ultimate goal as Thomas Jackson's 1810 sermon, *Marriage and Adultery Considered*. All three "preachers," Brontë, Fullerton, and Jackson, seek to define a "godly" marriage, and each presents secular marriage—or marriage which is only nominally Christian—as a nightmarish state of living death. Jackson portrays profane marriage as a man united to a corpse; Fullerton describes Gertrude, newly married to Maurice, as "looking more like a corpse than a bride"; and Jane's zombie-like double, Bertha, dons Jane's wedding veil prior to Jane's adulterous wedding ceremony. Figures evoking both marriage and death may well be an enduring cultural archetype (consider Dickens's ghoulish Miss Havisham, or more recently, Tim Burton's 2005 movie, *Corpse Bride*), but for these Victorian preachers, the death imagery seems colored by fears about secularization. The ideal modern marriage, as so many preachers lamented, privileged every sort of compatibility *except* that of religious doctrine; Brontë, Fullerton, and Jackson all express genuine concern that the wrong marriage partner could sabotage one's journey to heaven.

But leaving the possibility of eternal damnation aside, popular ideals of secular marriage conveyed other nightmarish undertones. The bar for modern marriages was set dizzyingly high. Marriage was to provide individuals with unprecedented levels of physical, emotional, *and* spiritual gratification: a tall order to fill, especially in a society with a documented shortage of eligible male partners. Marriage framed as a religious duty could be deemed successful if both partners went to heaven. Secular marriage, however, depended upon sexual passion, emotional bliss, and lifelong mutual attraction. Suddenly, getting to heaven may have seemed relatively easy. Marriage to Maurice Redmond, for Gertrude, and a potential marriage to St. John Rivers, for Jane, may be framed as spiritually deadening, but each author is much more convincing at portraying the *earthly* consequences of choosing marriage partners unwisely.

CHAPTER TWO

"Sick Souls"

Love, Guilt, and the Catholic Confessional in Victorian Women's Fiction

> [As] the confessional *is* an immoral, and *therefore,* unscriptural institution, can any woman whose purity should be above suspicion, have the boldness to defend, or even palliate it? [. . .] I have more respect for the poor outcast on our streets, who makes no profession of religion, than for the female (woman, I dare not call her,) who, in the sacred name of Christianity, frequents the Confessional [. . .].
> —H. J. Brockman, *Letter to the Women of England on the Confessional* (1867)

THIS chapter further develops the juxtaposition between Charlotte Brontë and Lady Georgiana Fullerton, from the commission of sin (idolatry, or erotic "creature worship") to its consequences and punishment. For all their differences, *Jane Eyre* and *Lady-Bird* both posit the existence of a jealous God who violently, even vengefully, punishes violations of the First Commandment through sudden death (Maurice Redmond) and dismemberment (Rochester). Early nineteenth-century Evangelical tracts, such as those circulated by *Jane Eyre*'s Reverend Brocklehurst, instilled in an entire generation of children the terror of punitive, physical annihilation, whether in this world or the next. Writings by Brontë and Fullerton, however, whether fiction, autobiography, or correspondence, suggest that the most violent consequence of, and penalty for, sin (whether real or imagined) was the torture imposed by one's guilt-stricken conscience: a disciplinary force more powerful and more determined than any Old Testament representation of outraged deity. As William James suggested as early as 1902, this theologically pessimistic worldview—a conviction of one's unworthiness, the omnipresence of evil, and the likelihood of eternal damnation—appears, from a modern, secular perspective, as a manifestation of severe pathology. James, in his famous Gifford lectures on "The Varieties of Religious Experience," contrasted this "sick-souled" worldview with the increasingly popular orientation toward "healthy-mindedness," which emphasizes, among other things, "*getting away from* the sin, and not groaning and writhing over its commission" (110; emphasis in original).

I include in this chapter on confession a few vignettes of the "sick-souled" worldview, as exemplified by Fullerton, Brontë, and other female contemporaries. A full understanding of the importance and controversial nature of confession in Victorian culture requires us to make a cultural leap into the mind-set of the "sick-souled." Protestant Victorian opposition to the practice of auricular confession has been well documented by scholars, and although we may now consider Victorian arguments against confession quaint and outdated, Catholic confession seems to retain a sinister aspect even for many modern scholars. Taking the lead from Michel Foucault—who in *The History of Sexuality* (1978) describes the discourse of confession as an "internal ruse," an "immense labor to which the West has submitted generations in order to produce [. . .] men's subjection" (60), contemporary literary scholars have focused almost exclusively on confession's potential to unnerve, frighten, or even horrify the average Victorian Protestant.[1] This approach is classically exemplified by feminist readings of Lucy Snowe's trip to the confessional in Charlotte Brontë's *Villette*. Despite Lucy's complex attitude toward Catholicism and the centrality of the confessional in her erotic and spiritual quest, critics tend to read Lucy's confession to Père Silas as one more symbol of patriarchal domination in her suffocatingly narrow world.

1. Denis Paz's *Popular Anti-Catholicism in Mid-Victorian England* (1992) is surprisingly thin on the topic of confession, merely listing some examples of anticonfessional rhetoric without much analytical commentary. In contrast, John Shelton Reed's *Glorious Battle: The Cultural Politics of Anglo-Catholicism* (1996) provides an excellent overview of anticonfession sentiment in Victorian England, but Reed does not develop his passing speculation that confession's threat to domestic authority "must surely have appealed to those who found parental and husbandly authority stifling" (201). Susan Bernstein's *Confessional Subjects: Revelations of Gender and Power in Victorian Literature* (1997)—a study of the gender politics inherent in Victorian novelistic representations of confession—provides a similar historical background, but professes little interest in confession as a religious rite, preferring to focus on its appropriation as a pervasive, secular discursive practice. In her literary analyses, Bernstein does acknowledge confession's potential as a site of cultural critique and an opportunity for liberating disclosure, but these possibilities are dwarfed by her overriding preoccupation with confession as "largely a site of [patriarchal] coercion" (1). More recently, Susan Griffin's *Anti-Catholicism and Nineteenth-Century Fiction* (2004), while mentioning Lucy Snowe's ambivalent attitude toward the confessional, focuses almost exclusively on traditional anti-Catholic representations of confession through her analyses of British novels published well after Villette's debut (1853).

But what do we make of the fact that female writers, even Protestant ones, were so fascinated with the confessional? That many Anglo- and Roman Catholic Victorian women confessed regularly?[2] Finally, considering the virulence of anticonfessional rhetoric in the Victorian period, what might induce a woman writer "to have the boldness to defend, or even palliate" what H. J. Brockman referred to as the "foul satanic institution" of auricular confession?

To uncover some of the complexities of Victorian women's attitudes toward confession, this essay examines Brontë's *Villette* alongside an 1844 novel by Lady Georgiana Fullerton, *Ellen Middleton*. Fullerton, prior to her conversion to Roman Catholicism in 1846, wrote *Ellen Middleton* to argue in favor of the reinstatement of auricular confession in the Anglican Church. Although almost no modern literary criticism exists on *Ellen Middleton*, the novel made a sensational debut in both England and America.[3] The novel's portrayal of Ellen, an outwardly respectable and virtuous young lady contending with her inner demons of murderous aggression and sexual longing, riveted and enthralled Victorian readers. Despite the fact that Protestant and secular ideals of marriage designated husbands as women's spiritual guides and superiors, Ellen cannot find salvation until she flees home for the confessional. Ultimately, *Ellen Middleton* challenges secular ideals of the home as a sacred space and makes a radical affirmation of the importance of women's spiritual and moral autonomy. When placed alongside *Villette*, *Ellen Middleton* exhibits some striking, even ironic parallels with Brontë's novel, despite the strident anti-Catholic over-

---

2. In *Glorious Battle: The Cultural Politics of Victorian Anglo-Catholicism* (1996), John Shelton Reed states that, although he cannot locate any nineteenth-century listing of Anglican churches that offered confession, other evidence suggests that it was a regular practice among Anglo-Catholics: "As early as 1847 one observer claimed that confession was 'practiced very extensively, and, as we believe, most beneficially, in the English Church,' but he noted that 'it was scarcely ever spoken of, even in the most confidential intercourse'" (qtd. in Walsh 89). Reed also notes that "Pusey, Manning, John Mason Neale [. . .] are known to have heard confessions with varying degrees of secrecy to keep the practice hidden from hostile parents, spouses, or bishops, and many lesser lights among Tractarians did the same" (49).

3. William Ewart Gladstone published a substantial essay on *Ellen Middleton* in the *English Review* (1844) in which he lauded the "rare pleasure [. . .] [of finding] the mastery of all human gifts of authorship" (356). *Ellen Middleton* was also reviewed warmly in *The Times* (29 May 1844, p. 3, col. F). In America, where Fullerton's books were also popular, Edgar Allan Poe and Emily Dickinson both expressed, in writing, their enthusiasm for Ellen Middleton (see Jaeger, "Lady Georgiana Fullerton [1812–1885]", 176–77). *Ellen Middleton* has received only scant mention in twentieth-century criticism (with the exception of a few doctoral dissertations), and most of these references are dismissive. Joseph Ellis Baker, for example, states that the novel is worth noting because its plot "turns on a Catholic principle," although he also describes the work as "contemptible" (19). Robert Lee Wolff (in addition to Kathleen Jaeger) offers a more generous assessment of the novel, remarking that Gladstone's glowing assessment of Fullerton's novel does not, even "131 years later, [. . .] seem hyperbole" (79).

tones of the latter. In their respective, and at times contradictory, engagements with Catholic confession, both writers sustain a consistent criticism of Victorian domestic values.

"Her confessor, her priest, her God"
Protestant Anxieties about Auricular Confession

Even in an era suffused with religious controversy, the Victorian debate over the nature and purpose of auricular confession was remarkable for the passion that it inflamed. Since the time of the Reformation, the rite of confession had been, among English Protestants, one of the most feared and misunderstood sacraments of the Roman Catholic Church. The Catholic Church had for centuries taught that serious sins could only be forgiven through the rite of confession, a confidential exchange between penitent and priest. After freely confessing his or her sins, the penitent would receive an absolution from the priest, who claimed his authority and power to forgive sins as Christ's representative on earth. To many nineteenth-century Protestants, this ritual suggested an illegitimate and dangerous exercise of ecclesiastical power. The debate over confession raged with heightened virulence at midcentury, in part due to the increasing visibility of the Roman Catholic Church in England. Even more alarming was the possibility that the ritual of confession could infiltrate the sacred confines of the Church of England itself. Supporters of the Oxford Movement in the 1830s and 1840s, in an effort to bring the Anglican Church more closely in line with its Catholic roots, urged for the reinstatement of auricular confession.[4] While the controversy over confession raged among male preachers and tract writers, women also took part in the fray through domestic fiction, the genre deemed most appropriate for their sphere.

It is particularly illuminating to explore women's writing on confession, because the confessional controversy was fueled by anxieties about Victorian constructions of femininity, marriage, and domesticity. Opponents of confession often portrayed the ritual primarily as a means for Catholic priests to weaken, even destroy, the bonds between fathers and daughters, husbands and wives. Anti-Catholic propaganda assured men that to allow women to avail themselves of confession was to invite ruin and scandal:

---

4. The Anglican *Book of Common Prayer* included a rite of confession, which became a linchpin of doctrinal debate. Supporters of confession used the rite to justify the reinstatement of confession, while opponents charged that the rite was meant to be used only in exceptional cases.

wives who rebelled against their husbands; daughters seduced and impregnated by evil Jesuits. William Hogan, in *Auricular Confession and Popish Nunneries* (1846), described the priest as "an incarnate fiend [standing] between man and wife, mother and daughter," who violated "all the ties of domestic happiness and reciprocal duties" (58). Jules Michelet, whose *Priests, Women, and Families* (1845) was translated and widely circulated in England, painted a startling picture of the female penitent revealing to priests not only her own deepest secrets, but those of her husband, who would henceforth live in a "glass dwelling." "How humiliating," Michelet said, addressing the penitent's husband, "[. . .] to be seen and followed into your most retired privacy, by an invisible witness [. . .], to meet in the street a man who knows better than yourself your most secret weaknesses, who bows cringingly, turns and laughs [. . .]" (11).

Opponents of confession argued that the procedure was not only invasive, but immoral. As Walter Farquhar Hook asserted in an 1848 sermon against confession, "[T]he Romanists are commanded to unlock their hearts to the priest, and persons of all ages and both sexes, standing before him in their *moral nudity,* are required to submit [. . .] to the most minute and searching questions as to their inmost thoughts" (24; emphasis added). Such arguments insinuated that priests' questioning of female penitents about possible sexual transgressions (whether in thought or in deed) was tantamount to a moral rape, which would ruin women as effectively as any physical one. Indeed, many implied that proper women had no need of confession at all; the priests' questionings would only plant the seeds of vice where none had previously existed. In an 1852 sermon, Thomas Hill Lowe reviled "the disgusting details of the minute questionings" to which priest subjected female penitents, "thus suggesting to their minds thoughts of evil, which otherwise would never have been harboured there, and making them familiar with images of pollution [. . .] and too often lead them on to the commission of open acts of impurity and sin" (11–12).[5] Accordingly, anti-Catholic propaganda was rife with "real" accounts of women who had been seduced and impregnated by their confessors. Such lurid descriptions of the vile outcomes of confession can also be found in midcentury novels such as Catherine Sinclair's *Beatrice* (1852), which hints at a sexual relationship between a young woman and her confessor. Bessie, with an "expression of abject terror [. . .] stamped on every feature," confides to her Protestant friend that Father Eustace "comes

---

5. Defenders of confession insisted that priests exercised the greatest caution in questioning women and children; some denied that such questioning occurred at all. See *Letters on the Confessional* by T. M. McDonnell, and C. W. Russell, review of J. Michelet's *Priests, Women, and Families.*

[...] every day for an hour to see me [...] I must see him alone!—always alone!" (2:145).

Secret Desires of the "Sick Soul"

> I want to assure you that however harassed by memory or anxiety you may be, I have (more or less) heretofore gone through the same ordeal. I have borne myself till I became unbearable by myself, and then I have found help in confession and absolution and spiritual counsel, and relief inexpressible. Twice in my life I tried to suffice myself with measures *short* of this, but nothing would do: the first time was of course in my youth before my general confession, the second time was when circumstances had led me (rightly or wrongly) to break off the practice. But now for years past I have resumed the habit, and I hope not to continue [to use] it profitlessly. (emphasis in original)

In this 1881 letter to her brother Dante Gabriel, Christina Rossetti consoles him on his depressed state of mind, and hints that perhaps he might, like herself, benefit from a regular course of private confession. Anti-Catholic polemics against confession nearly always focused upon victimized female, rather than male, penitents, implying that women as the weaker sex were less susceptible of resisting either the sophisticated recruitment tactics or the sexual magnetism of charismatic Jesuit priests. Rossetti, along with female contemporaries of all denominations, demonstrated a deep fascination with confession; their interest with this rite seems to have derived, at least in part, from more complex cultural factors. Female virtue was the linchpin of Evangelical constructions of sacred domesticity, and, as many scholars have pointed out, cultural expectations of womanly perfection generated enormous psychological stress for thousands of conscientious middle-class women.

As autobiographies reveal, a popular method of moral training for Protestant girls and young women was an emphasis upon constant self-monitoring and the regular examination of conscience. While confessing transgressions outside the home was of course out of the question, children—especially girls—*were* encouraged to confess to their parents. Evangelical novelist Charlotte Elizabeth Tonna recalls in her autobiography how, as erring children, she and her brother "Never rested until [...] we had encouraged each other to confession. We then went, hand in hand, to our mother, and the one who stood clear of the offence acknowledged it in the name of the transgressor, while both asked pardon" (25). Similarly, Frances Power Cobbe, also reared in an Evangelical home, recalls

> [. . .] once when I felt driven like a veritable Cain, by my agonized conscience to go and confess to [my mother] that I had said in a recent rage (to myself) *"Curse them all!"* Referring to my family in general and to my governess in particular! The tempest of my tears and sobs on this occasion evidently astonished her, and I remember lying exhausted on the floor in a recess in her bedroom, for a long time before I was able to move. (86; emphasis in original)

Elizabeth Missing Sewell's account of her childhood confessions is presented far less nostalgically and is even painful to read. In her autobiography, Sewell, a High Church Anglican, implies that even as a child, the expectation for her to self-examine and confess encouraged in her "strange, scrupulous fancies" and "a morbid and over-strained conscience" (27). One day, after mocking her teacher, Miss Crooke, behind the latter's back, young Sewell's powerful sense of guilt deepens further, generating not one, but multiple confessions of wrongdoing. As Sewell recalls: "I became very miserable, from the thought of what Miss Crooke would say if she knew the full extent of my naughtiness. [. . .] The following afternoon, after going through my usual reading lesson, I turned round to Miss Crooke, and said aloud, so that every one might hear, 'If you please ma'am, I called you a witch'" (26). Despite the punishment Miss Crooke metes out to Sewell as well as her classmates—weeks of remanded privileges resembling "a species of slow torture"—Sewell's guilt lingers:

> My conscience, however, went on working: having once begun to confess, the practice became a necessity, and I begged that I might be allowed to tell every day the things I had done wrong, because I felt so wicked. Miss Crooke at first treated me as a converted penitent, but by degrees she must have become alarmed. My confessions verged on the ludicrous, and the climax must have been reached when having received an order in common with my companions to mention if we saw any black beetles in the schoolroom, I made it a subject of confession that I had seen a black beetle crawl out from under a large bureau. (27)

Indeed alarmed, Miss Crooke informs Sewell's mother, who in turn requests her daughter to "leave off all confessions, and not tell any one but herself my conscience worries" (27). While this admonition seems to have cured Sewell of the worst of her "scrupulous fancies," she reports being plagued, well into middle age, with a persistent "sense of guilt, and the dread of not being forgiven, and the being followed about [. . .] by a spectre of evil from which I could not escape" (39).

James, of course, would consider Sewell a perfect example of the "sick-souled" personality, with a conscience so burdened by moral scruples and guilt that it seemed distorted even to Sewell's strict teacher and her pious mother. Today we might diagnose Sewell's behavior as symptomatic of obsessive-compulsive disorder. More to the point, however, particularly significant is that Sewell suffered the tortures of an oversensitive conscience well into adulthood, as did Charlotte Tonna, who, early in her married life, took up the practice of writing down all her perceived transgressions: "I then made a little book, wrote down a list of offences, and commenced making a dot over against each, whenever I detected myself in the commission of one." Tonna's husband was not a religious man, and newly arrived in Ireland, she seems to have had no one else in whom she could confide. Her book "became a mass of black dots" before she gave up the practice in desperation, sinking into religious melancholia: "an abyss of gloomy despair" (*Life of Charlotte Elizabeth* 109).

Although I have not found any explicit instruction to women to confess their sins to husbands, men's roles as their wives' spiritual superiors (as outlined in the sermons discussed in chapter 1) suggest that husbands, not parents, would be considered the most appropriate confessors for married women. And as *Ellen Middleton* illustrates vividly, not all husbands (if any) are cut out to be confessors for their wives. The spiritual isolation that Tonna suffers, as the wife of a man to whom she could not unburden her conscience, also permeates Fullerton's *Ellen Middleton*, fueling its argument in support of auricular confession. As Rossetti's letter, Sewell's and Tonna's autobiographies, and Fullerton's novel suggest, many Victorian women craved formal auricular confession as a convenient, and completely secret, respite from the afflictions of the "sick soul." As William James explains, perhaps a bit too blithely:

> The Catholic practice of confession and absolution is in one of its aspects little more than a systematic method for keeping healthy-mindedness on top. By it a man's accounts with evil are periodically squared and audited, so that he may start the clean pages with no debts inscribed. Any Catholic will tell us how clean and fresh and free he feels after the purging operation. (110)

Not surprisingly, both Fullerton's and Brontë's fictional engagements with confession appear to have been colored by the "sick-souled" personality of each writer and her own real-life experience with the confessional. In her brief autobiographical sketch, Fullerton recalls reading, at age fourteen, *Father Clement: A Roman Catholic Story,* a novel published in 1823 by the Evangelical writer Grace Kennedy. Despite the obvious anti-Catholic message of the novel, Fullerton recalls how the character of the Jesuit chaplain, whom Kennedy had intended to malign, excited her "admiration and sympathy": "I sided entirely with the girl in the family, who was a devout Catholic, and wished that I could, like her, have gone to confession from Father Dormer, and thought how exactly I would have obeyed him" (Henry James Coleridge 21). For Fullerton, by all accounts a serious young woman who "from her earliest childhood [. . .] dreaded sin" (Taylor 166), confession must have appeared as a potentially comforting and direct salve to the perpetual gnawings of her conscience—albeit an application which needed to be continually repeated. After her conversion to Catholicism, and when her life took a more markedly ascetic turn in middle age, Fullerton, according to her biographers, confessed twice a week (Coleridge 341).

Like Fullerton, Brontë possessed a painfully sensitive conscience, as well as an outsider's fascination for the mystery of the confessional. In a late 1836 letter to her friend Ellen Nussey, Brontë expresses profound anxiety over the state of her soul:

> [T]he melancholy state I now live in, uncertain that I ever felt true contrition, wandering in thought and deed, longing for holiness, which I shall *never, never* obtain, smitten at times to the heart with the conviction that ghastly Calvinistic doctrines are true [. . .]. If Christian perfection be necessary to salvation, I shall never be saved; my heart is a very hot-bed for sinful thoughts (qtd. in Gaskell 152; emphasis in original).

In a letter of 1843 to her sister Emily, Brontë describes how she made an actual confession to a Catholic priest in Brussels, an episode clearly reflected in Lucy Snowe's confession in *Villette.* Although the priest initially refused the sacrament to a Protestant, Charlotte reports that "I was determined to confess, and at last he would allow me [. . .]. I actually did confess—a real confession [. . .] the adventure stops there, and I hope I shall never see the priest again. I think you had better not tell papa of this" (qtd. in Moglen 209n). Why Brontë chose to go to confession (and what she confessed there) remains a mystery, but her fictional recreation of this incident in *Villette* suggests—despite the anti-Catholic resonances of the novel—that the confessional could offer genuine, if dangerous, comfort to women in the midst of spiritual turmoil.

Although Brontë's and Fullerton's novels engage with a variety of mid-century arguments against the confessional, both writers seem to have been especially intrigued by the widespread accusation that confession was tantamount to idolatry. Although the Catholic Church taught that the priest in confession was merely a *representative* of Christ, Protestant writers such as H. J. Brockman regarded the priest's role as a "substitution of the man-god for the God-man" and an "insult to His Divine Majesty" through "the idolatry involved in the act" (2). Yet as Fullerton's novel suggests most emphatically, confession could actually help women *avoid* idolatry—that is, idolatry defined as an all-consuming passion for husbands that rivaled or even eclipsed women's love for God. Fullerton was not alone in suggesting that marriage could become idolatry; Charles William Russell, a professor of ecclesiastical history at Maynooth College, wrote an essay for the Catholic *Dublin Review* in which he derided Michelet's implication that "the wife should give her husband not only her body, her heart, and her love, but her soul above all; that she should make him her director, her priest, and even her god, for she must give him her soul, which God alone can claim" (463).

Whereas confession represented idolatry to many Victorian Protestants, it is the "sin" of idolatry that causes spiritual turmoil for both Lucy Snowe and Ellen Middleton, and the sin that sends each to the confessional. While it is impossible to know all the reasons Victorian women sought confession, it seems significant that both novels focus on a sin that is essentially sexual in nature. Anti-Catholic depictions of confession, in all their prurience, implied, or directly stated, that the entire transaction between female penitent and priest was sexually charged, and that priests questioned penitents most aggressively about sexual sins. Both Lucy Snowe and Ellen Middleton are passionate, energetic women trapped in societies that deem passion, energy, and sexuality as incompatible with female virtue. This psychic split generates enormous tension for each character, and confession helps each to reconcile the conflicting elements of her identity. While female idolatry, aggression, and sexual desire must be confessed and absolved within the confessional, two points bear emphasis: First, the practice of secret confession validates for each heroine the existence of a "secret" self at odds with her public persona; and second, the very existence of this fragmented self seems to receive absolution through confession, as much as any specific transgression. In a culture that divided women into angels or fallen creatures, the confessional was possibly the only realm in Victorian culture that recognized that female sanctity was *not* incompatible with real, constant struggles against natural human drives of aggression and sexuality.

"Reprove me as often as you please"
Confession and Atonement in Ellen Middleton

Although the overt Tractarian sympathies of *Ellen Middleton* have led scholars of our own time to dismiss it as a mere "religious novel," these religious preoccupations infused Ellen's narrative with an emotional realism and psychological depth extraordinary for its period. The book's vivid, unsparing depictions of Ellen's guilt-ridden psyche resulted in an instant best seller. The novel drew rave reviews from such notables as Harriet Martineau, William Gladstone, Queen Victoria, and even Edgar Allan Poe. "A remarkable work," wrote Poe of *Ellen Middleton* in his *Marginalia*, "and one which I find much difficulty in admitting to be the composition of a woman" (34).[6] Despite widespread anti-Catholic sentiment—and the fact that even pious reviewers condemned overtly "preachy" novels—*Ellen Middleton*'s obvious religious sympathies did not detract from its widespread popularity. "The Puseyism of Ellen Middleton," marveled a reviewer for the Catholic *Rambler*, "could not keep it out of the circulating libraries; and we suspect that few recent novels have been so much read by the more intelligent and critical class of novel-readers" (Stothert 17). Most remarkably, these "intelligent and critical" readers were apparently unfazed by the book's strong argument in support of auricular confession. Yet, even if, in their lust for a good story, Fullerton's readers overlooked its doctrinal fine points, the concept of confession is crucial to understanding its appeal. *Ellen Middleton*'s use of confession as a rhetorical and narrative strategy allows for one of the most compelling, sympathetic, and believable representations of a violent, passionate woman to be found anywhere in Victorian fiction. Because confession is the only discursive practice which allows Ellen to acknowledge the disparate shards of her fragmented subjectivity—virtuous niece, devoted wife, idolatrous lover, and jealous murderess—the reader receives Ellen's entire story as a first-person narration from the penitent herself in the confessional.

Although most critical reviews did not describe *Ellen Middleton* as a novel of religious controversy, anyone familiar with contemporary anti-Catholic literature would have recognized that Fullerton had written a direct rebuttal to the most popular and widespread arguments against auricular confession. In response to arguments that confession could weaken or destroy the bonds of marriage and family, Fullerton paints in

---

6. For other praise of Fullerton's novel, see Coleridge, *Life of Lady Georgiana Fullerton*, 155–58, 160–61, which quotes the 1844 review by Gladstone in the *English Review* as well as remarks by Queen Victoria and Harriet Martineau.

Ellen Middleton a portrait of a family rent apart by the weight of a single, unconfessed sin. The novel's tragic heroine, Ellen Middleton, is a beautiful, intelligent, well-bred, and well-intentioned young woman who, at the age of sixteen, accidentally kills her cousin Julia in a fit of rage, knocking her off a staircase at the family estate. Guilt-stricken from the first moment, but terrified that her family will abhor and spurn her as a murderess, Ellen fearfully guards her dark secret throughout most of the narrative. Her situation becomes even more desperate when the adored and saintly Edward Middleton, her cousin, proposes marriage. Ellen considers confessing all to her beloved, but remains silent for fear of losing him. Shortly after the marriage, new complications arise for Ellen. A frustrated suitor, Henry Lovell—one who happened to witness Julia's murder years beforehand—uses his knowledge of Ellen's crime in order to manipulate her into accepting his passionate and selfish love. Although Ellen staunchly resists Henry's advances, he forces her into incriminating situations, leading Henry to accuse Ellen of adultery. Heartbroken, Ellen flees to a faraway English cathedral town, where she contracts consumption and confesses her sad history (i.e., the entire flashback that comprises *Ellen Middleton*) to Mr. Lacy, the canon of the cathedral. She writes her confession after revealing by degrees to Mr. Lacy that she has something terrible to confess, as Mr. Lacy reads the service for visitation of the sick—the portion of the prayer book that supporters of confession held up as empowering Anglican clergymen to grant absolution to penitents. Mr. Lacy effects a reconciliation between Ellen and her family, and Ellen dies peacefully in Edward's arms.

By making Ellen a highly sympathetic (and *almost* morally irreproachable) character who commits one horrible act in a moment of extreme anger, Fullerton refutes popular assumptions that women were naturally incapable of truly heinous crimes. Ellen is not, of course, the only depiction of a violent woman in mid-Victorian fiction, but her representation is a rarity in that her character is not rendered "monstrous" or "unnatural" by such an act. In Dickens's fiction, for example, violent, heartless, or sexually aggressive women generally carry with them tell-tale signs of mental abnormality or illness: *Great Expectations* (1860–61) shows us Miss Havisham and her delusions, along with Mrs. Joe's eventual imbecility; and, closer to the publication date of *Ellen Middleton*, *Dombey and Son* (1848) presents two related, mother-daughter pairs whose aggression and "unwomanliness" suggest that their female natures have, in one degree or another, all been warped beyond what God intended. In contrast, one violent act on Ellen Middleton's part does not mark her as a mentally unstable or unfeminine being. While the novel's depiction of the murder scene clearly demonstrates that Julia's death is an accident, not murder,[7] it also takes care to emphasize that Ellen retains her mental presence throughout the act and, therefore, bears moral accountability for the crime. In striking Julia, Ellen had not intended to murder her, but she makes no excuses for her deliberate act of violence: "I did not go mad," she states, "for I had not an instant's delusion" (1:68). Fullerton's portrayal of Ellen as natural, normal, and feminine in all respects other than her crime, suggests her belief in a universal fallenness: women could sin just as easily as men, and Ellen is no less a woman for having succumbed to her fallen nature.

Since the reader's identification with Ellen is made easier by the naturalism of the character's portrayal, the reader would likewise be able to imagine herself as capable of committing a great crime, and the psychological detail of the narrative invites the reader to partake of the same guilty tortures that Ellen suffers throughout the story. The reader is made to *feel* Ellen's guilt and, like her, to long for absolution: "I felt such an infection of criminality," reported Harriet Martineau after she read the book (qtd. in Coleridge 161).

Ellen refuses to confess her crime for years because the possibility of discovery and punishment terrifies her. Equally painful, however, is her conviction that her crime has cut her off from all other human beings, and, most important, from God himself: "I dared not address God as I had done the day before," she states. "I thought myself as of a guilty wretch, unworthy to live, unworthy to lift up her voice in prayer" (1:75–76). Only confession, by absolving Ellen's sin and removing her burden of guilt, can restore her to a sense of oneness with her Creator, and only in this way might Ellen, with a newly clean conscience, repair the intimate confidence she once shared with her aunt, one to whom "my heart had become as a sealed book" (1:257). Implicit in this passage is an argument that confession can actually repair familiar bonds rather than destroy them.

Ellen fears that a confession of guilt to her aunt would only estrange them further, and, for the sake of her marriage, she goes to great lengths to hide her secret from Edward as well. *Ellen Middleton* effectively argues that women should confess to priests rather than husbands. Certainly, Ellen's husband lacks nothing in holiness, but his excessive virtue—like that of St. John Rivers in *Jane Eyre*—renders him a rigid and unsympathetic character. His head filled with religious and romantic idealism, Edward invests both women and marriage with impossible expectations. For Edward, female violence or aggression is disgusting and completely incompatible

---

7. Ellen insists throughout her narrative that her act was not premeditated: "I had not murdered my cousin.... [W]ithout thought, without intention, I had struck her" (1:76).

with his idea of pure womanhood—even when exercised for a presumably just cause. Furthermore, as he makes clear to Ellen shortly following their marriage, a far less serious offense on her part might diminish his love for her. "[A] fault in you," he tells her, "would seem to me as a crime in another. [. . .] [T]o discover that you were not pure and good and true, beyond any other woman in the world, would be so dreadful to me, that I doubt [that] [. . .] my love could survive" (3:9).

Because a confession of murder would clearly destroy Ellen's marriage, she seeks to unburden her soul "to one who neither loved nor hated me" (1:209), for, if her husband loves her with excessive zeal for her virtue, Henry Lovell, the one man who witnessed her crime and knows her secret, loves her with a jealous ferocity that causes him at times "absolutely to hate me" (1:225). Henry, out of selfish love for Ellen, persists in his attempts to woo her even after she has married Edward. The love of both Henry and Edward for Ellen is tantamount to idolatry; although they cherish very different ideas of her, in neither case is the ideal approximate to the real, and in both this idolatrous desire drives Ellen one step closer to ruin. While Henry's idolatry merits severe narrative retribution (he dies suddenly without a deathbed repentance), Edward's fate seems surprising, considering his own significant role in bringing about Ellen's ruin and untimely demise. He experiences the conventional bout of remorse and grief over his wife's death, but, otherwise, he is never called upon to atone for his own injurious behavior.

Although several reviewers expressed dismay that Edward's "bullet-headedness," as Poe described it, escapes retribution, the novel identifies Ellen's idolatrous passion—not Henry's or Edward's—as the great sin at the root of her novel-length confession, and, therefore, Edward's sanctimonious behavior is left unpunished in spite of the novel's disapproval. Ellen's crime is murder, but what leads up to the act is her all-consuming hunger for human love. An orphan, Ellen spends her earliest years in the care of her distant and undemonstrative uncle. When Mr. Middleton takes a wife, however, Ellen's adoration of her new aunt takes on "the exclusive nature of a passionate attachment" (1:52). Thus, when, in the moments before her death, Julia, Mr. and Mrs. Middleton's daughter, suggests to Ellen that her aunt no longer loves her, it is the prospect of a seemingly loveless existence that goads Ellen into a violent rage.

The same fears of lost love which prompt Julia's death also prevent Ellen from revealing to anyone her own part in the accident. Hence she creates a situation in which her guilt feeds on itself and becomes all-engrossing. Ellen's conviction that she deserves punishment stokes her growing love for her cousin Edward, who, although ignorant of Ellen's crime, is nonetheless unsparing in his constant correction and criticism of her smallest faults. "From a child I had been afraid of Edward," she notes; "I felt in his presence as a criminal before his judge; his sternness was justice, his kindness was mercy" (2:7). Throughout the novel Edward represents for Ellen a divine and wrathful father figure, in addition to his role as her lover and husband. These two aspects of Edward's character become so intertwined in Ellen's psyche that his harsh moral chastisements begin to seem almost indistinguishable from lover's caresses: "Reprove me as often and as severely as you please," Ellen asks Edward immediately after their engagement, "treat me harshly when I deserve it: I shall never be weary of *your* reproof, nor complain of *your* severity" (2:252; emphasis in original). All tortures—physical as well as emotional—that Ellen might suffer at Edward's hands are nothing compared to the prospect of losing him and his love: "His words of love," she recalls, "sunk into my heart, like the rain of heaven on the scorched and burning sands of the desert, as I gave utterance to the long-subdued and deeply-tried passion of my soul, prostrate in spirit before him, living in the light of his eyes, and *almost longing to die in his presence, and by his hand,* ere aught in earth, or heaven, should divide us" (2:214; emphasis added).

Ellen's passionate desire is represented as a wild, unregulated force which brings harm not only to herself, but to others. Ellen, convinced of her unworthiness, resolves never to marry Edward. Yet passionate desire defeats her good intentions. In an extraordinary scene involving a rabid dog (seeming to symbolize the madness of Ellen's passion), Ellen suddenly decides to marry Edward after all (2:165-66).[8] Yet her consent to Edward's proposal is tantamount to committing another crime, which the text represents as a second murder. Ellen's repressed, guilty awareness of this fact expresses itself through a horrifying nightmare the evening before the wedding. Ellen sees herself standing before the altar as a bride, but the priest begins to read the burial service:

[T]he book in his hands grew larger and larger, and the words "For the

---

8. A scene remarkable for its Freudian implications. Edward, in the course of protecting Ellen from the dog, is left with a bloody bite on his hand; Ellen seizes his hand and sucks the poisoned blood from the wound:

[As I] pressed my lips again on that hand [. . .] there was such a suspension in my soul of everything but deep, boundless, inexpressible love, which thrilled through every nerve and absorbed every faculty, that I could have wished to die in that state of blissful abstraction. . . . The blood had ceased to flow; the task of love was over, and still I knelt by Edward's side; still his arm supported my head; still he murmured words of tenderness in my ear. (2:165-66)

Burial of the Dead," stood out in bloody letters, and seemed to rise from the page. I looked up into the priest's face [. . .] the thin lips moved, and said—"Julia's murderer—Julia's murderer!" And then the book and the altar were gone, and a coffin stood in its place; and the same voice said, "Open it!"—and the lid rose, and there was a corpse in its shroud. [. . .] I looked and it was Edward. Over and over again, during the night, I awoke in speechless terror; and when I went to sleep again, the dream haunted me anew. (2:280–81)

Although the novel criticizes Edward's unrealistic expectations of Ellen, this passage places the greatest blame for the fatal marriage once again squarely on her shoulders: the marriage is "fatal" in that Edward's unknowing espousal of a murderess jeopardizes not only his earthly happiness, but the welfare of his immortal soul.

Ellen's macabre dream also suggests, however, an alternate reading, which figures Ellen not as so much as a murderess, but as a victim of her own marriage. Marriage in this as in many other "religious" novels is portrayed as a compromise in terms of one's religious life, in that marriage signals the advent of sexual relations between husband and wife.[9] In this case, however, Ellen's foreboding about marriage in her dream, amid her repeated declarations that she wishes to die in Edward's presence or at his feet, could prefigure her own spiritual and emotional strangulation as the wife of a man who makes his love contingent upon her virtue, one who demands complete, unquestioning submission in every matter, and who even reads all her letters.

Far more than a subconscious affirmation of Ellen's guilt, this dream is one of the novel's more explicit warnings of the potential spiritual dangers of matrimony and domesticity. Such pointed social critique—expressed here and elsewhere throughout the book—seems enabled through the rhetorical practice of confession, which, whether religious or secular, as Susan Bernstein points out, allows women in Victorian novels to articulate their own social victimization (2). In *Ellen Middleton*, not only does confession form the structural framework of the novel itself, but it also offers apparently the only rhetorical vein in which Ellen can legitimately critique the social, religious, and literary conventions that have contributed to her ruin: Victorian ideals of angelic women; Evangelical notions of female religious subordination; and—most insistently—the selfish, destructive

---

9. As St. Paul warned his followers in Corinth, "the married woman is anxious about worldly affairs, how to please her husband," an admonition he delivers "to promote good order and to secure your individed devotion to the Lord" (1 Corinthians 7:34–35).

emotions which masqueraded in popular fiction as true love and salvation for women. As Bernstein also notes, however, Victorian representations of confession tend to recast women as transgressors rather than as victims (5). Despite all the ways in which Ellen is harmed by popular ideals of gender, love, and matrimony, she must, the novel insists, be held personally accountable for her moral failings—in particular, her destructive hunger for human love. Ellen's confession and absolution in a distant cathedral town presumably save her soul, but not her life: her subsequent death from consumption ultimately seems no different from the narrative retribution accorded to most other sexually and violently transgressive women in Victorian fiction.

Admittedly, it would be hard to imagine Ellen both repentant *and* alive at the novel's conclusion. If Ellen's critical voice cannot be sustained outside the confessional, neither, really, can Ellen herself. Absolution is to provide Ellen with "great depths of repose" (3:25) but "repose"—considering the heights of mental torment Ellen reports experiencing throughout her tale—is hardly something we come to associate with her character. From a reader's standpoint, in fact, it is worth considering whether Ellen's repentance and the repose that it offers are so desirable after all. In her guilt-ridden and unresolved state, Ellen's suffering invests her character with a tremendously engaging originality and vividness; more significant, as a sinner whose staunch refusal to confess alienates her from God and humankind alike, Ellen takes on the aura of a Byronic hero. She is not so majestically independent in her torment as Manfred or Childe Harold, but the association seems significant, particularly in light of her creator's adolescent crush on Lord Byron, a "strange infatuation," reported Fullerton in her autobiography, that "lasted nearly a year" (Coleridge 25). Cast in a Byronic light, Ellen's suffering—the direct outcome of her self-imposed exile from virtuous humanity, resulting from her deliberate choice to remain (throughout most of the book, at least) unrepentant—serves no lofty spiritual purpose, as it does for so many other Victorian heroines. Yet this "unholy" suffering still suggests an autonomous, even masochistic, self-mastery, one certainly at odds with Victorian norms of femininity.

Ellen's long-deferred confession does, however, restore her to the realm of Victorian womanhood. Whereas Ellen's fierce reticence eventually leads Edward (who mistakes her mysterious behavior for adultery) to cast her from their home, her confession facilitates her return to the domestic sphere. Despite the novel's construction of confession as a safe haven from potential domestic tyranny, Ellen's confessor, Mr. Lacy, arranges for her also to confess to, and beg forgiveness from, Edward and her aunt. So much for the secrecy of the confessional. The gesture does effect a reconciliation between Ellen and her family, providing her with the spiritual and emotional tranquility that she craves, although the confession ultimately silences her critical voice, recontains her dangerous (albeit energizing) impulses, and strips her character of its heroic, Byronic appeal. In the end, *Ellen Middleton* represents a most paradoxical—yet entirely comprehensible—attitude toward sin and evil. Just as Fullerton, in her youth, "dreaded sin" yet was fascinated by the scandalous Byron, *Ellen Middleton* upholds the value of confession and spiritual renewal—all the while inviting the reader, throughout most of Ellen's narrative, to experience vicariously the glamour of unregenerate evil. This fascinating tension raises *Ellen Middleton* above "mere" novels of religious controversy and renders it an important contribution to Victorian fiction at midcentury.

"I want to tell you all"
Confession in Villette

Among the many differences between Fullerton's *Ellen Middleton* and Brontë's *Villette*, most striking is the novels' divergent treatment of the relationship between human love and divine love. In contrast to *Ellen Middleton*, which piously affirms the primacy of divine love over potentially idolatrous human passion, *Villette* shows Lucy Snowe finding salvation only through the love of M. Paul Emmanuel. Yet, despite the ultimate emphasis in *Villette* on the transcendent potential of human love—as opposed to the distant, uncertain comforts of a future paradise—the Catholic rite of confession still plays an important symbolic role in Lucy's erotic redemption.

Most critics have overlooked the multivalent significance of the confessional in *Villette*, preferring to read Lucy's confession to Père Silas as, for example, one more symbol of patriarchal domination in the web of surveillance that confines her.[10] Although the novel does suggest that confes-

---

10. Many critics agree with Sandra Gilbert and Susan Gubar's assessment that confession is at best an unsatisfactory solace for Lucy, who "can only confess that she does not belong in this narrow space which cannot contain her," a realization that contributes to Lucy's growing conviction that "the church is a patriarchal structure with the power to imprison her" (415). Analyses that deal specifically with the topics of confession and anti-Catholic rhetoric in *Villette* take a similar stance. Rosemary Clark-Beattie defines Lucy's entire relation to others as "an ongoing resistance both to the temptation of the confessional and the power embedded in the confessor" (824). Although acknowledging Helen Moglen's apt observation that, in confession, Lucy acknowledges "the necessity of recognizing a part of herself too long rejected and denied" (*Charlotte Brontë* 209), Susan Bernstein concludes that "textual rebukes of the religious rite of

sion can be employed to manipulate and control women, confession also represents for Lucy Catholicism's most compelling aspect: its acknowledgment and understanding of female desire, in contrast to the austerity of English Protestantism, which recognizes only pure angels or corrupt whores. Catholicism, however, would still have Lucy repress these desires; ultimately she chooses a different "confessor," the Catholic layman M. Paul, who will, through his own passion for Lucy, "absolve" her of the necessity of hiding her less angelic self. In choosing a confessor who stands outside the auspices of institutionalized religion—one who fosters her tendency toward human idolatry—Lucy remains, unlike Ellen, to the very last page a rebel and a heretic.[11]

Unlike *Ellen Middleton*, which upholds auricular confession as a refuge for guilt-stricken women, a spiritual oasis removed from the prying eyes of fathers, husbands, and lovers, Brontë's *Villette* presents it, in many ways, in a manner similar to contemporary anti-Catholic novels. Brontë's depiction of confession, as a site for unlawful and destructive surveillance, is hardly an original one. Yet Lucy's attitude toward confession is far more nuanced and ambiguous than that demonstrated by the virtuous Protestant characters of more conventional anti-Catholic fiction. During her lonely "long vacation" (227) in Villette, Lucy acts upon her desperate need to confess to another human being—insisting, however, that her "confession" is not a revelation of sin but simply the acknowledgment of her silent sufferings: "I said, I was perishing for a word of advice or an accent of comfort. I had been living for some weeks quite alone [. . .] I had a pressure of affliction on my mind of which it would hardly any longer endure the weight" (233). Lucy's confession does bring her relief: "The mere pouring out of some

---

confession all underline the institutional subordination of women to patriarchal rule" (71). Most recently, Diana Peschier's 2005 study of anti-Catholicism in Charlotte Brontë's fiction also echoes conventional readings of the confessional in *Villette:* "Bronte extends the image of the confessional as presenting danger for Lucy Snowe who is vulnerable because of her loneliness and her repressed sexual feelings" (160).

11. Lucy's longing for confession and absolution does not end with her visit to Père Silas but persists to the final page of the novel. This spiritual and religious dimension of Lucy's quest has also been overlooked by critics, who generally read religious references, scenes, and characters either in terms of Lucy's struggle with patriarchy or as mere metaphors for self-development. "[T]he central problem in [*Villette*] is not denominational or religious but psychological," asserts Kate Lawson (53). Although, like Moglen in *Charlotte Brontë*, Lawson acknowledges confession's attractiveness to Lucy as "a place where emotion and desire may be safely expressed" (56), her emphasis on its "psychological" benefits overlooks Lucy's desperate need for religious counsel and spiritual cleansing. Similarly, Peschier argues that "when [Lucy] goes to make her own confession she is using the confessional more as a psychiatrist's couch than as a channel for the forgiveness of her sins" (158). What neither Lawson, Peschier, nor Moglen considers, however, is that, in the context of Victorian evangelicalism, Lucy's craving for human love is a sin, and a formidable obstacle to holiness and personal salvation.

portion of long accumulating, long pent-up pain into a vessel whence it could not be again diffused—had done me good," she acknowledges. "I was already solaced" (234). Unfortunately, however, Lucy's confessor immediately seizes upon his exclusive knowledge of her plight to gain for his church yet another convert. "You were made for our faith," he states, "[D]epend upon it our faith alone could heal and help you—Protestantism is altogether too dry, cold, prosaic for you" (234). Although Lucy would sooner "walk into a Babylonish furnace" than make a return visit, she admits that had she returned to him on the following day, "I might just now, instead of writing this heretic narrative, be counting my beads in the cell of a certain Carmelite convent in the Boulevard of Crecy in Villette" (235).

Why does Lucy admit to this startling inclination to Catholicism and to the rigors of monastic life? Possibly because Catholicism at least acknowledges—and consequently, in some fashion validates—Lucy's overweening desire. Although scholars have long speculated about the possible contents of Lucy's confession, when this scene is examined in the context of *Villette* as a whole, little doubt remains that Lucy's "dreary, desperate complaint" (258) centers upon her crushing loneliness and her desperate hunger for love. Although she insists that her revelation is no sin, female desire is continually represented as a potentially destructive force. The clearest embodiment of this danger is not a rabid dog, as in *Ellen Middleton*, but Madame Beck's violent and ungovernable child, who is appropriately named Desiree:

> This was a vicious child. [. . .] Amongst her other endowments she boasted an exquisite skill in the art of provocation, sometimes driving her *bonne* and the servants almost wild. She would [. . .] wantonly tear their best caps and soil their best shawls; [. . .] she would smash articles of porcelain or glass—[. . .] plunder the preserves, drink the sweet wine [. . .]. (157–58)[12]

In her response to Desiree's antics, Madame Beck in turn embodies the Catholic Church and its attitude toward the sins confessed by female penitents. As Lucy describes the confessions of her wayward young charges, she notes that "the priest heard unshocked and absolved unreluctant" (145). For the Church, surveillance and control are enough. In a like man-

---

12. My thanks to Nicole Knapp, a friend and fellow graduate student at Indiana University, who helped me appreciate the significance of this easily overlooked character and passage in *Villette*.

ner, Madame, when told of Desiree's latest transgression, simply states that "Desiree a besoin d'une surveillance toute particulière [Desiree needs a very special watch kept on her]" (158).

Although on the one hand Lucy resists the control that the Catholic Church would assume over her most private longings, on the other hand the very fact that it recognizes her sexuality as normal (albeit potentially dangerous) seems to provide her with some measure of consolation. The Catholic Church admits, despite its sinister intentions in the novel, a complex, well-rounded view of female human nature, in the midst of a culture which recognizes only angels, whores, or madwomen. For example, when Dr. John brings Lucy to the art museum, she is greeted by two images that underscore society's rigid, impermeable distinction between two kinds of women—purely sensual and wanton "slug[s]" as represented by the grossly voluptuous Cleopatra, as opposed to the "cold and vapid," "bloodless, brainless nonentities" Lucy so despises in the flat depiction of a virtuous wife and mother, as represented by a series entitled *La Vie d'une femme* (340, 277–78).

Yet Catholicism cannot, in its institutional auspices, help Lucy. Having recognized the physical and sensual desires possessed by *all* men and women, the Jesuitic Catholics of Villette pamper and indulge the cravings of the body in order to control the mind and the spirit. As Lucy states of Madame Beck's system of education, "Each mind was being reared in slavery; but, to prevent reflection from dwelling on this fact [. . .] [t]he CHURCH strove to bring up her children robust in body, feeble in soul, fat, ruddy, hale, joyous, unthinking, unquestioning. 'Eat, drink and live!' she says. 'Look after your bodies; leave your souls to me'" (195–96). Lucy's vision of herself as a nun suggests, moreover, that, rather than stamping out her desire, this most sensual of faiths would sublimate it, turning it into an eroticized yet otherwise wholly immaterial worship of God the Father and Son—a life that would be for Lucy tantamount to a live burial, as the legend of the nun and the pear tree suggests.[13] In reaction against the gross sensuality of Catholicism, Lucy clings to the austere faith of her childhood. Still, Protestantism is, as Père Silas aptly notes, a faith "too dry, cold, prosaic" for her. Lucy's "strange, self-reliant, invulnerable creed" (512), as M. Paul describes it, seems to provide her little or no consolation; she "went by turns, and indiscriminately, to the three Protestant Chapels of Villette" (513). Lucy's church attendance may reinforce her Protestant

---

13. Lucy explains that Madame Beck's house was presumed to have been a convent in former times, and she describes an old pear tree in the garden that, according to legend, sheltered "the bones of a girl whom monkish conclave of the drear middle ages had here buried alive, for some sin against her vow" (172).

identity, but her detached wanderings from one chapel to another suggest that she has found no community, no human connection, at any one chapel in particular.

Unable to find succor through either Catholicism or Protestantism, Lucy ultimately finds her redemption through an "erotic faith" (to borrow Robert Polhemus's term) which, heterodox as it is, nonetheless seems more Catholic than Protestant. While in *Ellen Middleton* Catholicism is an antidote to human idolatry, in *Villette* its most attractive aspects—its understanding of an integrated human nature and its emphasis upon absolution through confession—are incorporated through Lucy's idolatry. Although Lucy at first clings to the redemptive possibilities of her love for Dr. John, his attitude toward her reflects the blindness of English Protestant culture at large: even if Dr. John could *see* Lucy (he describes her, as a spinster, as virtually invisible, "a being inoffensive as a shadow" [403]), he could never help her reconcile body with spirit. Laboring under "an entire misapprehension of my character and nature," Dr. John attempts to treat Lucy's natural human desire as an illness.

Despite Lucy's horror of rendering herself vulnerable to the surveillance of Madame Beck and Père Silas, she cannot be redeemed until her soul is laid bare before one who will understand and absolve her desire. In contrast to Dr. John, who "did not read my eyes, or face, or gestures" (404), M. Paul, with his prying eye and penetrating insight into Lucy's character, can redeem her. Unlike the vast majority of Lucy's fellows, "who have something else to do than to read hearts and interpret dark sayings," a neglect allowing her to "be [her] own secret's sovereign" (545), M. Paul makes it his business to read the depths of Lucy's soul, starting with the contours of her physiognomy. As he peers at her face, Lucy recognizes that "he meant to see through me, and that a veil would be no veil for him" (128). Indeed, M. Paul prides himself on his intimate, privileged knowledge of everyone dwelling in Madame Beck's establishment. Trained by his Jesuit upbringing in the art of espionage, M. Paul points out to Lucy his special observation post above the garden, boasting: "My book is this garden; its contents are human nature—female human nature. I know you all by heart" (453). That post, a small room with a lattice, calls to mind what Lucy later describes as "that mystic lattice [. . .] the sliding panel of the confessional" from which Catholics "were under the surveillance of a sleepless eye" (503). Just as the Catholic priest reads the deepest secrets of the human heart in the sacrament of confession, M. Paul sees beyond women's feminine exteriors, uncovering in them what society might deem unforgivable—acts of violent aggression, displays of appetite. "[M]y pupils," he states, "those blondes jeunes filles—so mild and meek—I have seen the most reserved—romp like boys, the demurest—snatch grapes from the walls, shake pears from the trees" (454). While nearly all Lucy's acquaintances regard her as, at best, meek, retiring, and devoid of spirit, M. Paul insists to her that "you want so much checking, regulating, and keeping down" (452).

Mere surveillance, however, is not sufficient for redemption. In the confessional, the Catholic priest represents Christ, yet, according to Catholic teaching, even Christ in all his omniscience will not absolve sin until the penitent expresses sincere recognition of and repentance for her transgression. For this reason, as long as Lucy remains resistant to M. Paul's gaze, his spying is mere espionage and a mode of surveillance that is at once manipulative and unreliable. On the basis of his observations of Lucy's considerable erudition, for example, M. Paul becomes convinced that she is well versed in classical languages. This false impression is corrected only after he clumsily and cruelly attempts to extract from Lucy a confession of her knowledge in front of his two learned but boorish colleagues—a confession that would serve only M. Paul's selfish desire to impress his fellow scholars. Yet, despite her professed horror at these manipulative tactics, Lucy is no innocent victim. She actively participates in countersurveillance, and her own failures also threaten the precarious trust existing between herself and M. Paul. During the midnight festival, for example, Lucy, who is spying from a distance on M. Paul, Madame Beck, and their party, becomes convinced that she has stumbled upon the deepest secret of M. Paul's heart. Lucy's unreasoning desire—along with the information she has gathered from Père Silas regarding Paul's eternal devotion to the dead Justine Marie—leads her to believe that the young girl at Paul's side, his ward and Justine's namesake, is also his intended bride.

Snared in a tangle of espionage, suspicion, and secrecy, neither Paul nor Lucy can freely love until *each* has made a voluntary and sincere confession of desire to the other. While Ellen Middleton dies hoping to reach paradise, Lucy seems to attain it on earth—however briefly. Her redemption relies upon the attainment of full truth and knowledge in regard to her lover; in this regard, at least, her heterodox paradise fits St. Paul's description of heaven, where "then [we shall see] face to face [. . .] then I shall know even as also I am known" (1 Corinthians 13:12). Just as Christ promised to prepare heavenly dwellings for his apostles, Paul leads Lucy to her long-awaited home—in this case her new house in the Faubourg Clotilde. Immediately upon entering the house, Paul feeds Lucy—an act significant for its resonance of the Holy Eucharist but also indicative of the way in which Paul's love has reconciled Lucy's physical hungers with her spiritual longings. Appropriately, the meal is simple—rolls, fruit, chocolate—refreshing, but not cloying, to the body as well as the spirit.

The union of body and soul is further emphasized by the date of this event: 15 August, the Catholic feast of the Assumption, commemorating the day on which Christ lifted up the Virgin Mary, *body and soul*, into heaven. According to Catholic tradition, Mary was, among all human beings, the only one entitled to the privilege of immediate bodily resurrection, as she was conceived without sin.

Lucy's salvation, of course, is contingent upon confession: she must reveal to Paul the extent of her love for and devotion to him. As they walk toward the new house and school, Lucy obtains from Paul something tantamount to an absolution of what, for Lucy, has long marked her as doomed by Fate in her quest for erotic love: the deficiencies of her physical appearance:

> "Do I displease your eyes *much*?" I took courage to urge: the point had its vital import for me.
>
> He stopped, and gave me a short, strong answer—an answer which silenced, subdued, yet profoundly satisfied. Ever after that, I knew what I was for *him*; and what I might be for the rest of the world, I ceased painfully to care. (583; emphasis in original)

Although Paul's response brings Lucy one step closer to redemption, it also suggests that *his* salvation is at stake. By coyly withholding the exact content of Paul's response from the reader, Lucy endows his revelation of his physical attraction to her with the status of a secret confession.

The notion of Paul confessing to Lucy has the potential to overturn the power dynamic which Lucy (and undoubtedly, so many Victorian readers) abhorred: the control wielded by male priests over female penitents in the confessional. But Paul cannot convincingly take on the role of penitent, for, as a man, his desire is not perceived as sinful or transgressive. Therefore, although Paul obviously must unfold his heart to Lucy in order to elicit disclosures in turn, the climax of the afternoon in Fauborg Clotilde resides in Lucy's dramatic and passionate confession, one which goes far beyond the protestation of sisterly devotion she had made previously:

> "I want to tell you something," I said; "I want to tell you all."
>
> "Speak, Lucy; come near; speak. Who prizes you if I do not? Who is your friend, if not Emmanuel? Speak!" (590–91)

As Paul's mention of his surname calls to mind Christ and the means by which a Catholic priest derives from him the authority to absolve sin in the confessional, Lucy narrates to Paul all the heartrending details of her trip to the park: her drug-induced state, her obsessive spying, her reason warped by passion, her fierce jealousy of a simple schoolgirl. The dark torrent that pours out of Lucy's soul surprises her: "Warm, jealous and haughty, I knew not till now that my nature had such a mood" (591). Paul, however, careful student of human nature that he is, reveals that he knows Lucy better than she herself does. Rather than be shocked or offended by Lucy's disclosure, he embraces her. "I think I deserved strong reproof," she states, "but when have we our deserts? I merited severity; he looked indulgence. To my very self I seemed imperious and unreasonable. [. . .] [H]e gathered me near his heart. I was full of faults; he took them and me all home" (591).

Lucy's "sins" have been forgiven, but her absolution differs drastically from the one Ellen Middleton receives at the end of her narrative. Although, in *Ellen Middleton*, female desire and appetite are natural, not warped or monstrous, elements of female nature, these cravings disrupt the social order and destroy both self and others and, hence, must be strictly regulated and controlled. The desire itself may be natural, but any failure to rein in this desire for the love of God and one's fellow human beings is a transgression against divine law, and the errant woman (or man) must confess and renounce this sin in order to maintain a close relationship with God. In *Villette*, however, Lucy never alludes to a close union with God—nothing, at least, analogous to the sacred tie that Ellen Middleton longs to restore through confession. Lucy, through her confession, receives not so much absolution for her desire as a validation that this desire is, when accepted by another, no sin at all.

Lucy, who invests human love with divine transcendence, might seem, from a modern secular perspective, to have achieved a satisfactory reconciliation between the competing demands of flesh and spirit. This idyll does not last, however. In a plot development that has long baffled readers, M. Paul dies in a shipwreck. Feminist critics sometimes interpret Paul's death as a necessary condition for Lucy's full maturation as an autonomous being: "There was no man in Lucy's society," argues Kate Millett, "with whom she could have lived and still been free" (40). Yet the spiritual and religious integrity that Brontë and her female contemporaries craved is largely incompatible with twentieth- and twenty-first-century notions of freedom and empowerment. For all the radical individuality of her heroines, Brontë herself expressed a constant fear that her actions and beliefs might contradict a higher, divine will. Indeed, her letters reveal a woman no less preoccupied with the perils of human idolatry than Fullerton herself: "Why," lamented Brontë to her friend Ellen Nussey, "are we to be divided? Surely it must be because we are in danger of loving each other too well—of losing sight of the *Creator* in idolatry of the *creature*" (qtd.

in Gaskell 146; emphasis in original). Considering, then, that Lucy's situation as she narrates her story parallels that of the aged Miss Marchmont, tragically bereaved of a man whom she thinks of "more than of God," to the extent of committing blasphemy (101), M. Paul's death could be read (unattractive as such an interpretation seems today) as a divine condemnation for Lucy's sin of idolatry. In this sense, therefore, *Villette*, like *Ellen Middleton*, is a novel-length confession—one made, however, by an unrepentant sinner, an outcast and a heretic.

This chapter's juxtaposition of Brontë's *Villette* with Fullerton's *Lady-Bird* highlights how controversies over spiritual authority and auricular confession could help writers articulate concepts of female identity and vocation and represent the challenges women confronted in reconciling spiritual integrity with popular domestic ideals. As in the comparative analysis of *Jane Eyre* and *Lady-Bird* in chapter 1, Brontë's and Fullerton's novels, considered in tandem, also challenge simple dichotomies of "religious" versus "secular" fiction. Within the context of *Ellen Middleton*, readers gain a deeper understanding of the profoundly religious elements of *Villette*. Conversely, an analysis of the presumably conservative *Ellen Middleton* with *Villette* unveils a radical critique of domestic ideology within Fullerton's text. Once more, Fullerton's social critique could be considered more powerful and effective than Brontë's. While both women frustrate the marriage plot in killing off a major character, the "painfulness" of Fullerton's fiction (a quality which irked her reviewers) resides in her staunch refusal to compromise women's spiritual integrity with romantic sentiment or readerly expectations.[14] Ellen cannot love both Edward and God; God, it seems, jealously takes her to His bosom in the final pages. Lucy's God, in taking M. Paul, may be all too similar to Ellen's. Nonetheless, by clinging to earthly love at her soul's peril, Lucy epitomizes a dilemma facing so many female Victorian readers: the difficulty of accommodating an otherworldly, more traditional religious worldview represented by Fullerton's fiction, with the temporal expectations, demands, and desires imposed by an increasingly secular society.

Brontë's and Fullerton's engagements with auricular confession, like their "sermons" on marriage, once again demonstrate how the religious debates of the day spilled well beyond male clerical circles. Protestant male preachers and tract writers insisted that auricular confession victimized women and destroyed homes, but *both* Fullerton and Brontë, ironically,

14. While John Henry Newman would likely have approved of the arguments made in *Ellen Middleton* in support of confession, he reported that the novel "distressed" him: "I hardly know whether I ought to have read it. [. . .] I wish people would not write sad things—they make ones [sic] head ache; there are sad things enough in the world" (Newman qtd. in Sugg 129).

present the confessional (in one way or another) as a potentially liberating space for women. The one element tying together *all* these Victorian texts on confession is an acknowledgment of the fragility and precariousness of the middle-class British home. Asserting, like Jules Michelet, that a few feminine whispers in the ear of a Catholic priest transforms a man's castle into a "glass dwelling" hardly demonstrates confidence in the strength or solidity of the domestic establishment. Home is also a fragile entity for Fullerton and Brontë, but confession, in their novels, shores up the home rather than threatens it. Ellen Middleton, an orphan, is driven to murder when her cousin challenges her primacy in her aunt and uncle's establishment; later she is exiled from her marital home by a rigid, vengeful husband. Only confession can restore her to home and Edward. For Lucy Snowe, also an orphan, "home" remains an abstract concept throughout much of *Villette*. So traumatic are her memories of her earliest home that Lucy conceals them from readers. She longs for a home with Graham Bretton and his mother, but is denied it. As in *Ellen Middleton,* confession in *Villette* does not carry one away from home, but brings one toward it. Only after confessing her love for M. Paul does Lucy receive her little house and school, her paradise on earth, soon to be marred by the act of a vengeful, jealous God.

CHAPTER THREE

Narratives of Female Celibacy

> Charles Darwin's daughter Henrietta was, recalled her niece, "a very fierce anti-Catholic." One evening about the turn of the century she wrangled about Rome with her young relation until bedtime, till both went to bed with headaches. "I was lying peacefully reading, and beginning to feel a little calmer, [recalls the niece, Gwen Raverat] when the door burst open and a tiny frail figure, in a red dressing-gown and white shawl, appeared at the end of my bed. Fixing me with eyes burning out from under her shaggy brows, she began without preamble: "I could SWALLOW the Pope of Rome, but what I can NOT swallow is the Celibacy of the Clergy."
> —G. F. A. Best (quoting Raverat, 126)

THE aspect of Catholicism that most directly contributed to its popular designation as an "antidomestic" religion was surely its privileging of celibacy over matrimony. If the Victorians were famously prudish about sex, they were even more horrified at the thought that Catholic priests, monks, and nuns systematically renounced it. In 1840, William Wordsworth writes, "I reckon the constrained celibacy of the clergy the monstrous root of the greatest part of the mischiefs of Popery. [. . .] If we would truly spiritualize men, we must take care that we do not do so by unhumanizing them, which is the process in respect of all those who are brought up with a view to the making of that unnatural vow" (qtd. in Best 126). Wordsworth's vocabulary is telling: "[un]true," "unhuman," and "unnatural." As Best notes, Victorians accepted the fact that some mellow bachelors "could be happy and virtuous" outside the married state, but "they must have the freedom to choose the single life" (125).

If the Victorians had difficulty "swallowing" male celibacy (to the point that an elderly woman was still picking arguments about it with her niece half a century after the "Papal Aggression"), how much more "untrue, unhuman, and unnatural" might they consider female celibacy? Popular depictions of both Catholic nuns and Protestant spinsters suggest that in the opinion of many Victorians, no sane or healthy woman would *voluntarily* choose to live without a husband and children. Anti-Catholic literature constantly evokes the specter of young women being kidnapped, brainwashed, or inveigled into the convent; and spinsters, it was widely assumed, merely resigned themselves to a shabby lot in life. As an anonymous 1869 poem, "The Spinster's Dream," says of its protagonist,

> In gloomy idleness her time she passed,
> Blaming the lot in which her life was cast:
> Accusing Fate in bitter tone,
> For having left her thus—unloved—alone!

Despite the fact that many differences could, and did, exist between Anglo- and Roman Catholic nuns and Protestant spinsters (indeed, Catherine Sinclair, a model of virtuous Protestant spinsterhood, spent much of her time excoriating nuns in print), in nineteenth-century England both occupied what Frederick Roden describes as the "culturally queer" category of the Victorian celibate.[1]

Beyond their shared designation as Victorian celibates, another link between nuns and spinsters is the types of stories told about them. This is the only chapter in the book that discusses "forgotten" fictional texts exclusively; they are "forgotten," in part, because in the nineteenth century it was particularly difficult to write women's fiction that was not preoccupied with romantic love, matrimony, and heterosexual domesticity. The texts I discuss here—a handful of novels attacking Catholic convents, and *The Experience of Life* (1852), Elizabeth Missing Sewell's fictional apologia for spinsterhood—at times sit awkwardly within the genre of domestic fiction. These narratives of Victorian celibates rely on Catholic imagery and discourse to make radically different points. Anticonvent novels employ Catholicism to condemn lifelong female celibacy as "unnatural," whereas Sewell's novel invokes Anglo-Catholic veneration of virgin martyrs to "recuperate" spinsterhood as a spiritually empowering, freely chosen vocation for women. Perhaps the most interesting connection between these anti- and pro-celibacy novels, however, is that both, in very different ways, call into question the sanctity of conventional, heterosexual models of Victorian domesticity.

1. In designating Victorian celibates as "culturally queer," Roden does not necessarily imply homosexuality; queers, he notes, are "cultural dissidents, deviant or non-standard in some way" (2).

A Home That Is Not a Home
Victorian Women's Representations of the Convent

In her autobiography, Charlotte Elizabeth Tonna describes how she once made the acquaintance of a young nun, the director of an Irish convent who sought Tonna's advice in teaching a deaf student. Tonna describes how, on her first visit to the convent, she is alternately enchanted and horrified by the beautiful Mother Superior:

> The nun was indeed a most engaging young lady: in personal appearance, in manner, in feeling, realizing the visions of my girlish romance when reading idle stories in novels in such topics. She had, moreover, all the animated warmth of a genuine Irishwoman, and her fine countenance, beaming with benevolent joy at our successful beginning, and with affectionate gratitude for my services, quite won my heart. [. . .] I [. . .] unhesitatingly mounted the stairs with my sweet conductor. Judge what was my dismay when, on passing the folding-doors, I found myself in a splendid Popish chapel, opposite the altar, over which shone a richly gilt cross, while my poor nun was prostrated in the lowliest adoration, touching the ground with her forehead before the senseless idol! (*Personal Recollections* 152–53)

Shocked by the nun's "act of idolatrous homage rendered to a thing of wood and stone," Tonna decides to try saving her soul. "With all my heart I loved the gentle, affectionate, elegant nun, she notes, "and earnestly did I pray for help in bringing her back, as I was resolved to do, from the path of destruction. While I deliberated on the best means of commencing the work, the difficulty was removed by her openly attempting to convert me" (154). Tonna receives from the nun a book on Roman Catholic theology, reads it, and is, expectedly, repulsed by it: "[H]ow disgusting," she exclaims, "the painted face, the gaudy trappings, and the arrogant assumptions of the Great Harlot appeared in my eyes" (155).

Tonna's description of this incident suggests much about nineteenth-century Protestant women's encounters with Catholicism. Tonna arrives at the convent with certain expectations. Her "visions of girlish romance" nurtured by the "idle stories" she has read predispose her to view the nun at first as an alluring, yet entirely familiar and comfortable figure, who later betrays a frightening, incomprehensible tendency toward idolatry. The nun's idolatry marks her as radically other to Tonna's virtuous Protestant self, yet the nun's attempt to convert Tonna—simultaneous with Tonna's decision to convert the nun—renders her Tonna's mirror image or double.

The nun's threat, therefore, resides not just in her exoticism, but also in her familiarity. The tension between familiar and foreign is, of course, a common trope in nineteenth-century anti-Catholic literature. Perhaps nowhere, however, was the tension between familiar and foreign so obvious and so fraught with anxiety as in Victorian women's representations of the convent. While women writers attempted to maintain a sharp division between the corrupt convent and the wholesome Victorian home, implied similarities between the two continually threatened to undermine their project. Rather than valorize the home at the expense of the convent, women's anti-Catholic novels ultimately call the ideology of Victorian domesticity into question. Novels such as Mary Martha Sherwood's *The Nun* (1833), Catherine Sinclair's *Beatrice* (1852), Eliza Smith Richardson's *The Veil Lifted* (1865), and Jeanie Selina Dammast's *St. Mary's Convent* (1866)[2] help demonstrate that in attacking the convent, British Protestant women writers presented a nightmarish vision of domesticity gone wrong: a desacralized, nonreproductive domestic space overrun by the forces of materialism, atheism, imperialism, and industrialism.

British historians have documented the rapid establishment of both Anglican and Roman Catholic convents at midcentury, as well as the Protestant backlash against them.[3] Susan Mumm, in describing reasons for the "enormous popular opposition" against sisterhoods, emphasizes their challenge to the domestic ideal of women—both married and single—remaining within the bosom of the family (175). Jenny Franchot, in her analysis of nineteenth-century American convent exposés, describes Protestant constructions of the convent as a threatening, "alternative family" which "voiced anxieties about [. . .] domesticity, its gender dis-

---

2. Catherine Sinclair (1780–1864) was an Edinburgh philanthropist and writer, best remembered for her children's book *Holiday House* (1839) and for *Beatrice, or the Unknown Relatives* (1852), described by Gabrielle Ceraldi as "one of the most popular of the so-called Papal Aggression Novels" (361). Mary Martha Sherwood (1775–1851) was of course among the most prominent Evangelical writers of the nineteenth century. Her works include the highly successful *History of the Fairchild Family* (in three parts: 1818, 1842, 1847), in addition to approximately four hundred other titles. Eliza Smith Richardson and Jeanie Selina Dammast are extremely obscure figures, and I have been unable to find reliable biographical information for either. Both, however, seem to have been fairly prolific writers. The British Library catalogue lists ten other titles for Richardson, besides *The Veil Lifted* (mostly anti-Catholic works), ranging in dates from 1848–1873; there are six other works (besides *St. Mary's Convent*) by Dammast, at least two of which appear to be children's books.

3. See Peter F. Anson's *The Call of the Cloister: Religious Communities and Kindred Bodies in the Anglican Communion* (1955); A. M. Allchin's *The Silent Rebellion: Anglican Religious Communities 1845–1900* (1958); Walter L. Arnstein's *Protestant versus Catholic in Victorian England: Mr. Newdegate and the Nuns* (1982); and Susan Mumm's *Stolen Daughters, Virgin Mothers: Anglican Sisterhoods in Victorian Britain* (1999); and chapter 8 of Michael Wheeler's *The Old Enemies: Catholic and Protestant in Nineteenth-Century English Culture*.

symetries, its isolation from the public sphere, its polarized adulation of sentimental womanhood and entrepreneurial manhood" (117). Franchot focuses her analysis on two accounts by "escaped nuns," Maria Monk and Rebecca Reed. In writing their sensational, salacious narratives, Americans Monk and Reed, who were clearly inspired by Gothic thrillers, also drew upon the basic formula of the British anticonvent novel, one that remained more or less unchanged throughout the century.[4] The heroine is usually a young girl who, through ignorance, extreme circumstances, or the machinations of a Jesuit priest, finds herself trapped behind convent walls. Through the girl's narration, the reader gains privileged access to the forbidden, exotic world of the convent, in all its excesses, cruelty, and worldliness. The girl remains captive just long enough for the novelist to expound her views, and then she escapes, preferably into the arms of a Bible-toting Protestant hero.

One can, however, trace a subtle evolution in the British anticonvent novel between the early and middle decades of the nineteenth century. It began to exhibit more qualities of the domestic novel and less of the gothic. The "true" accounts by Monk and Reed resemble early British anti-Catholic Gothic novels, such as *The Italian* (1797) and *The Monk* (1796), in their sensational, salacious detail. But in Britain by the middle decades of the nineteenth century, the public was no longer to be frightened by wolfish priests, prostitute-nuns, or murdered babies. Frightening enough was simply the notion of women living "unnatural" lives in celibate female communities. As Hobart M. Seymour argued in an 1852 lecture against convents, nuns "must spend their life-long existence, wearisome to themselves, and useless to others, for they are without one object to interest or occupy them." He concludes "that the inner life of a nunnery is a life of monotony, wearisomeness, disappointment, contention, bitterness, and despair" (5). Like Seymour's lecture, midcentury anti-Catholic novels focus primarily on the nun's "unnatural" mode of life, and the psychological torments it entails.

While the convent novel's new emphasis on the inner lives of nuns resulted in a somewhat higher level of character development and psychological depth, they retained all the flaws that George Eliot so harshly condemns in "Silly Novels by Lady Novelists." Eliot, of course, insists that a novel should portray a realistic depiction of life, one drawn from personal experience and observation. In contrast, anticonvent novels remained the stuff of sheer fantasy. Protestant women like Sherwood,

---

4. Wheeler lists nine other eighteenth- and nineteenth-century British anticonvent novels of this genre, not discussed here (214).

Dammast, and Richardson had, at best, limited access to the convent, and they drew their information largely from anti-Catholic propaganda and hearsay.[5] While this ignorance did not make for good fiction, it did leave room for telling inventions. Just as the Irish nun, in Tonna's recollections, became the mirror image of Tonna and her own spiritual strivings, the fictional nuns in midcentury anticonvent novels eerily represent unhappy housewives. British women writers intended to demonstrate how Anglo and Roman Catholicism threatened the integrity of the Victorian domestic sphere. In their novels, however, women and domestic spaces are not threatened so much by Catholicism as by the larger, more pervasive, and unavoidable social forces it represents, such as industrialism, materialism, and secularism.

In the Victorian convent novel, the primary distinction between the domestic and commercial spheres is dismantled. Although some novels, such as Catherine Sinclair's *Beatrice,* depict nuns in arduous, degrading tasks—such as the novice who must clean wooden floors with her tongue (II:145)—others show nuns engaged in pleasant, if frivolous and mundane, tasks. Cecile, the heroine of Sherwood's *Nun* who decides to join a convent, states that "some of us made sweetmeats, and dried them in the sun; others artificial flowers; some made purses, and bags, and covers of books, adorned with beads; these were sent to Turin and sold" (65). Emily, the heroine of Dammast's novel, describes a similar scene, with "a number of the sisterhood [. . .] occupied in embroidering robes for priests, and dressing up little figures of the Virgin and St. Joseph" (61). Both novels are critical of this type of silly work: "Emily [. . .] wondered how women in the full possession of their faculties could occupy their time in so frivolous a manner" (61). On one hand the nuns' work seems so insignificant that it is mere play, like the dressing of dolls, yet these scenes also call to mind sweatshop labor, which serves to fatten the coffers of the Church of Rome. The nuns' fascination with trinkets is a most worldly wallowing in materialism, one that might easily call to mind ornate middle-class Victorian homes. Finally, one cannot help but observe that the work of beading and embroidering, as frivolous as the heroines describe it, was precisely the kind of occupation that proper Victorian women were expected to pursue in their drawing rooms. The conflation between domestic and commercial continues as the nuns, workers in the Romish factory "system," themselves resemble dumb pieces of machinery. "I could enumerate a dozen or more

---

5. Richardson claimed to have spent five years in the Roman Catholic Church and had direct experience of convent life (*Five Years a Catholic: with incidents of foreign convent life* [1864]). Even if this claim is true, her representations of convent life are as flat and stereotyped as those by Tonna, Sherwood, and other Protestant writers.

of these good honest bodies," confides Sister Pauline to young Cecile, "who never think at all" (60). Dammast's novel continually describes the nuns as performing actions "mechanically" (69); and "at the end of the year Emily found herself, as it were, part of the machine, whose regular movements seemed *clock-like in their perfectness*" (116; emphasis added). Apparently life in the convent did not lead to a higher, ethereal existence, but one engulfed by the grinding, soulless cycle of manufacture and consumption.

The factory imagery in anticonvent novels of course raises the question of products, aside from beaded bags and wax dolls. While the business of the domestic family was to produce babies, there were certainly no babies (legitimate ones, at least) produced in these depictions of the convent. Indeed, their message is that women who do not produce babies are themselves infantilized. "An old nun is like an old baby," states Catherine Sinclair in *Popish Legends and Bible Truths*, "her mind reduced to a mere second childhood by leading a life of unreasoning obedience" (liii). Aside from this most unnatural production of "babies," the primary function of the convent "factory" seems to be the transformation of living, thinking, feeling women into mindless automatons stripped of all feminine traits, in particular, the all-important capacity for feeling. "I thought you knew," remonstrates another nun to the naïve Emily, "that a Jesuit is bound not to possess human feeling [. . .]. It is one of their most binding rules that all love and humanity are to be trampled upon when they threaten to interfere with any duties imposed by the order" (Dammast 99). These nuns "are not naturally more unfeeling than others," explains the narrator of *The Veil Lifted*, "but their feelings have been repressed and blunted, and their finer susceptibilities deadened, by years of practical stoicism" (151). These female Scrooges in black habits have become hardened by their association with the Catholic Church, presented here as a global moneymaking enterprise.

The one feeling that these accounts do not deny is sexual attraction: sexuality diverted, however, from its "natural" channels. Despite the enduring popularity of the figure of the lascivious priest, in novels such as *The Nun* and *St. Mary's Convent*, the sexual predator is the Mother Superior, and the primary sexual tension is between women. Dammast, in *St. Mary's Convent*, describes the Reverend Mother as a classic femme fatale:

> [Reverend Mother] was tall and slight, long flowing black robes setting off the graceful outline of her figure [. . .] but in her eyes and smile lay the fascination that made her irresistible. Usually the lids drooped over those lovely eyes, and the long black lashes literally rested on her cheeks [. . .] two lurking dimples near the corners of her mouth gave an almost magi-

cal sweetness to her expression! Then the raised eyelids gave to view the soft black velvet-like orbs, that seemed to enchain the gaze, and draw the beholder as by a hidden power or spell under their marvelous influence.

Reverend Mother's beauty has an almost hypnotic effect on the young female visitor to the convent: "[H]er eyes seemed to penetrate into Emily's very soul, and draw forth as by magnetism a responsive thrill" (21). Cecile, the narrator of Sherwood's *Nun*, describes the "particularly pleasing" appearance of the abbess, remarking upon "a most encouraging and even caressing manner, and of a sort which, had I previously been balancing respecting my vocation, would, I felt, have instantly decided me" (10). "I did not," she concludes, "feel able to resist her" (12). The Reverend Mother is typically presented as the center of her "home," but it is a female power unsoftened or untrammeled by any higher male authority. For the young, orphaned female narrators of *The Nun* and *St. Mary's Convent*, the Mother Superior initially is presented as a version of the Household Angel, a substitute for the lost mother. But each girl soon discovers the anti-Mother lurking beneath. Sherwood's abbess sows dissension among the nuns in her charge, choosing favorites among the novices (the most beautiful ones), and persecuting those who have fallen out of favor. *The Veil Lifted* describes a Mother Superior blind to all "natural" family ties and obligations, who refuses to let a dying nun see her sister. This same Mother feels morally obligated to cultivate a "heart of bronze" when punishing any infractions of her rule.

Sexuality in these communities, although undeniably present, is fairly well suppressed (no nun-prostitutes here). However, the convent is frequently made to resemble another site of female lasciviousness—the harem. Descriptions of the convent resonate with Eastern allusions. This comparison is particularly marked in the writing of Catherine Sinclair, whose heroine, Beatrice, compares one of the convent rituals to a "secret Hindoo rite," and tells the nuns that they "seem in all respects like the Vestal virgins of a heathen temple" (III:131). Another character, Lady Edith, sees a nun prostrating herself in church one day, and "almost expected to see the black face of a Hindoo worshipper" under her veil (II:271). In this sense, the convent also appears as a nightmarish version of the Victorian home despoiled by Britain's exposure to the "heathens" and "pagans" of its far-flung empire. As Susan Griffin argues in her chapter on Sinclair's novel, Beatrice "attempts to shore up a unified, homogenous British identity by descrying and describing foreign "Others," only to uncover how the foreign has already infected contemporary Britain" (132).[6] Here the

---

6. Griffin's chapter on *Beatrice* includes an interesting discussion of the novel's implicit com-

Imperial Other has, quite literally, come home to roost in English domestic spaces.

Sherwood, Dammast, Richardson, and other opponents of convent life worked particularly hard to point out the differences between the Victorian home and the convent. Yet what leaps out from the pages of their narratives is a tremendous anxiety about the resemblances between them. Just as anti-Catholic polemicists condemned Catholicism for "posing" as Christianity, writers of anticonvent narratives were eager to disabuse young female readers of the error that the convent could provide them a loving, supportive, or happy home.

While the figure of the Reverend Mother was exposed as one point of false parallelism between the home and the convent, what writers focused on in even greater detail was the nuns' profession ceremony, which, in both Anglo and Roman Catholic sisterhoods, did indeed resemble that of a marriage.[7] Apparently these ceremonies greatly appealed to the public imagination; in her autobiography, Charlotte Tonna describes how, when a nun took her veil at the nearly Irish Catholic convent "Every body [...] was trying for tickets to see the unhallowed show" (*Personal Recollections* 156). Writers of anticonvent novels appealed to this curiosity by providing copious details of the ceremony, "marked by all the pomp and glittering pageantry which the Church of Rome has ever at command, and all those dangerous appeals to the senses which she knows so well how to direct and organize" (Richardson 12). Sinclair describes the profession ceremony of a Miss Turton, majestic in "brocaded white silk, trimmed round the skirt with festoons of Honiton lace, looped up with bunches of white jessamine and lily of the valley" (III:127). Crowned with a wreath of orange flowers and diamonds (the property of the convent), Turton performs "a pantomime of devotion," "having practiced over the whole scene of her profession in various rehearsals before a mirror" (III:129–30). Protestant writers obviously feared that young girls would be attracted to the convent by the lavish ceremony, just as a young woman might jump into marriage for the excuse to wear a splendid gown. Their descriptions, however, only increase the allure of the profession ceremony. Naomi Ryde Smith comments on this dimension of Sherwood's novel, wryly stating: "It is possible that The

---

parisons between Jesuit priests and the "secret Hindu cult of Thuggee[...] discovered and subsequently prosecuted by British officials in India during the 1830s" (135). Gabrielle Ceraldi, in "'Popish Legends and Bible Truths': English Protestant Identity in Catherine Sinclair's *Beatrice*" (2003), also discusses how Beatrice's condemnation of the Catholic other betrays subliminal anxieties about aspects of the collective self—in particular, English Protestant identity.

7. Mumm describes profession ceremonies as "the high festival of [Anglican] sisterhood life [...]. These ceremonies were closely modelled on their Roman Catholic equivalents. At profession, the novices would wear wedding dresses at the beginning of the ceremony, which would be changed for the dress of a professed sister after the taking of the vows" (29).

Nun, intended to dissuade, may actually have persuaded some women of their vocation" (148).

These novels portray girls and women who, attracted by the romantic veneer of the convent, make a lifetime commitment to a life that they do not understand. Soon after profession they are stripped of their illusions. However, the worst most nuns suffer is not rape or other physical brutality, but a long, dreary life unrelieved of any "female" interests. "Oh! Who, that has not felt it," exclaims Sherwood's Clarice, "can conceive the horrible monotony of the mode of life I had precipitately adopted, in which there was gloom without privacy, dullness without ease, idleness without rest [...], society without amusement [...]" (78). Richardson's novel also focuses on the mental, rather than physical, trials of nuns, who, she argues, suffer from homesickness, preoccupation with the state of their souls, intense feelings of guilt, callousness, and a sense of entrapment. Yet the specter of women driven to psychological neuroses out of enforced idleness calls to mind in our own time not nuns, but Freud's bored, hysterical *hausfraus*. And surely, feelings of regret, boredom, and entrapment could plague the Victorian housewife just as easily as her "cloistered" counterpart. While Sherwood, Dammast, and Richardson never acknowledge this liability of the domestic sphere, defenders of the convent seized upon it. In *Five Years in a Protestant Sisterhood and Ten Years in a Catholic Convent* (1869), Mary Margaret Cusack, a Catholic convert and nun, states that "[u]ndoubtedly some few nuns may be drawn into the cloister unwisely, but how few are they in comparison with the thousands who make unhappy marriages" (271). In response to a proposed bill requiring government inspection of all religious houses,[8] the Catholic archbishop of Birmingham, William Bernard Ullathorne, also transforms criticisms of the convent into an exposure of the weaknesses of the institution of marriage. After explaining the long, careful process of discernment required of all novices, Ullathorne asks, "[Is this] like the lottery or the bondage which a lady subjects herself to in entering the married state? [...] [I]s [...] not [marriage] accompanied with a far less degree of probation, if previous acquaintance can be called such, and with infinitely smaller checks and reserves against the despotism of authority? And if the one state implies a final decision, and that for life, so does the other" (9).

Victorian women's representations of the convent were, for the most

---

8. Arnstein notes that parliamentarians Henry Charles Lacy and Thomas Chambers both urged for the government inspection of convents, without success. "Chambers's attempt in 1853 to institute a system of convent inspection won one test vote but was ultimately defeated, as were separate attempts in 1853 and 1854 to establish a parliamentary select committee to consider whether the inmates of such institutions and their property required additional legislative protection" (63).

part, troubled by the sensationalism of the subject matter and their lack of information about it. Ignorance, however, left room for other kinds of revelation. In their novelistic depictions of corrupt convent interiors, these women simultaneously project their darkest apprehensions about secularized English homes. Novelists worked hard to establish the nun as radically alien to everything the Victorian woman valued. Yet in their eagerness to "contain" the nun, by presenting her as powerless, feeble-minded, materialistic, and childlike, they inadvertently presented her as a distorted caricature of the Victorian domestic angel.

Spinsters in Popular Fiction
Brontë and Yonge

Victorian women writers may not have had much firsthand knowledge about nuns, but they certainly did about spinsters. Even so, the spinster proved a difficult topic, especially for novelists. In a literary form conventionally determined by the courtship plot, and in a society in which marriage, motherhood, and femininity were intimately linked, how might one construct a convincing, realistic single heroine with an autonomous identity? While the Household Angel owed her existence to Evangelical Protestantism, which framed marriage and motherhood in the context of a religious vocation, Protestant discourse was at best an impoverished medium for representing the plight and the identity of the Victorian spinster. In many cases, conduct literature presented the ideal spinster simply as a more mobile version of the Household Angel—one who places *everyone*'s needs above her own, and whose character is ennobled by passive suffering. In response to the rigid, unimaginative role allowed for single women in Protestant culture, some writers turned to Catholicism—with its emphasis upon worldly renunciation and its privileging of celibacy over marriage—in writing about spinsterhood.

This difficulty of representing the perpetually single woman plagued Charlotte Brontë, who tackled the issue of spinsterhood more directly than any other midcentury canonical novelist. In contrast to conduct books that preached religion and self-denial as reliable substitutes for husbands and children,[9] Brontë's fiction attempted to show that, as she insisted in her

9. The desire to neutralize, soften, or contain the potentially threatening figure of the single woman is evinced by a growing number of advice manuals at midcentury aimed specifically at spinsters. Anne Ritchie, in an 1861 essay for *Cornhill Magazine*, complained of "those unmarried ladies whose wail of late has been so constantly dinning in the ears of the public [. . .]. Old maids, spinsters, the solitary, heart-broken women of England, have quite a little literature

correspondence, "even a 'lone woman' can be happy, as well as cherished wives and proud mothers" (qtd. in Gaskell 247). She was, however, less than successful. In *Shirley*, we see potential spinster Caroline Helstone rejecting pious, long-suffering spinsters Miss Ainley and Miss Mann as role models; similarly, *Villette's* Lucy Snowe is only happy when she feels secure in the love of a man—whether that of Graham Bretton or M. Paul Emmanuel. Caroline Helstone's depression and Lucy Snowe's hysteria are, in the end, cured only by the promise of love and matrimony.[10]

Catholicism informs the construction of nearly all Brontë's spinsters. She uses Catholicism, however, not to elevate the condition of spinsterhood, but to cast it as an unnatural condition for women. In *Jane Eyre*, for example, one of the only women who does not marry, Eliza Reed, embraces at first Anglo-Catholic asceticism, and then enters a Catholic convent, "where punctual habits would be permanently secured from disturbance, and place safe barriers between herself and a frivolous world" (264). Although *Shirley* presents Christ-like Miss Ainsley in a positive light, her life—implicitly compared to that of a nun—strikes Caroline as an impossible model for her. "Does virtue lie in abnegation of self?" she reflects, while pondering what old maids should do with their lives. "I do not believe it. Undue humility makes tyranny; weak concession creates selfishness. The Romish religion especially teaches renunciation of self [...] and nowhere are found so many grasping tyrants as in the ranks of the Romish priesthood" (190). In *Villette*, the misery of spinsterhood is even more explicitly and extensively compared to that of the cloistered life, as Lucy Snowe identifies herself with the nun once buried alive in Madame Beck's garden.

While Brontë's suspicion of Catholicism seems to have influenced her negative construction of spinsterhood, Anglo-Catholic novelists were more successful in depicting the single life as an honorable vocation in its own right. Charlotte Yonge's spinsters are far more interesting than many others in Victorian fiction. In *Heaven and Home*, June Sturrock notes that Yonge's "concern with the spiritual life, [...] and the Tractarian emphasis on 'good works' and her personal experience of absorption in her own work, led to a foregrounding of aspects of female life beyond the erotic and

---

of their own" (318).

10. There are, of course, Elizabeth Gaskell's contented spinsters in *Cranford* (1853). Yet this novel hardly makes an effective comparison, as Gaskell situates her spinsters in a community in which marriage is not the norm. One might also consider Eliot's Dinah Morris in *Adam Bede* (1859), who initially renounces marriage for her vocation, but the force of this renunciation seems heavily compromised by the fact that Dinah eventually does marry.

the domestic" (16). Sturrock also notes that Yonge frequently provides her female characters with "interesting alternatives" to marriage, which Yonge never treats as an "inevitable resolution" (50). In the *Daisy Chain* (1856), for example, the brilliant and ambitious Ethel May and her cousin Norman fall in love—the two are presented as a perfect match—but each one renounces the other. Norman marries another out of duty to his parents, and parental duty motivates Ethel as well, who feels called to remain home and care for her aging father:

> For herself, Ethel looked back and looked on. Norman Ogilvie's marriage seemed to her to have fixed her lot in life, and what was that lot? Home and Cocksmoor had been her choice, and they were before her. Home! but her eyes had been opened to see that earthly homes may not endure, nor fill the heart. Her dear father might, indeed, claim her full-hearted devotion, but, to him, she was only one of many. Norman [her brother] was no longer solely hers; and she had begun to understand that the unmarried woman must not seek undivided return of affection, and must not set her love, with exclusive eagerness, on aught below, but must be ready to cease in turn to be first with any. Ethel was truly a mother to the younger ones; but she faced the probability that they would find others to whom she would have the second place. To love each heartily, to do her utmost for each in turn, and to be grateful for their fondness was her call; but never to count on their affection as her sole right and inalienable possession. She felt that this was the probable course, and that she might look to becoming comparatively solitary in the course of years—then tried to realize what her lonely life might be, but broke off smiling at herself, "What is that to me? What will it be when it is over? My course and aim are straight on, and He will direct my paths." (666–67)

Although Yonge's novel resembles popular conduct books for spinsters in that it counsels fortitude and faith in God for the trials of single life, what is unusual here is Ethel's choice of potentially lonely spinsterhood over the attractive Norman Ogilvie. This presentation challenges the Victorian stereotype of spinsters, who were generally presented as women who, through bad luck and lack of personal charms, were forced into lives of solitude. Because freely chosen, Ethel's spinsterhood takes on the nature of a divinely ordained vocation equally (if not more) dignified than marriage or the convent.

Heroic Spinsterhood
Elizabeth Missing Sewell's The Experience of Life

For the purposes of this chapter, I have chosen to focus on Sewell, who, even in her own lifetime, was regarded as a less talented version of Charlotte Yonge.[11] While Yonge's depictions of spinsters are uncharacteristically positive for her era, none of them, in my opinion, equal Sewell's semiautobiographical creation of spinster Sarah Mortimer in her compelling and sophisticated characterization. Elizabeth Missing Sewell (1815–1906), a celebrated writer of children's books, turned her attention to adult fiction in 1852, with the publication of *The Experience of Life*.[12] This novel, her most popular work, is a spinster *bildungsroman* whose heroine, after a lifetime of struggle and renunciation, eventually achieves a self-sufficiency, material and moral agency, and a respectable, defined role within her community. The novel, which appeared a year before Brontë's *Villette*, contains some striking parallels to Brontë's novel: each is narrated by an unattractive, insignificant heroine; each directly grapples with the difficulties facing the single woman; after many trials and much suffering, each woman develops a firm sense of who she is and her place in the world. Unlike Lucy Snowe, however, Sewell's Sarah Mortimer accomplishes this without relying on a traditional courtship plot, or indeed, any romantic attachments at all.

Sewell's dispensation of the courtship plot allows her to make a forceful critique of middle-class family life. In the midst of a culture which traditionally placed home and family at the center of all that was most sacred and holy, Sewell's novel suggests that the traditional, patriarchal home could be in fact a stumbling block to an earnest, ambitious woman of faith. In contrast to the quarrelsome, worldly Mortimer household, Sewell's novel presents two alternative, overlapping spheres—the female world of her Aunt Sarah, and the idyll of a future heavenly home. Throughout the

---

11. In a *Dublin Review* essay of 1858, Fanny Margaret Taylor (who eventually cofounded, with Georgiana Fullerton, the Poor Servants of the Mother of God) states that "Miss Sewell and Miss Yonge have displayed sufficient talent to place them in the rank of the standard novel writers of our day, but they have by no means kept even pace with each other. Miss Yonge (author of the *Heir of Redclyffe*, &c.) fairly carries off the palm" (316).

12. Born in 1815 on the Isle of Wight, Sewell was the oldest daughter of a large, prosperous family, and the sister of William Sewell, a prominent figure in the Oxford Movement. Upon her father's death in 1842, she turned to writing in order to support her mother and dependent siblings. Sewell established her reputation as a writer of pious tales for children, but her later fiction—including *Margaret Percival* (1847), *Ursula* (1858), *Ivors*, and *The Experience of Life*—was intended for adults. Sewell's books sold extraordinarily well, and her most popular titles were successively reprinted (in English, French, and German) decades after their initial publication. Sewell's tendencies to moralize, however, frustrated some critics, who regarded her pious tone as a hindrance to her full literary potential.

FIGURE 3.1 *The rotogravure of Elizabeth Sewell from her 1908 autobiography. Image courtesy of Rare Books and Special Collections, Thomas Cooper Library, University of South Carolina*

novel, Sarah's spinsterhood is presented not as an inevitable affliction, but as a freely chosen, if arduous, vocation. Sewell, an Anglo-Catholic, constructs Sarah's vocation by drawing upon revived interest in the lives of early Christian saints.[13] Sarah seeks not a garland of orange blossoms, but a martyr's crown. While Victorian women were expected to suffer passively and silently, the female martyr's active embrace of her suffering suggested a dangerously unfeminine degree of autonomy and self-assertion. Sewell's spinster-heroine Sarah Mortimer, as a self-styled martyr, creates for herself a viable, even heroic, identity in the midst of a culture which defined the

---

13. Roman Catholics, of course, drew fire from Victorian Protestants for "worshiping" the saints. Saints' feast days and legends were an important part of the Anglo-Catholic revival; this is evident through such publications as Keble's *The Christian Year* (1839) and Newman's *Lives of the English Saints* (1844–45). Within the fold of the Roman Catholic Church, Newman and Cardinal Nicholas Wiseman each published a novel about early Christian martyrs—*Callista* (1853) and *Fabiola* (1854), respectively.

spinster as invisibility or lack. Moreover, in rejecting for its heroine earthly, domestic delights for an impending, transcendent heavenly home, Sewell's novel challenges not only the rhetoric of Victorian domesticity, but also existing standards of novelistic realism and the narrow confines of the marriage plot.

Literary posterity has not been kind to Sewell; she has been remembered only as a minor novelist affiliated with the Oxford Movement, and her novels dismissed by Joseph Baker as "juvenile in morality and experience" (116). Yet a few scholars, including Patrick Scott and Shirley Foster, have called for a reassessment of Sewell's work.[14] Indeed, Sewell's characters often are more complex, their inner lives more vividly represented, and her innovations with narrative structure more ambitious than that of her more famous contemporary Yonge. But perhaps most striking, Sewell's novels more often, and more directly, interrogate the rules and expectations governing women's lives. Sewell, more religiously and socially conservative than Brontë, would never have considered herself an advocate of women's rights. In many ways Sewell's novels offer very conventional images of Victorian womanhood. Yet even in the cases of Sewell's heroines who quietly resign themselves to suffering, so vividly represented is their pain that the reader's focus inevitably shifts from the presumed value of religious resignation to the social conditions underlying the spinster's plight. As a reviewer for the *Christian Remembrancer* complained of Sewell in 1857,

> The troubles incidental to [Sewell's] own sex especially weigh on her heart and feelings; and life after life of patient self-sacrifice [. . .] pass before us, all told with an air of truth that ensures conviction, till her male readers [. . .] must feel ashamed of themselves for being at the bottom of so much suffering; and the advocates of the rights of women would certainly claim her as one of their sisterhood, but that her pious resignation and her course of active religious remedies might be, we fear, worse to their taste than the original disease. (292)

As this passage indicates, any stark display of pain might challenge a reader's complacency with the status quo. All the more so, however, when

---

14. Despite Sewell's reputation as a writer of children's fiction, Patrick Scott calls attention to "the much more exploratory, sympathetic and ironically multiperspectival complex of attitudes taken in [Sewell's] autobiographical writing and her adult fiction" (20). Shirley Foster asserts that "[Sewell's] attitudes are often surprisingly unorthodox, and, without overt radicalism, she champions a far more challenging vision of independent womanhood than many of her contemporaries dared or wished to assert" (Foster 1985, 110).

a character fashions herself as a martyr by deliberately choosing suffering. In Catholic hagiography, martyrdom is never exclusively a matter between the sufferer and God; it is also a political gesture, a simultaneous rejection of a corrupt social order. In so many hagiographies, for example, a woman chooses martyrdom rather than worship the false gods or ideals of her culture. This heroism was celebrated by Victorian Anglo-Catholics, women in particular. The martyr was, without exaggeration, the only truly heroic literary prototype for women, suggesting a courageous, active femininity which legitimately transgressed traditional gender norms and expectations. Christina Rossetti wrote a number of poems about martyrs (among them "The Martyr" [1846], "A Martyr" [1856], and "Martyrs' Song" [1863]), and all feature female protagonists similar to the martyr-heroine of John Henry Newman's 1853 novel *Callista*.[15] Newman's Callista, a third-century Christian, deliberately renounces both her brother and her earthly lover to embrace martyrdom, thereby gaining a heavenly love which far surpasses any familial or matrimonial tie: "A loved One," she exclaims, "yet ideal; a passion so potent, so fresh, so innocent, so absorbing, so expulsive of other loves, so enduring yet of One never beheld;—mysterious!" (221). Callista, like Rossetti's martyrs—led by "sublime desire" for the love of Christ—must face torture and death stoically and completely alone. Certainly, the martyr's all-consuming, eroticized love for Christ and her willingness to suffer for him suggests some resemblance to the suffering household angel. Unlike this ideal, however, the martyr's suffering is finite; the angel is plucked from the hearthside and delivered to an all-perfect Lover, and a heaven in which no suffering exists. Apparently, this idea was irresistible to many little girls of religious temperament. In her autobiography, Annie Besant (who became enamored of the Tractarian Movement in her teens) recalls how she read tales of the Christian martyrs "and passionately regretted I was born so late when no suffering for religion was practicable—no chance of preaching and suffering for a new religion" (42).[16]

Despite the martyr's invocation of religious devotion to justify her potentially unfeminine acts, the erotic intensity of her religious passion, her rejection of marriage and domesticity, and the public spectacle of her suffering continued to defy Victorian gender norms. While the angel was

15. In her journal Sewell mentions having enjoyed excerpts from Newman's *Lives of the English Saints*, despite its "extreme" [unflattering] portrayal of the Protestant Reformation and the Church of England (*Autobiography* 126).

16. It must be noted, of course, that martyrdom was hardly a foreign concept to Evangelical Protestants. In another childhood reminiscence, Evangelical novelist Charlotte Elizabeth Tonna recalls reading *Foxe's Book of Martyrs* with her father, and asking, "Papa, may I be a martyr?" Tonna's father assured her that if Catholic Emancipation succeeded, she would have ample opportunities (Tonna, *Life of Charlotte Elizabeth*, 22).

presumed to have no capacity for sexual pleasure, the erotic dimensions of the martyr's suffering cannot be overlooked. Just as Besant recalls flagellating herself "till I often felt that the very passion of my devotion would draw Him down from His throne in Heaven" (57), the martyr Callista declares to her tribunal, "He [Christ] came to me amid much pain; and the pain was pleasant, for He came in it" (362). As for the martyr's rejection of marriage, Agnes Smith Lewis declared in her book *Select Narratives of Holy Women* (1900) that the Syrian virgin martyrs "brought upon themselves and their friends a bitter persecution, not only by their steadfastness in the faith of Christ, but also by their *unchristian* renunciation of the marriage bond; a teaching which, if successful, would have upset all respectable society, and put an end to civilization" (vii; emphasis added).

While the martyr's sublimated but powerful sexuality and her rejection of marriage could prove unsettling, most threatening was the visibility of the martyr's suffering—a spectacle which, in effect, refuted popular notions that love, for women, could make all pain easy. In addition to treacherously unmasking the bleak, unromanticized trials of domestic life, both the martyr's striving and her tendency to flaunt her pain also suggested that most dangerous of female traits, that which Sarah Stickney Ellis called "the love of distinction." "In man," warns Ellis, "this passion is ambition. In woman it is the selfish desire to stand apart from the many, to be something of, and by, herself, to enjoy what she does enjoy, and to appropriate the tribute which society offers her, distinct from the sisterhood to which she belongs" (109). Simply stated, professional victimhood and a martyrlike resignation could bestow upon women a distinct identity, a means of constructing a freestanding selfhood. In *The Experience of Life*, the power conveyed by Sarah's role as a martyr—fortified by unshrinking observations of the imperfections of domestic life and Victorian matrimony—allows her not only to embrace life-in-death, but by so doing, to hold out for a more perfect love and a heavenly home.

Although spinsters, in the popular media, were occasionally (and mockingly) referred to as "martyrs," the use of the term "martyr" did not fit the popular stereotype of spinsters: women who were *forced* into lives of solitude. The passive endurance implied by this stereotype was at once unheroic and entirely compatible with Victorian gender norms. Such a figure appears in one of Sewell's own novels, *Ivors* (1856). Sewell, despite her earlier successes (including, of course, *The Experience of Life*), nonetheless felt compelled to attempt what she called "a regular novel, or a story in which love is the essential interest" (*Autobiography* 143). *Ivors* presents the reader with two cousins, Susan and Helen, who are in love with the same man. Although Sewell obviously intended for the reader to prefer pious, gentle Susan to the beautiful, wayward Helen, her decision to leave the former single at the novel's end (while Helen gets her man) disappointed and frustrated readers. As Sewell states of *Ivors* in her autobiography,

> Up to the time when I wrote it, I had always tried to show that life could be happy, and its events of importance apart from marriage. I thought, and I think still, that marriage is a beginning, not an end—and that it is very misleading to young people to represent it in a different light. But love is, of course, a very prominent factor in human existence, and having fairly well established my reputation as a writer of fiction without it, I thought that I might venture to introduce it, endeavoring, if possible, to avoid the usual ending—"and so they were married, and live happily ever after." But I did not quite succeed. My own interest lay with Susan, whom I left unmarried; but my readers did not, I think, as a rule, feel with me. (145)

So powerful was the courtship plot to Victorian readers that Sewell could hardly "venture to introduce it" without having it dominate the entire novel. Although the novel's primary goal is to uphold heartbroken Susan's patience and Christian fortitude as a model for single female readers, Helen's romance and marriage seem to push Susan to the margins of her own story. Left disappointed in love, the suffering that is supposed to ennoble and strengthen Susan merely renders her pathetic. The novel's conclusion shows us parallel images of the two cousins—Helen standing before the altar as a bride, and Susan praying at home, too ill with grief to attend the ceremony. As Susan hears the wedding bells, "one bitter cry, one agonised burst of human feeling escaped her; and the crushed heart offered its last lingering feelings to God, and Susan Graham had no worse pang to suffer" (II:429). For the reader who believes, with Callista, that Susan's pain "was pleasant, for He came in it," *Ivors*'s ending might indeed provide adequate religious consolation and assurance to the lonely single woman. Sewell's critics, however, could find no solace in Susan's suffering. Refusing to believe that such a pious and faithful mind as Susan's "could be surprised and disturbed by such a hurricane of earth-born grief," one reviewer concluded that "[w]e really do not see who [*Ivors*] is to do good to, or in what critical position of circumstances a young person can turn to this work for counsel" (*Christian Remembrancer* 346).

Ironically, however, *Ivors* contains one of Sewell's most forceful and direct affirmations of heroic martyrdom: the rejection of human suitors for a perfect, divine Lover. As Susan's mother attempts to console her, she states,

> A void has been created in our hearts which only one kind of earthly love can entirely fill. God has willed to deny you that [. . .] but he has not willed that you should go through life in loneliness. There is another love, before which all human affection fades into nothingness. [. . .]
>
> [God offers] a love which can never change, never misunderstand [. . .] which is more fond than the love of a husband, more watchful than the care of a parent [. . .] a real, earnest, living, intense love, and to which we may give, not mere duty, or reverence, or gratitude, but the warm, eager, absorbing affection, which is as intimate as the craving of our hearts, and lasting as the blessedness of eternity. (II:411–12)

Here Susan's mother suggests that her daughter has been specially chosen, singled out by God for an ecstatic divine romance. Although this passage transforms spinsterhood from a bleak misfortune to a passionate, ardent vocation, *Ivors* never convinces readers that Susan would rather have God than Claude Egerton. While the martyr suffers for God's love, at one point Susan insists that "I would cut off my right hand to make them [Claude and Helen] happy" (I:232). So much for Susan's integrity as a spinster.

Clearly, Sewell could not write a "regular novel" in which "love is the essential interest" without compromising the dignity and effectiveness of her spinster heroine. Not surprisingly, *Experience of Life* does not rely on a conventional courtship plot. Although many factors seem to have contributed to the novel's success, foremost among them is its close resemblance to Sewell's own life. "Nothing I have written," states Sewell in her memoirs, "has ever been as popular as The Experience of Life—probably because it is what its name denotes [. . .] the groundwork is constructed from facts which belong either to my own experience, or personal knowledge and observation [114]. [. . .] Sarah's troubled mind was a record of my own personal feelings [115]." Sewell's critics agreed with her assessment; the physically frail Sewell, who passed through life unmarried, and who did not "remember having been at more than half a dozen balls in my whole life" (46), was comfortably in her element in constructing the introspective and pious Sarah Mortimer, weak in body and timid in disposition.[17]

---

17. A rare firsthand description of Elizabeth Sewell can be found in the correspondence of Elizabeth Barrett Browning, who met the novelist in 1861. Barrett Browning, although admiring of Sewell, nonetheless describes her as a stereotypical spinster:

> She is a very nice, gentle-looking, cheerful, respectable sort of—single-womanish person (decidedly single) of the olden type; very small, slim, quiet, with the nearest approach to a poky bonnet possible in this sinful generation. I, in my confusion, did not glance at her petticoats, but judging a priori, I should predicate a natural incompatibility with crinoline. But really I liked her, liked her. There were gentleness, humility, and con-

The power of Sewell's personal experience helped her push past representational conventions in telling Sarah Mortimer's story. Challenging traditional ideas about the place of romance in the novel, the first paragraph of *Experience* is a sort of realist manifesto against romantic falsehoods. Sarah Mortimer, who narrates her autobiography, ambitiously promises the reader in their stead "a real representation of human existence":

> I am not going to write a tale, not at least what is usually so called. A tale is, for the most part, only a vignette, a portion of the great picture of life, having no definite limit, yet containing one prominent object, in which all the interest is concentrated. But this is not a real representation of human existence. For one person whose life has been marked by some very striking event, there are hundreds who pass to their graves with nothing to distinguish the different periods of their probation, but the changes which steal upon them so naturally as scarcely to occasion a momentary surprise. They hope and enjoy, they are disappointed and sad, but no one points to the history of their lives as containing warning or example. They are born unthought-of beyond their own immediate circle, and die lamented only by a few; and we pass over their names in the obituary of the day [. . .] forgetting that for each individual soul in the vast multitude there has been a special day of trial, a special providence and guidance, and there will be a special day of reckoning and doom. (1)

In this passage, through its assertion that the true stories of human life are, by traditional novelistic standards, unremarkable, Sewell anticipates the closing paragraph of Eliot's *Middlemarch*, composed nineteen years later. Of Dorothea Brooke, modern-day St. Theresa and "foundress of nothing," Eliot states,

> Her full nature [. . .] spent itself in channels which had no great name on the earth. But the effect of her being on those around her was incalculably diffusive: for the growing good of the world is partly dependent on unhistoric acts; and that things are not so ill with you and me as they might have been, is half owing to the number who lived faithfully a hidden life, and rest in unvisited tombs. (682)

Like Eliot, Sewell sets out to record the story of a woman noteworthy not for her personal charms, her romantic conquests, or the excitement of her life, but for her ethical import; that is, her subtle but nonethe-

---

science—three great gifts. (Qtd. in Kenyon 430)

less perceptible influence in promoting the well-being of others. Sewell's insistence upon altruism, even its "unhistoric" manifestations, as the truly noteworthy quality of her protagonist, defines a legitimate form of female heroism and female power based on moral and ethical agency. Thus Sarah Mortimer, who renounces earthly life in a much less dramatic fashion than Newman's Callista, can nonetheless take on a heroic, martyrlike stature.

Conveniently for an aspiring martyr, Sarah encounters difficulties and sorrows from an early age. Like Brontë's Lucy Snowe in *Villette*, Sarah narrates her own story toward the end of her life, as an elderly woman.[18] Describing herself as "one of that numerous race who are set apart from their earliest childhood for patient endurance" (8), Sarah also rivals Lucy Snowe in the extent to which her negative self-portrayal unsettles, even repels, the reader. "Sickly, plain, and indifferently educated," states Sarah at one point, "what better could I expect than to live in shade, whilst others glittered in sunshine?" (29). Sarah seems the only sensible and truly good-hearted member of a household populated by quarrelsome, shallow, and self-absorbed relations. When Sarah's father dies, leaving nothing but a legacy of debt for his wife, two unmarried adult daughters, and two younger children, Sarah takes it upon herself to start a school and be the financial savior of her family.

Despite Sarah's ill health, her willingness to be imposed upon and manipulated by greedy family members, and the loneliness of her unmarried state, her strength of character and her religious faith pull her through every crisis. By the story's end she has established a thriving school, successfully provided for her mother, and raised her younger brother and sister to be as sensible and good-hearted as herself. For all Sarah's self-dependence, however, clearly her success is directly aided by two important female role models in her life: Aunt Sarah Mortimer (her godmother and her grandfather's sister) and Lady Emily Rivers, a charitable-minded aristocrat who befriends and advises young Sarah. Lady Rivers, happily married, provides Sarah with the emotional sustenance of her friendship and provides for her a model of benevolence to the poor. It is Aunt Sarah, however, who most profoundly influences "Sally" (her pet name for Sarah), emphasizing to her the importance of self-sufficiency. As she tells her niece "never be a burden" to others, the words give to Sally "a brave, determined, independent feeling, such as one might imagine to inspire a soldier with courage on the eve of a battle" (22).

18. We do not know if Charlotte Brontë read *The Experience of Life*. However, in an 1852 letter to her friend and former teacher Miss Wooler (a close family friend of the Sewells), Brontë requested her to "tell me how you liked The Experience of Life." Unfortunately, Miss Wooler's response is lost to history. (Qtd. in Shorter 275)

Moreover, Aunt Sarah, herself a lifelong spinster, provides Sally with a religious rationale for her unmarried existence: "The unmarried woman careth for the things of the Lord," Aunt Sarah says, as she quotes St. Paul, "that she may be holy in body and spirit; but she that is married careth for the things of the world, how she may please her husband" (199). Upon hearing this proclamation, Sarah's sister Joanna exclaims, "Oh! then, aunt Sarah is going to turn Roman Catholic, and say that people ought not to marry" (199). Aunt Sarah informs Joanna that she will do no such thing, "in a tone of unusual severity, which made poor Joanna shrink" (199). "[T]o be an old maid," she concludes, "is to be able to live to God, and work for your fellow-creatures in an especial manner" (200).

Sarah's conscious desire to live for God rather than this world seems to emerge on Sarah's confirmation day—also the day of her older sisters' first dinner party. This marks the first time in which the increasingly pious young woman realizes that the world and the spirit are perpetually at odds. "And yet in the midst of all this distraction and even vanity," recalls Sarah, "I was very much bent upon collecting my thoughts, and sadly distressed when I found myself wandering from my confirmation vow to the question, how all the people who were expected at luncheon would manage to find room in our small dining-room" (35). When Sarah returns from church, rather than join the family luncheon downstairs, she practices her first deliberate act of self-denial, apparently choosing the spirit over the world: "I should have liked very much to see the luncheon, and I thought to myself several times what a cheerful party there must be down stairs, but I felt that it would do me harm to be with them, for it would untone my mind, and I could not bear the thought of placing myself voluntarily in the way of temptation" (37). In retrospect, Sarah remarks that she remembers that first act of self-denial "with great gratitude [. . .]. It gave me [. . .] a consciousness of moral strength; and with strength came hope and happiness" (37).

This is virtuoso asceticism indeed.[19] But it is not an isolated moment in the novel. On the contrary, Sarah's lacerating self-denial manifests itself throughout her narrative in her continual efforts to take on the burdens of others and to deny herself pleasure, even when these sacrifices are not called for. A self-fashioned "Cinderella," Sarah helps her mother and sisters dress for a party one evening, all the while taking it for granted that she will stay home, alone with her younger sister Hester, and nurse a headache.

---

19. James Eli Adams, in *Dandies and Desert Saints: Styles of Victorian Masculinity* (1995), notes that heroines such as Maggie Tulliver and Dorothea Brooke often embrace "a virtuoso ascetic regimen," to enact "a decidedly masculine self-fashioning" (9).

When Hester protests against Sarah's unfair treatment at the hands of her mother and older sisters, Sarah simply replies, "[Y]ou must go to sleep, and I must be miserable." "Must you?" asks Hester. "Who told you you must?" (44). Later in the novel, Aunt Sarah also chides Sally for her martyrlike acceptance of her older siblings' unwillingness to help support their widowed mother. "[C]ontrary to the dreams of self-sacrifice in which I had for years indulged," Aunt Sarah orders her to ask the rest of the family for help, her aunt all the while pointing out that "good people sin in their virtues, as well as bad people in their vices" (315).

Clearly, Sarah also resembles Dorothea Brooke in that she "likes giving up." Just as *Middlemarch* suggests that Dorothea's youthful penchant for needless self-sacrifice is misguided, Aunt Sarah's description of her niece's ambition as a "sin" questions the true motives of Sarah's extraordinary altruism. While Sarah seems aware that extreme self-renunciation might be a paradoxical attempt at self-aggrandizement, it is one scruple she does not agonize over. In *Middlemarch*, Dorothea's love match with Ladislaw indicates her evolution away from futile renunciation, and toward an acknowledgment of her own needs and desires. Sarah, in contrast, renounces an attractive offer of marriage that would effectively strip her of her cherished martyr role. Sarah, who claims to submit to God's will, seems in this case particularly determined to control her own life. Although wise Aunt Sarah acknowledges the religious benefits of spinsterhood, she tells Sarah that marriage is also a divinely ordained vocation. In case of a proposal, instructs Aunt Sarah:

> If you don't care for the man, or if your parents object, or if there's any other very good reason for saying no, why those are plain marks that it's not meant you should marry; but if a man comes to you and says he's fond of you, and he's a good man, and your parents like the notion, and you like him, it would be just setting yourself against the ordering of Providence to declare that you would be better for a single life. (201)

Eventually, Sarah receives a proposal that seems, by her own description, to fit Aunt Sarah's definition of a marriage proposal willed by Providence. Sarah's suitor is—like all worthy suitors in Sewell's novels—a clergyman:

> [. . .] [A] person whom I thoroughly esteemed, and liked, personally, more than any one I had ever seen. If we had met when we were respectively twenty and thirty, instead of nearly thirty and forty, I might probably have given him a still warmer feeling. As it was, I will not pretend to say that the necessity of refusing him did not give me a great pang. But to leave

my mother and sisters was impossible; and he was not rich enough to offer them a home, or give them, indeed, any assistance. If we had married we must have lived for ourselves alone. (354)

Sarah, consistent with her "dreams of self-sacrifice," seems completely unaware that she has just provided the reader with a detailed account of family finances, which demonstrates that her mother is already adequately provided for through a legacy from Aunt Sarah, and that another unmarried sister, Joanna, is perfectly capable—as capable, at least, as Sarah herself—of earning her own living. The most telling evidence that self-will has usurped God's will in this instance, however, is the fact that the proposal "was the only very important event in my life which I ever kept from Aunt Sarah" (355). Although Sarah claims that she has no fear of Aunt Sarah's disapproval, "It was just possible [. . .] that she might have tried to induce Caroline to come forward more largely with assistance, and then the whole thing would have become known to my mother, which was what I especially wished to avoid" (355). Although Sarah does not explain her reasons for this sentiment, clearly, if she became less financially necessary to the family, she would no longer have a reasonable excuse to refuse the marriage proposal. As it is, Sarah professes to have made her decision in the best interests of the family, all the while overlooking any possible heartache she might have caused the poor clergyman. Claiming that he was "not desperately in love" with her (354), she next mentions the fact of his immediate departure to Australia with no overt acknowledgment of what his emigration might imply (355).

While Sarah's attachment to her role as family martyr influences her decision to remain single, her choice also reflects her belief in the exclusivity of perfect Divine love. To love in this world, Sarah seems to believe, would be to render oneself ineligible for an analogous, yet immensely more perfect, kind of love in the next. "My spirits had been so worn [at the time of the proposal]," she states, "that I actually dreaded the thought of any change, even though it might be for happiness. I felt as if I had not the power of beginning life again,—as if it would be, in a certain way, going backwards, creating interests for this world, when all my object, hitherto, had been to loosen them" (354). Sarah's dismissal of the clergyman's suit allows her to channel all her desire upon the prize of a heavenly consummation with her Divine Lover. When Aunt Sarah finally passes on, her deathbed scene—immediately following Sarah's description of her sister Hester's wedding—suggests a consummation even more wonderful than that between Hester and her own clergyman, and also prefigures the sort of union Sarah herself also anticipates. When Sally reminds Aunt Sarah of the long-dead family members she will soon meet again, Aunt Sarah simply replies, "One love, Sally, one all-sufficient love, is my comfort and joy,—the love which has blotted out sin" (441). By the closing pages of the narrative, Sally's preparation to receive this "all perfect" love in its fullness would seem to have eclipsed all worldly interests and occupations. Attending daily church services, morning and evening, Sarah also frequently finds herself meditating in the graveyard, "look[ing] forward to the time when I also shall be called to deliver my body to the dust, and my spirit in the gladness of its love 'to Him who gave it'" (470).

Implicit in female martyrs' rejection of marriage and motherhood for Paradise (as Agnes Smith Lewis realized to her dismay) is a bold challenge to societal expectations and norms for women. Appropriately, Sarah's narrative provides only a few, fleeting glimpses of happy marriages and contented families. Sarah's beautiful older sister marries a coarse, elderly banker solely for his money; the couple's subsequent misery paints a grim picture of the emotional, spiritual, and psychological degradation awaiting those who marry unwisely. As for Sarah's descriptions of life with her parents and other siblings, such representations led critics to complain of Sewell's tendency to "so constantly pictur[e] the home as the scene of disappointment, want of sympathy, uncongeniality, worry, weariness and pain" (Taylor 316). Here reviewer Fanny Taylor complains that Sewell's scenes of home life might lead young people to view their own familial situations with discontent. Hints that not all homes were happy ones were subversive enough; Sewell's portrayal of the pious Sarah being driven to distraction by her irreligious, worldly family, moreover, also boldly challenged Evangelical Christian notions that home was ever the center of all that was most sacred and holy. In short, marriage and family life, far from being the natural vocation of every woman, might in fact prove a dangerous stumbling block to women's moral, religious, and spiritual integrity. Robbed of such integrity, then, women like Sarah Mortimer—who defined personal agency as the ability to discern God's will and act upon it—would be stripped of their power entirely.

Because the martyr's rewards are beyond the representational scope of the novel, however, *Experience* cannot balance scenes of domestic misery with representations of an ideal heavenly home. Therefore, even though the narrative's conclusion thwarts the dominance of the courtship plot, it does not (or cannot) sustain Sarah's otherworldly focus to the very end. *Experience* is not, after all, a hagiography (in which we might expect to see Sarah Mortimer, in the final scene, sprout wings and ascend a heavenly throne), but a novel that seems to demand some sort of concrete, tangible gratification for its protagonist, even if she is a martyr. As Sarah, in the final paragraph, dictates her burial arrangements, the focus suddenly shifts from Sarah's exclusive relationship with God to a recognition of her honored and revered position in the eyes of her nieces and nephews:

> It seems as if it would be safe and blest still to be within reach of the prayers and praises I have loved; it soothes me to think that I may thus be connected in memory with the constant worship of the Church;—and most dear is the hope that those over whom I have watched from infancy, the children of my darling Hester, and it may be their children after them, may recall, as they pass my grave, the lessons I have labored to teach them, and speak of me with the love, though it can never be with the reverence, which must ever place amongst the dearest of my earthly memories, the name of—aunt Sarah. (471)

For all Sarah's insistence that her true happiness lies in the next world, her identification of herself as a second Aunt Sarah suggests the possibility that spinsters *could* achieve a measure of fulfillment on earth.

Sarah may aspire to a heavenly home, but in the meantime she seems to long for the existence enjoyed by her own Aunt Sarah. Throughout the novel, Sarah finds peace, quiet, sympathy, and religious guidance not in her own home, but in the well-ordered tranquility of Aunt Sarah's spinster household. In contrast to the tumultuous Mortimer household—ostensibly controlled by a father lacking in financial acumen and overall common sense—Aunt Sarah runs her home competently and efficiently. Although Aunt Sarah also has a limited income, she keeps her home and gardens in impeccable condition; she retains a personal companion as well as three servants, who efficiently prepare and serve five meals a day: "[N]o dinners," recalls Sally, "were ever so nicely dressed as aunt Sarah's" (18). Not only does Aunt Sarah exercise strict control over her own domestic affairs, but, as matriarch of the Mortimer family, she can, unlike Sally, speak her mind to the rest of the family, men included. Nothing but a strongly worded letter from Aunt Sarah to Sally's older siblings, for example, can induce them to contribute their financial share to the support of their widowed mother.

Aunt Sarah's most impressive power, however, is her power to do good unto others. Having taken upon herself the supervision of the poor people of Carsdale, Aunt Sarah possesses "a large manuscript book," which contains "a list of houses and inhabitants, the number of children, the occupations of the parents, their necessities and their characters" (75). With the aid of this book, Aunt Sarah and her friend Lady Emily Rivers—who, although married, provides Sally with another model of active, independent, benevolent womanhood—can determine which families in the parish most require financial assistance. Although Aunt Sarah is strong willed, her care for others adds "the charm of a woman's feeling to a character which was masculine in its strength of will and vigour of action" (17). It is Aunt Sarah's Christian love which tempers and softens the otherwise potentially unnerving fact of her power. In this regard she is set apart from other strong-minded, powerful female characters such as Horatia, a scheming, money-hungry pretend "cousin" of the Mortimers, who is repeatedly described as a mannish female. In regard to Horatia, Aunt Sarah acknowledges that a fine line exists between masculine love of power for its own sake and a more feminine power born of love itself: "[Horatia] knows quite well, that if she rules herself first, she may rule the world afterwards. If she had but one grain of honesty, and two of kindheartedness, in her composition, she might, with such self-command, become a saint" (392).

For all Sarah's longing after her transcendent God, it is Aunt Sarah who embodies for her God's wisdom, his knowledge (witness the fact of her great book, chronicling the lives of her poor people), his goodness, and even his severe judgment. At one point, Sally, plagued by what she considers to be a sinful excess of religious doubt, almost takes her "sin" to Aunt Sarah. "I fancied I could better bear my doubts if they were not secret," she states, "and a sudden impulse urged me, and I stopped at the parlour door and thought I would go to Aunt Sarah—go to her, confess what I was, beg her to hate me, to send me from her, to give me any suffering, but only to listen to me and know me" (87). Aunt Sarah's power extends to even more than the absolution of sins, however. At the end of Aunt Sarah's long afternoons of planning charitable projects for the poor of Carsdale, she orders the frail Sally to rest on the couch during household prayers: "I lay down, weary with the day's exertions [. . .] and generally at last fell asleep, with a happy, tranquil sense of reposing under the shelter of an Infinite Power" (80). Although Sarah's use of the term "Infinite Power" refers to the prayers and to the One to whom the supplications are addressed, Sally's happy and tranquil sense of absolute protection no doubt owes as much to Aunt Sarah's judicious care as to her own sense of divine omnipotence.

Considering both the temporal and spiritual influence Aunt Sarah wields, both in Sarah's life and in the overall narrative, young Sally's gradual metamorphosis into a second Aunt Sarah to her own nieces and nephews emphasizes her acquisition, in old age, of increasing wisdom, self-assurance, and autonomy. Having been left a legacy of five thousand pounds in her uncle's will, white-haired Sarah, in the final scene, is financially independent, now able to devote herself to charitable projects and to the maintenance of a separate household, a peaceful cottage adjoining that of her sister Hester and Hester's children. Sarah, a spinster looking on from the margins of her own narrative—a narrative she fills up largely with accounts of the trials and tribulations of others within her family—has by the novel's end moved to the center. As the new "Aunt Sarah," Sally has become not only the centrifugal force for goodness and piety in her autobiography, but also a sort of glorified, saintly figure, her considerable "Experience of Life" now authorizing her to narrate her own story. Even though Sarah spends these final days meditating on the site of her burial and, like Susan in *Ivors*, fastens her heart's desire onto an anticipated, blissful union with God in the next world, by the final chapter the temporal benefits of her spinsterhood cannot be denied. While *Ivors* requires of Susan (and its readers) absolute faith in God and his heaven to conjure up a convincing "happy" ending, *The Experience of Life* satisfies more conventional expectations of novelistic closure. Sarah, much like any romantic heroine who marries into money and social status by the novel's end, at long last achieves financial stability, the respect of the community, and most important, a well-defined social role. Rather than derive these benefits from marriage, however, Sarah owes her temporal well-being at the novel's end to God and to her aunt. Uncle Ralph's deathbed bequest to Sarah seems nothing short of providential; as the novel implies, the stingy uncle's uncharacteristically generous gesture springs from an awakening conscience, a terror of impending divine judgment. It is from Aunt Sarah, however, that Sarah receives her most priceless inheritance—a precedent by which to define her identity and purpose as a single woman, one who gains power not from the passive exercise of receiving love, but from actively loving others.

Although Sewell's narrative seems less conflicted in many ways than other novelistic treatments of spinsterhood, one might ask whether her representation of Victorian women is really superior to or more desirable than others. The notion of embracing suffering is of course repugnant in our own culture, as it was for many Victorians. Yet to label the religious beliefs espoused by the Tractarian Sewell as morbid or "sick-souled" would bring us no closer to understanding them. The integrity and validity of such worldviews demand to be acknowledged on their own terms, rather than being forced into (or negated by) our own cultural frames. As a woman and a writer Sewell had to function within the constraints imposed by her society—in particular, a construct of womanhood defined by passive, invisible suffering. The spinster-martyr, then, although not a feminist figure, was a radical one nonetheless. This assessment is confirmed by *The Afternoon of Unmarried Life*, an 1858 conduct book that—despite its attempts to cheer and console unmarried women—emphatically resists the notion that single life could be preferable to the married state. Its author, Anne Judith Penny, may well have had Sewell's novel in mind when she passionately argued that

> we should do wrong to believe this state of detachment from earthly love to be decidedly the *best*. [. . .] [T]his assumption that single life is in *itself* holiest and best has caused an incalculable amount of misery among Christian people during many successive ages. In the feebler sex it has occasioned morbid excitement of a perverted impulse. Instead of a meek submission to the temporary disadvantages of single life, and a clear-sighted recognition of its sorrow and deprivation, how often has there been among virtuous women an attempt to exalt and glorify this separate and unfinished life as being holier and more desirable in the abstract, as well as in their own particular case! [. . .] Would it not be better to allow that some right feelings must lack their completion, some pure desires their scope, rather than to confound devout joy and holy confidence with the passionate tenderness of a woman's lonely heart? (286; emphasis in original)

Cold consolation for spinsters, indeed. Sewell's ideology, in comparison, is certainly radical and—on some level—much more appealing.

Even if *The Afternoon of Unmarried Life* does not respond directly to Sewell's work, surely Catholic ascetics are the miserable "Christian people" its author had in mind. Sewell, in writing *The Experience of Life*, drew upon her Anglo-Catholic beliefs to make statements at once radical and countercultural. Sewell, unlike most of her female contemporaries, managed to produce a sympathetic, realistic narrative of female celibacy, and a novel in which "love is not the central interest." This was no mean feat in an era which, as Robert Polhemus explains in *Erotic Faith*, novels became "cathedrals" which enshrined and disseminated secular notions of erotic love as the source of ultimate transcendence (3). The other narratives of female celibacy discussed in this chapter are less satisfying and less ideologically consistent. The anticonvent novels, of course, are doomed by a combination of religious bigotry and an utter disregard for real life. Works by Yonge and Brontë, and even Sewell's *Ivors*, fall into the mistake of presenting spinsterhood as a calamity that is passively endured and nowhere near preferable to the married state. The spinster may cling to God for solace, but this is meager comfort for the reader convinced—as Brontë's Lucy Snowe seems to be—that one can only be saved through human love. In the logic of erotic faith, the spinster remains a reprobate and an outcast. Of course, Sarah Mortimer also clings to her Christian faith. But more than passive resignation, her faith provides her with models of active female heroism in the tales of the Christian martyrs. And unlike other narratives of female celibacy, *Experience* does not overlook or abandon the rich possibilities of female community, as sustenance for its heroine. While Sarah Mortimer does not join a formally organized female community, strong bonds between female characters contribute significantly to the success of her *bildungsroman*.

Sewell and other Anglo-Catholic women did not set out to challenge the status quo. But in an era in which women defined their agency in moral, spiritual, and ethical terms, not even the most entrenched social institutions or expectations could quench the desire of so many women to live, act, and even write as their consciences demanded. Florence Nightingale, herself a lifelong "spinster" who at one time nearly converted to Roman Catholicism, once criticized popular romance novels for promoting a "false idea" of life, as they always concluded with two people "wrapped up" solely in each other, in "an abyss of binary selfishness" (64). Sewell would undoubtedly have agreed. In her attempt at creating what she deemed a more ethically responsible representation of women's lives, Sewell challenged the dominance of the courtship plot, interrogated her culture's definitions of female sanctity and identity, and presented an exposé—not of profane convents, but of profane Victorian homes.

CHAPTER FOUR

"Hoc est corpus meum"

Aurora Leigh, Goblin Market, *and Transubstantiation*

> [Y]ou must compare calmly the [. . .] doctrines of our real, eternal Christ, recorded in the New Testament, with the disgusting tenets of the Catholic false Christ, whom silly and wicked priests have the power, as they assert, to squeeze into a wafer, and swallow like an oyster. By doing so, I trust you will finally understand and discover the difference between that spiritual faith, [. . .] and the gross, material, and absurd performances of what is called the catholic religion.
> —John Teodor, *Eliza Barry, the Child of a Cloister* (1850) (3)

> It is true, that God is a Spirit, and must be worshipped in spirit and in truth; but man is a compound of body and spirit, so intimately blended, that whatever affects the one affects also the other. [. . .] The great art is to make the body subservient to the spirit, which is not to be done by annihilating [it, but] by sanctifying [it], by employing [it] so that, instead of impeding, [it] may contribute to the great end of our existence, the salvation of our souls.
> —Alexander Dick, *Reasons for Embracing the Catholic Faith* (1848) (171)

AS WOMEN novelists have shown, Victorian constructions of the Angel in the House—as a wholly spiritualized, ethereal being—were incompatible with the material and physical realities of middle-class domestic life. Jane Eyre, for example, is uneasy with the creature comforts of her domestic spaces, as well as the potential of "creature worship" inherent in popular ideals of marriage. Georgiana Fullerton denies Gertrude Lifford a second marriage in the interests of her soul; Elizabeth Missing Sewell constructs spinsterhood as spiritual freedom from the worldly cares of matrimony; and a series of Protestant women writers projected their fears of material domesticity onto their representations of "real" convent establishments. The dichotomy between material world and ostensibly spiritual woman is no less a concern for poets such as Elizabeth Barrett Browning and Christina Rossetti. In *Aurora Leigh* (1856) and *Goblin Market* (1862), anxieties about the material world center most emphatically on the claims of the body. Unlike much of the fiction discussed in this study, however, *Aurora Leigh* and *Goblin Market* do not resolve the problem of the physical by abolishing it (Fullerton, Sewell), but by embracing it and celebrating it as vital to the heroine's fulfillment of her divine calling.

Although the conclusion of each poem betrays some lingering apprehensions of the body and its demands, each resolves the tension between spiritual and material more effectively and completely than any of the novels examined in this study. As poets, Barrett Browning and Rossetti invoked the Romantic precedent of perceiving and celebrating the transcendent in nature; such was the poet's unique and divine calling. As Barrett Browning's heroine reflects of her vocation, "Earth's crammed with heaven, / And every common bush afire with God; / But only he who sees, takes off his shoes, / the rest sit round it and pluck blackberries [. . .] (7:821-24). Had Barrett Browning and Rossetti limited themselves to writing about topiary, they might have claimed sufficient authority to elevate base matter as poets in the Romantic tradition. But each chose as her subject the female body: hungry, sexualized, and frequently fallen. In order to assert the integrity of the sexual female body, these women invoked another, more mysterious power—specifically, the highly controversial Roman Catholic doctrine of transubstantiation. According to this doctrine, at the moment of consecration the bread and wine *literally* become the actual, *physical* body and blood of Jesus Christ. While neither Barrett Browning nor Rossetti would have personally sanctioned this doctrine, a distinctively Roman Catholic interpretation of the Eucharist plays a vital role in each of their poems. At the heart of each poem, women *and* their bodies are miraculously transformed: wayward, dying Lizzie becomes a happy wife and mother; raped and brutalized Marian Earle turns into a Madonna; and Aurora Leigh descends from her Palace of Art (Leighton, *Victorian Woman Poets,* 90) to embrace a more corporeal existence as Romney's wife. These transformations, resonant of Roman Catholic transubstantiation, ultimately support a moral common to both poems: a woman who ignores the body does so at her spiritual peril. Only in embracing the created world in *all* of its manifestations can the woman, poet, and sister find her true calling in the world.

Transubstantiation, or "A gross carnal feeding"

Many scholars have identified the Eucharistic imagery in both *Aurora*

Leigh and *Goblin Market* as a significant Christian symbol. Few, however, have considered how Protestant anxieties about the Roman Catholic doctrine of transubstantiation inform each poem.[1] Eucharistic imagery does not, of course, necessarily imply Roman Catholicism. The sacrament of the Lord's Supper was also central to the rites of the Church of England and other Protestant denominations. Indeed, the great importance accorded by *both* Protestants and Roman Catholics to the Lord's Supper resulted in particularly fierce and complicated arguments over different interpretations of it. This controversy seems to have generated some of the deepest anxieties—and the most vicious rhetoric—among Protestant clergymen and anti-Catholic propagandists at midcentury.[2] Cardinal Wiseman, in his 1836 lectures outlining Catholic teachings on the Eucharist, noted that despite the many differences between Catholics and Protestants, "[W]e may safely assert, that not one is more frequently discussed, or more frequently made the touchstone of the two systems' respective claims, than their doctrine respecting the Sacrament of the B. Eucharist" (Wiseman 11).[3]

In these same lectures, Wiseman quotes from the documents of the Council of Trent to define transubstantiation:

> Whereas, our Redeemer Christ did declare that to be truly his body which he offered under the appearance of bread, therefore hath it always been held in the church of God [...] that by the consecration of the bread and wine, a change is wrought of the bread's *whole substance,* into the substance of Christ our Lord's body, and of the wine's *whole substance,* into substance

---

1. Although some critics have pointed out the significance of Eucharistic imagery in *Aurora Leigh* (see Marjorie Stone, *Elizabeth Barrett Browning,* 150; and Margaret Reynolds's editorial comments on page 8 of *Aurora Leigh* [1996]), I have not found any in-depth discussions of the topic. Far more extensive commentary can be found on the Eucharistic imagery in *Goblin Market.* Recent criticism, discussing the influence of Tractarian/High Anglican doctrines and/or Rossetti's personal religious convictions on the depiction of the Eucharist in *Goblin Market,* includes work by Mary Arseneau, Linda E. Marshall, Mary Wilson Carpenter, and D. M. R. Bentley. The possibility that Rossetti may have been intrigued or influenced by Roman Catholic (rather than Anglican) Eucharistic doctrine is typically left unaddressed or, in the case of Diane D'Amico's *Christina Rossetti: Faith, Gender, and Time* (1999), dismissed outright (77). Frederick Roden's analysis of *Goblin Market* in *Same-Sex Desire in Victorian Religious Culture* (2002), however, does describe the communion scene between Lizzie and Laura in unmistakably Roman Catholic terms as a "transubstantiation" (44).

2. I had no idea of the extent or vehemence of Victorian Protestant-Catholic Eucharistic controversy until I began reading the wealth of primary materials outlining the issue. The neglect of this topic in standard works on Victorian anti-Catholicism (Norman, Paz, Wheeler, etc.) is surprising and puzzling.

3. Anglican clergyman John King, in an 1843 sermon, also notes that "on no other question [than the real nature of the Eucharist] have greater differences existed, or warmer disputations been carried on. How large a portion of the controversy with Rome turned on this point, is well-known to all, who have the least acquaintance with the history of the 'Blessed Reformation' [...]" (5).

of his blood's; which change, hath been, by the Holy Catholic Church, suitably and properly called Transubstantiation. (12; emphasis added)

The controversial nature of this doctrine hinged upon the phrase "whole substance." That is, according to Wiseman and the Council of Trent, although the bread and wine retain the *appearance* of bread and wine, they undergo a total elemental transformation. After consecration they are, literally and completely, the *actual,* physical body of Jesus Christ. It was the *physical* nature of the sacrament that Protestants emphatically rejected. This objection to transubstantiation was not, of course, new to the Victorian era; the Church of England had long ago written its condemnation of transubstantiation right into the Thirty-Nine Articles. Article Twenty-Eight (taken from an 1844 copy of the Book of Common Prayer) states that:

> Transubstantiation (or the chaunge [sic] of the substance of bread and wine) in the Supper of the Lord, cannot be proved by holy writ: but is repugnant to the plaine words of Scripture, overthroweth the nature of a Sacrament, and hath given occasion to many superstitions.
> The Body of Christ is given, taken, and eaten in the Supper onely [sic] after an heavenly and spirituall manner. And the meane whereby the bodie of Christ is received and eaten in the Supper, is fayth.

According to the Article, no change occurs to the physical substance of the bread and wine; "body" and "blood" are only used figuratively, as Christ intended them. Thus he is consumed spiritually, but *not* physically, by the recipient. In a note appended to the Order of Communion, the Book of Common Prayer also states that although communicants receive the bread and wine on their knees, the elements are not to be worshiped. "For the Sacramental bread and wine remain still in their very Natural Substances, and therefore may not be adored, (for that were Idolatrie, to be abhorred of all faithful Christians)." To worship the elements in an Anglican Communion service, therefore, would be to adore—that is, idolize—nothing but flour, water, and wine.

There exist, in British archives, hundreds of anti-transubstantiation tracts, pamphlets, and sermons dating back to the seventeenth century. Many of the arguments employed against transubstantiation remained consistent over two centuries. The "unscriptural" character of transubstantiation was frequently asserted, with reference to the sixth chapter of John.[4] Aside from contradicting God's word, transubstantiation, as these

---

4. In John 6:54–56, Christ says, "[H]e who eats my flesh and drinks my blood has eternal life, and I will raise him up at the last day. For my flesh is food indeed, and my blood is drink

documents claim, was also a logical absurdity. For example, if the bread and wine *really* became Christ's physical body, how could he be in so many places at once? In an 1838 sermon, clergyman John Lyons mocks the Catholic teaching that each drop of wine and crumb of bread contains a "whole" Christ:

> The officiating priest, who alone partakes of the cup, [. . .] must then swallow at the least two perfect living bodies; and if the part of the wafer, received by the communicant, should break into smaller pieces in the mouth, each separated fragment becomes a separate entire Christ, and thus none can tell how many living human bodies may be contained within him at the same time. (308)

Lyons's tone is ironic, but his criticism is in earnest. And of course, how could the change possibly take place to begin with? In an anonymous pamphlet, *The Doctrine of Transubstantiation Refuted*, also published in 1838, the writer ("A Layman") takes issue with the Roman Catholic teaching that, after transubstantiation, nothing but the *appearance* of bread remained. He speculates on what would happen if arsenic were mixed into the communion wafers prior to consecration: "If the priest's words, '*Hoc est corpus meum,*' should have the power of expelling the arsenic, as well as the flour and water, from the consecrated wafer, I will acknowledge a miracle, and perhaps some worthy Papist may have the courage to run the risk of being poisoned, for the sake of converting a heretic" (19).[5]

Clearly, the doctrine of transubstantiation was an easy target for satire. If Protestants had merely found it ridiculous, however, there would have been little fuel for controversy. Especially worrisome to Protestants was the possibility that the doctrine of transubstantiation, by contradicting the senses, would overturn the evidence of Christianity altogether. "When the priest professes to change the paste with the words *Hoc est corpus meum,*" queries the Reverend W. K. Tatam in an 1850 sermon, "where is the body of Christ? I taste it to be paste—I feel it to be paste—I see it to be paste. [. . .] A true miracle must be such that our senses can take cognizance of it" (13). Recalling that all Christ's miracles could be seen, heard, and

---

indeed. He who eats my flesh and drinks my blood remains in me and I in him." The Church of England, and other Protestant denominations, insisted on a figurative rather than literal interpretation of these words.

5. In *The Priest and the Lady, or, Transubstantiation Exposed*, an undated pamphlet published by the Protestant Evangelical Mission, a cunning Protestant housewife dares the local Catholic priest to consume consecrated bread—after informing him that she had mixed arsenic into the dough before baking it. The priest flees in fear and confusion, and the wife's Catholic husband (who had invited the priest over in an attempt to convert his wife) immediately decides to turn Protestant.

tasted, opponents of transubstantiation could not accept that the host, after consecration, still looked suspiciously like bread. Alexander Carson, in an 1827 pamphlet entitled *Transubstantiation Subversive of the Foundations of Human Belief*, makes a similar, more detailed argument:

> To deny the authority of the senses is to overturn almost every truth. It overturns the Scriptures and the miracles of Christ. It overturns the evidence of his birth, life, death, and resurrection. [. . .] [I]f God has given us senses to deceive us, why may not all our faculties be equally fallacious? It overturns the evidence for the very existence of God, for this is derived from the senses. (20)

Carson's argument—that the doctrine of transubstantiation was a slippery slope toward atheism—would have been particularly compelling in an era in which scientific, historical, and geological discoveries increasingly challenged Christian faith.

The notion of God's absence was, of course, terrifying to Victorian Christians. Even so, the tone of these sermons and tracts passes from vehemence to near hysteria only when they consider the implications of blending the spiritual with the corporeal. Although Victorians could, in theory, accept the doctrine that Christ became flesh (Incarnation), these sermons and tracts—theological arguments aside—betray an absolute horror of the notion of Christ's divine spirit mingled with (or entrapped within) the gross human body.[6] It is this point of Protestant controversy, so pronounced in the Victorian period, that I find so relevant to women's appropriation of Eucharistic imagery in poetry. The Victorians' extreme anxiety regarding a corporeal Blessed Sacrament seems to have sprung, in part, from the same root as their tendency to hyperspiritualize the Household Angel. As Nina Auerbach and many others have argued, there was no *via media* in the Victorian conception of women. In order to deny the base physical qualities of the Angel, society had to displace them in another category created expressly for that purpose—including women who were fallen, "unnatural," demonic, and insane. In similar terms, anything physical that threatened to encroach upon the altar was banished as heathenistic, idolatrous, and profane. For example, the Reverend Melville Horne, in *The Great Mass Idol* (1822), declares that because of transubstantiation, Catholics worship not God but an idol far more abhorrent than

---

6. In making this argument, I do not mean to imply that Protestants' opposition to the doctrine of transubstantiation was due primarily to a fear of the body. Obviously, transubstantiation was (and is) a challenging doctrine on many fronts: logical, theological, and metaphysical. I simply wish to point out that controversies over transubstantiation provide a unique and fascinating insight into the vexed Victorian negotiations between body and spirit.

any fabricated in previous human history. "[I]t is obvious to *Protestant Men of understanding,*" he argues, "that we have here, raked together, such an incongruous Mass of monstrous nonsense and absurdity, of idolatry, blasphemy, tyranny and cruelty, as never disgraced the Priests of Jupiter, Seraphis, Woden, Brahma, Budhu [sic], or the Living Lama of Thibet [sic]" (3; emphasis in original). A pamphleteer by the name of "Paphnutius" also describes the Catholic, transubstantiated god as a terrifying, Frankenstinian creature, distinguished primarily by his corporeal bulk. Accusing the Catholics of cannibalism, Paphnutius contrasts them with other ancient peoples, who brought offerings of food for their gods to consume:

> [In contrast,] the Anthro-pophagan religion [Catholicism] makes the worshippers regale on *the god himself.* [. . .] [H]e delights in being eaten by his priests and worshippers. So immense is this god—such a hyper-colossal body of human flesh has he—that myriads of his votaries have been eating of his flesh and drinking of his blood every day for one thousand two hundred years, and yet there is no fear but that it will serve the same purpose for one thousand two hundred years longer. (*Cannibal Church* 6; emphasis in original)

Paphnutius next shifts his attention from the idolatrous mound of flesh to its contaminating effects on the mostly female congregation. "The sex," he notes, "'for softness formed, and sweet attractive grace,' displays a remarkable attachment to this revolting religion, the proportion of female [Catholics] being ten to one of the other sex [. . .]." Papnutius leaves his reader to imagine a congregation of dainty, ethereal ladies gorging on the idol's flesh and blood.

Most of the controversial literature on this topic was not quite as graphic or as sensational as Paphnutius's pamphlet. And rather than focus so much on the qualities of the idolatrous God, they tended to highlight the unworthiness of the recipient. How dare Catholics expect Christ to subject himself to our base human bodies? Clergyman Charles Bird Smith, in an 1839 sermon, declares it is "hard to be conceived, and painful to a devout mind, that the body of our Lord should descend into the stomach of the wicked, be digested, mix with their blood, and flow through their system, and yet do them no good? Is that pure and spotless body to be thus amalgamated with all that is vile?" (17). The author of *The Doctrine of Transubstantiation Refuted* also takes the reader on a virtual journey through the communicant's digestive tract:

> [A]n insignificant worm of corruption, a popish priest, in all the pride and presumption of his office, holds up a bit of wafer, and presents it to the

wretched dupe prostrated before him, telling him it is the body and blood, soul and divinity, of the great God of Heaven, who fills the interminable regions over his head; and he, as he is taught to believe, swallows that immaculate God down his throat, reeking most frequently with the fumes of stinking tobacco and spirits, and food in the process of digestion. (27)

Aside from the potential insult to Christ's divinity, this argument—like so many others opposing transubstantiation—seems to derive from a fundamental resistance to incorporating the body into religious worship in any real form whatsoever. Tatam plainly admits this to be the case. Describing Roman Catholicism as "a kind of organized imposture, just for carnalizing Christianity," Tatam insists that "[e]verything that the soul contemplates in the religion and in the worship of Christ is spiritual and invisible, in opposition to what is carnal and visible" (7). John Ward Spencer, in an 1853 sermon, similarly reminds his congregation that although they consume physical elements, they commune with Christ only in spirit. "By the power of the *imagination*" he notes, "we may *think* of Christ, *conceive* Him to be present; but it is only by *faith* that we can receive Christ, and so *realise* His presence [. . .] to think that without faith we may enjoy the eating and drinking of the Body and Blood of Christ, is but to 'dream a gross carnal feeding'" (28; emphasis in original).

It is, of course, beyond the scope of this chapter to represent nineteenth-century controversies over the Eucharist in all their variety and complexity. But even a broad brushstroke of the controversy suffices to demonstrate what was at stake for women writers when they appropriated Eucharistic imagery, especially that which smacked of Roman Catholicism. To say that Barrett Browning and Rossetti overtly represent the phenomenon of transubstantiation in their poems may risk placing too fine a point on the matter. Nonetheless, both Barrett Browning and Rossetti represent Holy Communion as a merging of bodies, as well as souls. And given that Barrett Browning—as a resident of Italy—and Rossetti—as a devout Anglo-Catholic—were exposed to Roman Catholic influences more than the average Englishwoman, it seems likely that the Eucharistic imagery in each poem was informed by the doctrine of transubstantiation.[7] In a Protestant culture that denied the corporeal in "good" women, just as it did in matters of faith and worship, the Catholic doctrine of tran-

---

7. Commenting on the meeting of Aurora's father and mother, Margaret Reynolds states, "As Aurora's mother goes to take communion in the [Catholic] church, celebrating the sacrament of the Eucharist by eating the wafer (see line 1.85) and drinking the wine (which represent the body and blood of Christ through the miraculous process of transubstantiation), so EBB takes over Catholic doctrine, applying that nexus of ideas to the discovery of sexual love, which also encompasses body and spirit" (*Aurora Leigh* 8, n.9).

substantiation could provide women writers with a conceptual tool—and a means of authority—by which to unify the fragmented female self into physical and spiritual wholeness.

Aurora Leigh

Although Elizabeth Barrett Browning professed to dislike sectarian controversy, she was deeply critical of Roman Catholicism, and incredulous that any of her fellow Englishmen and women could reject Protestantism for the allure of Rome.[8] Yet like many of her contemporaries, Barrett Browning demonstrated a fascination for Romanism alongside her uneasiness. On Christmas Eve, 1846, the Brownings attended Catholic Mass at the Duomo. Elizabeth described the incident in a letter to her sister: "The Duomo was very striking as we entered it, illuminated from end to end .. [sic] Galileo's great lamp glittering with a starry splendour. .then the choir & organ!—I was impressed for the first ten minutes! Afterwards it grew all weariness of the flesh & no edification of the spirit, certainly." The letter continues to express dismay at the customary "want of all reverence and decency" in the congregation, describing how the people wandered around and talked during the Mass.

> A dog that sate in the midst with his eyes gravely fixed on the altar, Robert pointed out as the most reverent member of the congregation. [. . .] The service in the meantime was carried on at the altar with the usual hoarse chanting of old priests, & curtsies & gestures of various sorts—all

---

8. Barrett Browning was reared a Congregationalist and, according to Linda Lewis, "classified herself as an Independent or Dissenter" (11). She grew "increasingly scornful of the narrowness of Protestant churches" (Mermin 179) and "for the most part [. . .] avoided established religion" (12). Lewis, Mermin, and other critics also discuss Barrett Browning's growing fascination with Swedenborgianism, beginning in the 1840s. Critics have said little about EBB's attitude toward Catholicism. In her correspondence, Barrett Browning struggles to balance a tone of respect and tolerance for Roman Catholics, with her obvious contempt for those who converted from Protestantism. "There is a great distinction," she writes to Mary Russell Mitford in 1842, "between a R Catholic by birth and education—and one by choice & *conversion—inversion* I would rather say! [. . .] I hope that your M.r De Vere [Irish poet Aubrey Thomas De Vere] may resist his impulse [to convert to Catholicism]" (*The Brownings' Correspondence* 6: letter 999; emphasis in original). After Mitford writes of attending Catholic vespers in 1843, Barrett Browning replies, "[G]ood sense & clear judgement predominate in you too much—you are not a woman to go over in a rapture & a puff of incense into the belief of an infallible Pope—& therefore I am not afraid—For the rest I w.d not willingly speak with disrepect of Roman catholic Christians" (*The Brownings' Correspondence* 7: letter 1231).

magnificent & feeble. .saying nothing to the senses even,—which mine could be impressed by. If they would have let the organ & the choir sing on, & the incense burn. .I like that cloud of incense floating about the brazen crucifix. .we might have felt an effect—but the priest dispossessed us of our own imaginations even! (*The Brownings' Correspondence* 14: letter 2645)

Barrett Browning's description seems no different, ultimately, from other Protestant descriptions of the Roman Mass: all sensual appeal, but no spiritual substance. Remarkable, however, is Barrett Browning's disappointment that she was deprived even of a sensual "effect." Like many other Victorian Protestant visitors to Italy, she at once condemned the sensual appeal of the Mass while simultaneously enjoying it. And Barrett Browning also seemed fascinated with the consecration of the host. In the midst of the mummery and irreverence, Barrett Browning noted an almost miraculous change pass over the congregation: "At the moment of the uplifting of the host, . . [*sic*] for the one *moment*. .there was attention & silence, & everyone knelt or stood still. That one moment of devotion was the only one for the *people*, observe [. . .]" (emphasis in original).

Despite Barrett Browning's conventional, critical view of the Catholic Mass as all sense and no spirit, ultimately she did embrace the ideal of a spiritual worship that also celebrated the material body. According to both Dorothy Mermin and Linda Lewis, one of Barrett Browning's primary attractions to Swedenborgianism in the 1840s and 1850s was that it was a theology of the body as well as the spirit (Mermin 179; Lewis 135ff). As Lewis notes, "St. Paul has taught Barrett Browning about the resurrection of the body, and Swedenborg makes the veil separating life and death more nearly transparent, allowing her to imagine the correspondences [between material and spiritual existence] beyond the veil" (142). Based solely on Barrett Browning's letters, it is difficult to tell whether Catholicism also influenced her desire to integrate body and spirit. In a letter of 1843, Barrett Browning reveals she thinks little of the Christian sacraments, including Holy Communion: "In truth, I can never see anything in these sacramental ordinances except a prospective sign in one (Baptism) and a memorial sign in the other. .the Lord's supper, & could not recognize either under any modification, as a peculiar instrument of grace, mystery, or the like" (*The Brownings' Correspondence* 7:211–12). But Barrett Browning's attitudes might easily have changed, especially after her prolonged residence in Italy. In any case, she clearly enjoyed Christmas Mass more in 1853, seven years after her first description of it. "The music was sublime, which, with the influence of the place and the sight of the crowding multitudes, carried me over everything I could otherwise have been schismatical upon. I was very much impressed and affected" (*Elizabeth Barrett Browning: Letters to Her Sister*, letter 55, p. 198).

Perhaps this was merely another sensual "effect," but there is other substantial evidence to suggest that Catholicism profoundly influenced Barrett Browning: the text of *Aurora Leigh*. Despite the fact that critics frequently mention Barrett Browning's interest in Swedenborgianism, Catholicism, as a source of inspiration for Barrett Browning's work, has received very little attention.[9] Like *Jane Eyre*, Barrett Browning's verse-novel is suffused with references to Catholicism that have remained largely overlooked or ignored. Catholicism in *Aurora Leigh* is no mere window dressing. The Catholic identity of Aurora's mother, the setting of Catholic Italy, and its overt Marian and Eucharistic imagery all contribute in significant ways to Aurora's development as both a woman and an artist. Although numerous critics have explained the nature of Aurora's quest, I find Joyce Zonana's reading particularly helpful, as she draws attention to the narrative's overwhelming preoccupation with merging body and spirit. Noting that Aurora initially regards herself as a disembodied, purely spiritual muse, Zonana states that "[h]er quest is to reclaim the material as an integral aspect of her already female, 'heavenly' being" (524). It is Aurora Leigh's quest for her own body—a body she can reconcile with her lofty poetic vocation—that renders Catholicism, with its emphasis on sacramental grace and transubstantiation—so vital to her story.

As if to set the keynote for her entire narrative, Aurora Leigh describes, within the first hundred lines, a Roman Catholic communion. Aurora's father, an "austere Englishman" (I:65), falls in love with Aurora's mother at first sight, as she processes to Mass:

A train of priestly banners, cross and psalm,
The white-veiled rose-crowned maidens holding up
Tall tapers, weighty for such wrists, aslant
To the blue luminous tremor of the air,
And letting drop the white wax as they went
To eat the bishop's wafer at the church;
From which long trail of chanting priests and girls,
A face flashed like a cymbal on his face

---

9. Despite its emphasis on Barrett Browning's engagement with "theological issues of her own time," and its assertion that "apart from the religious context, one cannot adequately interpret many works of the Barrett Browning canon" (4), even Lewis's study mentions Roman Catholicism only in passing, stating that Barrett Browning considered it "religion sensualized" (12).

And shook him with silent clangour brain and heart,
Transfiguring him to music. Thus, even thus,
He too received his sacramental gift
With eucharistic meanings; for he loved. (I:80–91)

Numerous Protestant accounts of the Roman Catholic Mass emphasized its sensual (and especially, visual) allure; a naïve, unguarded Protestant visitor to a Catholic country might, without due caution, find himself swept away by Rome's appeal to imagination and feeling rather than reason. On one hand, the "austere Englishman's" sudden conversion mimics this dangerous, potential effect of the Mass, but here he is converted to love, not Romanism. This love, which "transfigures" him, draws an obvious parallel between his emotional transformation (which will shortly lead to physical consummation) with Roman Catholic communion. This "transfiguration" prefigures Aurora's own eventual marriage with Romney.

This Mass procession is the only time the reader gets to "see" Aurora's mother—however fleetingly—still alive. And the setting—aside from reinforcing the sacramental, transformative nature of sexual love—is vital in that it firmly establishes Aurora's mother's identity as a Catholic. Catholicism endows the simulacrum of Aurora's absent mother with a constellation of multiple, often mutually contradictory, attributes. Critics frequently note how Aurora's mother's portrait (painted posthumously) conceals more than it reveals; Helen Cooper, for example, describes the portrait as "woman's identity [. . .] created by the cultural economy" and the "object of narratives formed from men's terror or adoration of her" (156). Aurora gazes upon the picture and sees not her mother, but multiple cultural constructions of femininity:

[. . .] I, a little child, would crouch
For hours upon the floor with knees drawn up,
And gaze across them, half in terror, half
In adoration, at the picture there,—
That swan-like supernatural white life
Just sailing upward from the red stiff silk
[. . .] Still that face,.. which did not therefore change,
But kept the mystic level of all forms
Hates, fears, and admirations, was by turns
Ghost, fiend, and angel, fairy, witch, and sprite,
A dauntless Muse who eyes a dreadful Fate,
A loving Psyche who loses sight of Love,
A still Medusa with mild milky brows

> All curdled and all clothed upon with snakes
> Whose slime falls fast as sweat will; or anon
> Our Lady of the Passion, stabbed with swords
> Where the Babe sucked [. . .] (I:135–40; 151–61)

Critics often discuss the dual image of womanhood in this portrait. "The composite maternal image in the portrait," states Dorothy Mermin, "then splits into two opposite figures: virtuous Marian Earle and wicked Lady Waldemar, the victimized innocent and predatory sophisticate, the good mother and the bad" (192). While the portrait clearly prepares the reader to encounter saintly Marian and demonic Waldemar, the Catholic identity of Aurora's mother adds an additional layer of signification to this portrait. Viewed in one light, the portrait shows us the Virgin Mary; from another angle, however, it is the Whore of Babylon, swathed in a red silk gown.[10] This picture shows us more than one mother; it is also Rome, the "Mother Church," in its most benevolent and terrifying auspices. Mermin points out how the text of *Aurora Leigh* expresses ambivalence toward the mother figure, and this ambivalence is reinforced by its doubling with Protestant ambivalence toward Rome. Protestants simultaneously acknowledged Rome's material, sensual comforts (apropos of the proliferation of maternal and sexual breasts in the text), while fearing spiritual annihilation in her embrace.[11]

The portrait's merging of femininity and Catholicism is all the more significant when we realize that almost *every* woman in Aurora's story is figuratively linked with Rome in either its attractive or repellent forms. Aurora's second mother figure is the Catholic servant Assunta, "Crossing herself whene'er a sudden flame / Which lighted from the firewood, made alive, / That picture of my mother on the wall" (I:125–27). Aurora's third "mother," her aunt, seems initially to break this pattern, as she (with her Anglican catechism, creeds, and Articles) is so clearly an austere Protestant foil to the sensual femininity of Italy. Yet so extreme is her austerity ("Her somewhat narrow forehead braided tight / As if for taming accidental thoughts " [I:273–74]) that she resembles in her black garments (I:314) a Catholic monastic. More specifically, she is a stereotypical "female Jesuitess" of anti-Catholic fiction, the same type that inspired Brontë's creation

---

10. Marjorie Stone notes that EBB "mines the book of Revelation for images for Aurora Leigh, including a 'dropped star' and the 'woman clothed with the sun'" (182).

11. Mermin notes "the large company of rejecting mothers who crowd the pages of the poem: Aurora's mother and aunt, Marian's mother, Lady Waldemar and her agent, as well as Marian's friend Lucy's grandmother and the various passing sights, voices, and images that stain the fabric of the text with the colors of maternal cruelty" (193).

of Madame Beck in *Villette*.¹² Indeed, Aurora's aunt strongly resembles Madame Beck, with her spying gaze and manipulative understanding of human nature. When Aurora first arrives, her aunt, "[W]ith two grey-steel naked-bladed eyes / Searched through my face,—ay, stabbed it through and through, / Through brows and cheeks and chin, as if to find / A wicked murderer in my innocent face" (I:327-30). Aurora's aunt has a penetrating gaze indeed, for she discovers Aurora's repressed love for Romney. After Aurora infuriates her aunt by refusing Romney's proposal, Aurora states the her aunt (whose looks "Still cleav[ed] to me, like the sucking asp / To Cleopatra's breast" [II:863-65]) intended "a commination, or at best, / An exorcism against the devildom/ Which plainly held me" (II:869-71).

While Marian's associations with the Virgin Mary and with Christ have been frequently noted, *Aurora Leigh*'s most fascinating appropriation of Catholicism relates to Lady Waldemar, who plays the Whore of Babylon to Marian's Madonna. Although Waldemar never reveals a religious affiliation, she compares herself to a wayward Catholic at her very first meeting with Aurora. Since Aurora's status as a poet elevates her, claims Waldemar, above ordinary women, Waldemar feels no shame confiding to her her love for Romney. "There's many a papist she," says Waldemar, "would rather die / Than own to her maid she put a ribbon on / To catch the indifferent eyes of such a man, / —Who yet would count adulteries on her beads / At holy Mary's shrine, and never blush" (III:414-18). Waldemar's act of confession to her chosen "saint" Romanizes her further; Aurora protests that she is "no Muse, still less [. . .] any saint; / [. . .] that Lady Waldemar / Should make confessions" (III:423-25).¹³ Another implicit comparison between Waldemar and sinister Romanism is her almost irresistible appeal to the senses. Glennis Stephenson notes that the text refers to her as an "eye-trap" (V:835), and that "[a]ll her dealings with others are conducted on a sensual level," including her interactions with Aurora, on whom she attempts a kind of "seduction" (100). Waldemar's sensual appeal is particularly pronounced in the text's description of her at Lord Howe's party; it is, in effect, an image mirroring the dark side of Aurora's mother's portrait. Aurora glimpses among Waldermar's tresses "a single gray hair," but beyond that,

---

12. Cora Kaplan states that Barrett Browning preferred *Villette*, which she described as "a strong book," to Brontë's other novels, despite the multiple, obvious echoes of *Jane Eyre* throughout *Aurora Leigh*. An attention to Catholic themes and imagery in *Aurora Leigh* highlights equally compelling resonances with *Villette*, especially when we consider Aurora's situation (later in the poem) as a lone Protestant wanderer in a foreign Catholic country.

13. Waldemar will confess a second time to Aurora (IX:90 ff) when she discloses her role in Marian's abduction and sexual fall.

> The woman looked immortal. How they told,
> Those alabaster shoulders and bare breasts,
> On which the pearls, drowned out of sight in milk,
> Were lost, excepting for the ruby-clasp!
> They split the amaranth velvet bodice down
> To the waist or nearly, with the audacious press
> Of full-breathed beauty. If the heart within
> Were half as white! [. . .] (V:618–25)

Lady Waldemar's alabaster shoulders and milk-white breasts, bursting out of a gown that is later described as red (V:634), clearly relates back to "[t]hat swan-like supernatural white life / Just sailing upward from the red stiff silk" (I:139–40) of Aurora's mother's portrait. Here Lady Waldemar, "immortal," represents something larger than herself, the same fusion of maternal, sensual, and demonic qualities long attributed to the Church of Rome.

Fittingly, Lady Waldemar's "demonic" qualities manifest themselves through the sexual corruption of innocent Marian. Although Marian's kidnapping, drugging, and rape in a French brothel were inspired in part by Richardson's *Clarissa*, the story also reads like the plot of a more prurient anti-Catholic novel.[14] Jesuits were, of course, frequently accused of seducing and kidnapping young women, and such literature also implicitly—or overtly—equated convents with brothels. After Marian's rape and release, she describes her wanderings through rural France as a passage through a nightmarish Romish landscape, as the lurid iconography of the French Catholics—rebuking, she thinks, her violated body—prolong her torture: "[. . .] every roadside Christ upon his cross / Hung reddening through his gory wounds at me, / And shook his nails in anger [. . .]" (VI:1247–49). Twice, well-meaning peasants hang an image of the Virgin around Marian's neck: "How heavy it seemed! as heavy as stone; / A woman had been strangled with less weight" (VI:1257–58). Marian gains temporary asylum at the home of a Frenchwoman who teases her for her gravity: "[. . .] mass-book still, and Lent? / And first-communion pallor on your cheeks, /Worn past the time for 't? [. . .] (VII:33–35). This frivolous mistress, her time divided "betwixt her lover and her looking-glass" (VII:25), is an overt Catholic echo of Lady Waldemar, particularly when she vents her hypocritical self-righteousness upon pregnant Marian, ordering her confession ("Confess thou'lt be a mother in a month, / Thou mask of saintship" [VII:47–48]), and turning her out on the street.

---

14. See Margaret Reynolds's note on *Clarissa* and other literary influences for Marian's kidnapping and rape (AL VI:214, n.4).

If other female characters in the text help to shape Aurora's emerging identity, what is the relevance of these Catholic associations? Just as Marian Earle and Lady Waldemar mirror contradictory aspects of Aurora's self, the many Catholic images that surround Aurora also speak to a particular dimension of her character. In *Jane Eyre,* Jane's basic human nature—namely, her tendencies toward "creature worship" and her sensuality—are coded Catholic and must be controlled or repressed before she can achieve maturity, and the novel, satisfactory closure. So also, in *Aurora Leigh,* is Catholicism a signifier for Aurora's deepest instincts. But while Jane Eyre must work to suppress her "inner Catholic," Aurora Leigh's primary challenge is to acknowledge and embrace hers. That is, Aurora must channel her sensitivity and sensuality into an understanding of material creation on two levels—one in regard to her own sexual nature and her repressed love for Romney, and the second in regard to her vocation as a poet who celebrates the material world.

When Aurora first begins to write poetry, she figures herself very much as a Romantic poet, celebrating the divine in nature. On her walks with Romney, "I flattered all the beauteous country round, / As poets use . . [*sic*] the skies, the clouds, the fields, / The happy violets hiding from the roads / The primroses run down to, carrying gold [. . .]" (I:1119–22). So confident is Aurora in the beauty and goodness of nature, that she cannot comprehend the reality of evil: "[. . .] see! is not God with us on the earth?" she asks Romney, "And shall we put Him down by aught we do? / Who says there's nothing for the poor and vile / Save poverty and wickedness? [. . .]" (I:1135–38). In stark contrast, Romney insists that "The world, we've come to late, is swollen hard / With perished generations and their sins" (II:263–64). Aurora, however, just emerging from her sheltered middle-class girlhood, cannot conceive what he means: "[I]s the world so bad," she says mockingly, "While I hear nothing of it through the trees? / The world was always evil,—but so bad?" (II:305–7). Although apparently Aurora has written some verse on social problems, Romney condemns it as the work of a lofty muse who merely appropriates others' suffering for the purposes of her art: "All's yours and you, / All, coloured with your blood, or otherwise/ Just nothing to you. / Why, I call you hard to general suffering" (II:196–99). Although it is tempting to demonize Romney and his self-righteousness, Leighton reminds us that this particular criticism is "not simply to be dismissed as examples of male prejudice. His attack on the narrowness, sentimentality, and ultimate self-centeredness of women's verse is one which, at the moment of her humiliation in the garden, Aurora takes to heart" (*Victorian Women Poets* 92).

Women, pronounces Romney, "give us doating [*sic*] mothers, and perfect wives, / Sublime Madonnas and enduring saints! / We got no

Christ from you, and verily / We shall not get a poet [...]" (II:222–25). Although Romney sees a female Christ as an impossibility, his words nonetheless predict Aurora's greatest challenge: how can a woman follow her artistic vocation and also her central calling as a Christian? That is, how is the female poet, Aurora specifically, to imitate Christ? It is not enough, as Romney's criticism has demonstrated, to show an interest in the poor, or even to exercise abstract philanthropy in their behalf. Christ manifested his love for humanity through the physical act of incarnation, sharing the very flesh of sinners. Similarly, Aurora must descend from her lofty chamber ("up three flights of stairs / Not far from being as steep as some larks climb" [III:158–59]) and understand, as intimately as possible, the lives and sufferings of the poor. And Aurora's challenge is formidable indeed. In the fashionable church of St. James, where Christ's incarnation is regularly memorialized, and his body and blood figuratively consumed, the bodies of the poor swarm to attend Romney's wedding, physically repulsive, as it would seem, past all redemption: "They clogged the streets, they oozed into the church / In a dark slow stream, like blood," says Aurora (IV:553–54). Her words describe the bodies of the poor as literally turned inside out, and their faces as barely human:

> Those, faces? 'twas as if you had stirred up hell
> To heave its lowest dreg-fiends uppermost
> In fiery swirls of slime,—such strangled fronts,
> Such obdurate jaws were thrown up constantly
> To twit you with your race, corrupt your blood,
> And grind to devilish colours all your dreams [...] (IV:587–92)

These people assault not merely the eye, but the nose as well: Aurora describes their stench as "Exasperating the unaccustomed air / With hideous interfusion. / You'd suppose a finished generation, dead of plague, / Swept outward from their graves into the sun" (IV:546–49). Aurora describes the upper-class women burying their noses in perfumed handkerchiefs and smelling salts, but her undisguised horror at the sight and smell of the poor seems to align her, at this point, with those same ladies of fashion.

Yet later, passing through Paris on her way to Italy, Aurora reflects, in relation to her poetic vocation, how "we are shocked at nature's falling off / We dare to shrink back from her warts and blains, / We will not when she sneezes, look at her, / Not even to say 'God bless her'?" (VI:178–81). Aurora condemns this tendency, noting that it stands in the way of art: "For that, she will not trust us often with / Her larger sense of beauty and desire,

/ But tethers us to a lily or a rose / And bids us diet on the dew inside, / Left ignorant [...] [of] the hungry beggar boy" (VI:182–86). Appropriately, as Aurora continues to muse upon the means of making poetry relevant to the common good, she suddenly spots Marian in the crowd: "God! what face is that?" (VI:227). This question, which Aurora repeats a few lines later, echoes her reaction to the poor in St. James at the aborted wedding ceremony. Only this time, rather than respond to the faces of the poor in horror, Aurora responds to this second apparition with a desire so intense that she longs to consume—almost literally—the body of the poor, now symbolized by Marian.

Angela Leighton, Marjorie Stone, and others have noted how Aurora's later encounter with Marian enables her to "humanize" her poetry and so become a true artist (Leighton, *Elizabeth Barrett Browning* 152). And at the level of the corporeal, Cooper argues that in such close contact with Marian as mother, "Aurora finally claims her female identity" (169). Aurora may rescue Marian from the slums and give her an honored position in her home, but it is Marian, through the literal sacrifice of her body, who "transfigures" Aurora into both a woman and an artist. It is fitting, then, that Aurora should use the language of Holy Communion upon meeting her again in Paris:

> I lost my sister Marian many days,
> And sought her ever in my walks and prayers,
> And, now I find her ... do we throw away
> The bread we worked and prayed for,—crumble it
> And drop it, .. [*sic*] to do even so by thee
> Whom still I've hungered after more than bread,
> My sister Marian?—can I hurt thee, dear? (VI.449-55)

To "crumble" and "drop" the bread of Marian's company seems tantamount, in this passage, to profaning the Eucharist. Through this implicit comparison between Marian and sacramental food, Aurora introduces a corporeal element into what Leighton describes as "an alternate love story" (*Victorian Woman Poets* 103). Furthermore, while Aurora's proposal to make Marian her household saint redeems Marian's tortured body, it does *not* deny it. Zonana argues that Aurora's attitude toward Marian at this point wholly spiritualizes her, and "strengthen[s] [Aurora's] already well-developed alienation from her physical self and her world" (526). I disagree here; Aurora's reunion / communion with Marian suggests that she is already well on her way toward embracing the full implications of the material world. More significant, however, is that Aurora wishes to turn Marian into a *Catholic* saint: "I am journeying south, / And in my Tuscan home I'll find a niche / And set thee there, my saint, the child and thee, [...] And ever at thy sweet look cross myself [...]" (VII:125–27, 129). In the Victorian Protestant imagination, Catholic veneration to the Virgin Mary was anything but a spiritual practice, as it was considered idolatrous. While Aurora clearly recognizes Marian's sanctity, her desire to set her up as a household Madonna compares the fallen woman to Mary, who, according to Catholic doctrine, ascended both body *and* soul into heaven.

The communion imagery would seem to imply a double transubstantiation; each woman is bodily transformed by the other. Aurora's redemption is as much spiritual as corporeal, for it is her encounter with Marian that allows her to realize her full powers and fulfill her divine calling of celebrating the sacred in the material world. Marian, through Aurora's "adoption" of herself and her child, is elevated to the status of a Madonna, but Marian's "redemption" is, at best, problematic. In the culture that produced *Aurora Leigh,* it would take nothing less than a total bodily transformation (in other words, a Catholic miracle) to redeem the fallen woman. Yet as the poem reveals to us, even that has its limits. Numerous critics have expressed unease that Marian, although an innocent victim of rape, is nonetheless denied the traditional happy ending accorded to women: the love of a good man. Of the several reasons that Marian gives for rejecting Romney, some are less objectionable than others. Marian implies that she no longer desires Romney's condescension. "[...] I, who felt myself unworthy once / Of virtuous Romney and his high-born race / Have come to learn, a woman, poor or rich, / Despised or honoured, is a human soul [...]" (IX:326–29). She also suggests that she never really loved Romney, but merely idolized him: "Did I indeed love once; or did I only worship? (IX:363). Yet alongside these protestations of high moral principle, are Marian's persistent expressions of self-loathing:

> I told your cousin, sir, that I was dead;
> And now, she thinks I'll get up from my grave,
> And wear my chin-cloth for a wedding-veil,
> And glide along the churchyard like a bride
> While all the dead keep whispering through the withes,
> You would be better in your place with us,
> 'You pitiful corruption!' [...] (XI:391–97)

Undeniably, *Aurora Leigh*'s treatment of the fallen woman was advanced for its time. In a letter to her sister, Barrett Browning explains how "Marian, subjected to the most hideous of trials [...], is made to emerge with a glory of purity & moral dignity [...]. You shall feel the virtue of chastity, in her, even more than in Aurora" (qtd. in Kenyon 334). Yet despite her attempts to redeem Marian, Barrett Browning seemed unable to relinquish wholly her culture's fear and suspicion of sexually violated women. As Linda Lewis points out, throughout history woman "has been associated with filth and death," and "Marian conveys this message, perhaps more than even her creator realizes" (160).

Aurora Leigh makes an earnest attempt to redeem Marian body and soul; Marian, however, continues to define herself in terms of her degraded body. This observation is hardly a new one, but what has received less attention are the troubling ways in which Marian is soon stripped altogether of her newfound *spiritual* agency. Marian's "murder," which indirectly leads to Aurora's redemption as woman and artist, also makes Marian into a female Christ. In the tradition of anti-Catholic Protestant discourse, however, Christ's sanctity is diminished by the corrupt, self-aggrandizing powers of the Romish priest. And in a manner certainly unintended by Barrett Browning, Aurora's appropriation of Marian's sacrifice and suffering for her own uses transforms *her* into a Protestant stereotype of a Roman Catholic priest. Even before this point in the narrative, we see Aurora performing "priestly" functions. Aside from creating poetry that, as Romney notes, has Eucharistic connotations (VIII:265–69), she is the confessor for every major character in the story. Lady Waldemar confesses to her twice (once of her love for Romney, and again of her role in Marian's fall); Marian tells her the story of her rape; and finally Romney appeals to Aurora in book 8: "I ready for confession— I was wrong, / I've sorely failed, I've slipped the ends of life, / I yield, you have conquered" (VIII:467–69).

Critics have remarked upon how Marian disappears from the final pages of *Aurora Leigh*. Perhaps this is because Aurora, like a priest consuming a Eucharistic wafer, almost literally *ingests* her. Aurora hungers after Marian "more than bread" because she possesses two things Aurora lacks—her motherhood and her affiliation with the lower-class body. Aurora's "communion" with Marian necessarily precedes both her marriage to Romney (and its potential for offspring) and the full development of her poetic genius. Once Aurora appropriates the necessary, corporeal elements of Marian's character, Marian's body might as well vanish altogether. After all, she is, like Lady Waldemar, only one fragment of Aurora's divided self. Bertha Mason left alive at the conclusion of *Jane Eyre* would somehow diminish Jane's triumphant ending, and Marian, although by no means a sinister character, must disappear as well. But even at the moment of Marian's spiritual apotheosis, when Aurora takes her into her home, it is important to bear in mind that Marian's salvific agency absolutely depends upon Aurora as priestly mediator. It is Aurora who seeks and finds Marian; Aurora who presents to the reader (almost as a memorial ritual) Marian's horrific story; Aurora who absolves Marian of wrongdoing and "canonizes" her; and Aurora who consecrates Marian's fallen body and gains both spiritual and corporeal benefits from her sacrifice. So great is Aurora's priestly power that Marian's spiritual agency is ultimately negated by it. So also did Protestants regard the unlawful, inflated power of the Romish priesthood as an insult to Christ's divinity. As the Reverend J. Aldwell Nicholson told his audience in an 1859 lecture, the Romish Christ was a false god, and a pathetically small and contemptible one at that:

> The Christ I believe in, is not the poor Wafer of the Mass; a God which, this Roman Mass-book tells me, can be blown away by the wind, carried off by an animal, warmed in a cloth, and melted in hot water! No; the Christ and the God I believe in, is a God inconceivably great and glorious. The heaven and the heaven of heavens cannot contain him. (44)

Elizabeth Barrett Browning deliberately framed her heroine as a quasi-divine prophetic figure, but she would never have consciously sullied Aurora with overt associations to the Romish priesthood. Yet the echoes are there. So pervasive was anti-Catholic discourse in the 1850s, and so exposed was Barrett Browning to Romanism in Italy, that *Aurora Leigh*'s unconscious framing of its heroine as a Catholic priest seems almost inevitable. The Catholic priest was, in the Protestant imagination, far more powerful, majestic, and intimidating than any other contemporary minister of religion, even if his power was deemed illicit and blasphemous. The author of *The Doctrine of Transubstantiation Refuted* (1838) presents just such an image:

> Behold them, on their high festivals, their high masses; [. . .] in all the pomp and pageantry of their mystic office, appearing to the laity like descended gods, blazing in gems and gold, amidst the luster of tapers and the floating splendour of an irradiated atmosphere alive with light, and all soft and delicate harmonies and delicious odours, [. . .] the intoxicated eye dreamt it saw them ascend to Paradise. Such was the scene; but what was behind? I saw it all; and when the delusion was over, I spurned them in my soul. (29)

Despite his horror of the priests, the writer is clearly fascinated by them as well; he did not "spurn" them until "the delusion was over." Something of this fascination with the Romish priest is also evident in *Aurora Leigh*. Cora Kaplan has suggested that *Aurora Leigh* be read "as an overlapping sequence of dialogues with other texts, other writers" (145). This analysis proposes that "corrupt priests" and other popular stereotypes of Catholicism were as influential in the composition of *Aurora Leigh* as "Tennyson, Clough, Kingsley, the Brontës, Gaskell, and Sand" (Kaplan 145).

Regarding *Aurora Leigh*'s intertextual dialogues, Kaplan also notes that "[n]one of these debates is finished and some pursue contradictory arguments" (145). This seems especially the case with Roman Catholicism, an entity which *Aurora Leigh* does not so much converse with but *absorbs*. Throughout most of the narrative, Aurora's incipient Catholicism is linked with her sensuality and her incarnational poetics and is, in this respect, something beneficial and even sacred. But just as the Janus-faced nature of Catholicism exhibits itself in the contrasting associations in Aurora's mother's portrait, Aurora's own Catholic lineage contains a sinister potential.

At the end of chapter 8, Aurora kneels alongside other women in an Italian church, "And prayed, since I was foolish in desire / Like other creatures, craving offal-food, / That He would stop his ears to what I said, / And only listen to the run and beat / Of this poor, passionate, helpless blood" (VII:1267–71). According to Joyce Zonana, this is a pivotal, positive moment in Aurora's self-identification as an embodied muse: "no longer striving, no longer reaching up to God [. . .] Aurora [. . .] has finally given in to the impulses of her own body; the impulses of desire and love [. . .] taking [her passion] to be, finally, divine" (529). Given the fact that Catholicism has, to this point, symbolized a healthy embrace of the corporeal world, Zonana's reading makes sense. But what seems more at issue in book 7 is not the divinity of Aurora's passion, but the fact that she has no one to expend it on. She has just described her visit to her old home, now inhabited by strangers, and reflected sorrowfully upon both her parents' graves and Assunta's death. "I was past," she reflects ruefully. "It seemed, like others,—only not in heaven" (VII:1158–59). Aurora's deep loneliness and figurative deadness are only intensified as she walks past a cluster of festival-goers, each lady with her "cavalier," listening "to his hot-breathed vows of love / Enough to thaw her cream and scorch his beard" (VII:1184–85). It is at this moment that Aurora, still believing in Romney's marriage to Lady Waldemar, commits a desperate act.

Aurora's fervent praying in a Popish church would have scandalized some readers, and it seems a deliberate echo of Lucy Snowe's visit to a

Catholic confessional in *Villette,* at the most painful part of her long, lonely sojourn in a foreign land. Lucy tells us that had she accepted her confessor's invitation to visit a second time, "I might just now, instead of writing this heretic narrative, be counting my beads" as the inmate of a Catholic convent (235). So also does Aurora's act, at this delicate moment, seem to indicate the risk of religious perversion. It's one thing for Aurora to embrace the Catholic *part* of her nature, but neither Barrett Browning nor her readers would have seen any point in Aurora becoming a Romanist. Although Aurora enjoys watching the Italian women pray "Toward's the altar's silver glory" (VII:116) and to the Virgin Mary and other saints (VII:1235–56), she also sees their religious error: "Such utterance from such faces," she thinks, "poor blind souls / That writhe toward heaven along the devil's trail" (VII:1258–60). But then reflecting that God might "pick them up" nonetheless, she joins them, praying "[t]hat He would stop his ears to what I said" (VII:1269).

According to this one line, not only is the *location* of Aurora's devotions suspect, but also the *form.* Has she said a prayer to the Virgin Mary? Given her figurative Madonna worship through Marian, this is a distinct possibility. Unlike Lucy Snowe, who does not repeat her visit to the confessional, Aurora seems to continue her Popish prayers: "So many Tuscan evenings passed the same [. . .] [I] would not miss a vigil in the church" (VII:1273, 1275). Although Aurora expresses confidence that "He heard in heaven," just a few lines later, she describes her encounter in church with Sir Blaise Delorme. Delorme, a minor character whom critics generally overlook, has a seemingly inexplicable effect on Aurora: "his thought disturbed my life: / For after that, I oftener sate at home / On evenings [. . .]" (VII:1295–96). What is it about Delorme, whom Aurora describes as a "scarce acquaintance" (VII:1292), that disturbs her and keeps her from returning to church?

Although at least one commentator has linked Delorme to the Anglo-Catholic movement, both Delorme's description and his comments suggest that he is beyond the pale of the English Church altogether, a convert to Rome.[15] Delorme refers to his church, "The catholic, apostolic, mother-church" (V:747), which allows no ambiguity in moral matters. She "[d]raws lines as plain and straight as her own wall; / Inside of which, are

---

15. Reynolds writes that "Sir Blaise is old in terms of his outlook on life, which is influenced by the fashion for things medieval that arose in the 1840s and 1850s and by the reactionary doctrines of the Anglo-Catholic movement led by John Henry Newman and Edward Pusey" (AL 162, n. 6). Mermin labels Sir Blaise as "conspicuously Catholic" but only mentions him as one of several minor figures that are remarkable for the "loving attention" (218) that EBB expended in describing them.

Christians, obviously / And outside . . [*sic*] dogs" (V:748–50). Delorme's physical description marks him both as a Catholic and an ascetic:

> But, though you miss his chin, you seldom miss
> His ebon cross worn innermostly, (carved
> For penance by a saintly Styrian monk
> Whose flesh was too much for him,) slipping through
> Some unaware unbuttoned casualty
> Of the under-waistcoat. (V:675–80)

Given Elizabeth Barrett Browning's own contempt for English converts to Rome (a sentiment Robert Browning shared), we are likely meant to regard the chinless Sir Blaise, an apostate to his faith, as spineless as well. Lost in religious mysticism, he is clearly alienated both from his own body and the world around him. Aurora recalls their brief encounter to Romney:

> By chance I saw him in Our Lady's church,
> (I saw him, mark you, but he saw not me)
> Clean-washed in holy water from the count
> Of things terrestrial,—letters, and the rest;
> He had crossed us out together with his sins. (VIII:145–49)

The letter Aurora refers to is the missive, entrusted to Delorme's care, which would have informed Aurora that Romney was still an unmarried man. Blaise's loss of the letter, which he "Has twisted to a lighter absently / To fire some holy taper" (VIII:178–79), places a slight complication on the progress of Romney and Aurora's courtship, reinforcing his ascetic character even further.

Blaise's unattractive character, and the unease he causes Aurora, suggests that he is a mirror of what Aurora could become, if denied a physical outlet for her passion. The fact that Aurora seems susceptible to otherworldly asceticism even after appropriating Marian's body diminishes the power of the female Eucharistic encounter even further. The text's anxieties about the female body are displaced onto Marian, which seems appropriate for her role as sacrificial lamb (or scapegoat). Yet until Romney arrives to claim his bride, Aurora's redemption—which seems to require "sexual passion, which devours the flesh / In a sacrament of souls (V:15–16)"—is incomplete. The rapturous kiss Aurora shares with Romney in book 9 consummates Aurora's redemption, as the two seem to merge into a single body:

> [. . .] were my cheeks
> Hot, overflooded, with my tears, or his?
> And which of our two large explosive hearts
> So shook me? That, I know not. There were words
> That broke in utterance . . . melted, in the fire,—
> Embrace, that was convulsion, . . [sic] then a kiss
> As long and silent as the ecstatic night,
> And deep, deep, shuddering breaths, which meant beyond
> Whatever could be told by word or kiss. (IX:716–24)

Only through the fleshly "sacrament of souls," Aurora's requited passion for Romney, can Aurora finally reconcile both her body and her mind and carry out the vocation she was put on earth to follow. To Romney's proposal that they "raise men's bodies still by raising souls, / As God did first," Aurora says they must "stand upon the earth [. . .] to raise them" (IX:853–56). By descending from the lofty pinnacles of social theory and art, respectively, to embrace and uplift humanity, Romney and Aurora both can imitate, in a sense, Christ's incarnation. The final lines of *Aurora Leigh* summon up a vision of the New Jerusalem they will help to build.

In its evocation of the Book of Revelation and its New Jerusalem, *Aurora Leigh*'s conclusion is yet another echo of *Jane Eyre*. Yet the contrast between the two images is stark: Jane's New Jerusalem is really the kingdom St. John aspires to, and as such, is not of this world. In contrast, Aurora and Romney's kingdom will be built—or at least established—in their lifetimes through their own sanctified efforts. While *Jane Eyre* never achieves a satisfactory reconciliation between the flesh and the spirit, seasoning its heroine's domestic bliss with a rigorous dose of asceticism and Evangelical moral earnestness, *Aurora Leigh*'s conclusion betrays no such anxieties. Aurora's erotic redemption through her marriage with Romney Leigh is as joyous and untroubled as the most passionate of the *Sonnets from the Portuguese*. The blissful merging of female body and spirit at *Aurora Leigh*'s conclusion is achieved, in part, through the verse-novel's appropriation of Catholicism and, in particular, its doctrine of transubstantiation. Although the "miracle" of transubstantiation still cannot redeem Marian, it renders her into a sacrificial victim who can bear the weight of Aurora's material anxieties, and in turn, transfigures Aurora into a woman, lover, and artist. Although Marian's representation and her fate in the poem is the great disappointment of *Aurora Leigh*, Barrett Browning at least carries off the argument that "legitimate," married domestic bliss need not induce spiritual anxiety for women.

Goblin Market, or, The Fruits of Romanism

Christina Rossetti was a great admirer of Elizabeth Barrett Browning, and *Aurora Leigh*'s influence on *Goblin Market* is evident in the latter poem's emphasis on sisterly love, its call to Christ-like sacrifice, and, most significantly, its pronounced Eucharistic imagery.[16] These two poems make a particularly interesting juxtaposition, for despite their obvious similarities, Barrett Browning and Rossetti differed markedly in religious backgrounds and preoccupations. Barrett Browning, in her poetic affirmations of this world over the hereafter, would probably have been described by William James in *Varieties of Religious Experience* as "healthy minded." In contrast, Rossetti—whose love for the natural world and her deep conviction of its fallen state create such a remarkable, consistent tension in her poetry—would certainly have fit the opposing Jamesean category of "sick-souled."[17] Yet despite these profound religious differences, the poems also demonstrate a remarkable similarity in how they define and employ Eucharistic imagery: unashamedly corporeal, and more Catholic in nature than Protestant.

A Catholic transubstantiation in *Goblin Market* might seem less surprising as the work of Anglo-Catholic Rossetti, until we realize that Anglo-Catholics had as much—if not more—reason than their contemporaries to condemn the notion of corporeal presence in the Eucharist. Because Tractarianism was marked by its emphasis on sacramentalism (God's grace working through the created world), and its particular reverence for the sacrament of the Eucharist, the Tractarians had to work especially hard to demonstrate their adherence to the Thirty-Nine Articles, and to refute charges of Romanist heresy. To squeeze *Goblin Market* into yet another allegorical reading is not my intention here. Rather, I wish simply to consider this poem in light of Anglo-Catholics' complicated attitudes toward the Eucharist, and the ever-present danger of Anglo-Catholicism shading into heretical Romanism. This contextual exercise throws into sharp relief not only the poem's obsession with the sin of idolatry, but also its remarkable insistence upon the centrality of the body—and in this case, the female body—as an agent of God's grace.

It is by now a biographical commonplace that Rossetti was deeply influenced in her teens by the teachings of the Anglo-Catholic movement,

---

16. Barrett Browning's influence on Rossetti has been discussed by both Angela Leighton and Catherine Maxwell (Maxwell 79).
17. I explain James's terminology in the first paragraph of chapter 2.

conveyed to her, in particular, through the sermons of William Dodsworth at Christ Church Albany Street.[18] Initially, Dodsworth, along with the leaders of the movement, upheld the Eucharistic doctrine of "Real Presence" as distinctly and emphatically separate from the Roman doctrine of Transubstantiation. In a series of *Discourses on the Lord's Supper,* published in 1836 (2nd ed.), Dodsworth criticizes those Anglicans who insist that the Eucharist is merely a symbol of Christ's sacrifice. "[T]he true doctrine of the Church is as far from this [viewing the Eucharist as mere symbol]," he argues, "as it is from Popish transubstantiation" (29). Dodsworth explains that Christ is "really and virtually present" in the sacrament (46), but only in a *spiritual* sense, as the bread and wine "undergo no change in their nature and substance" (45; emphasis in original). This *via media* in Eucharistic doctrine proved difficult to maintain. Peter Nockles, in *The Oxford Movement in Context,* points out that "Tractarian apologists increasingly implied an Objective if not material presence in the sacrament itself, rather than one confined to the heart of the recipient" (242). "Real Presence" was a complicated doctrine, and for some Anglo-Catholics, a slippery slope to Rome. In 1851, Dodsworth followed in the wake of Newman and Manning and became a Roman Catholic.

Surely Dodsworth's conversion would have been upsetting to his congregation. In her biography of Rossetti, Georgiana Battiscome notes that Tractarians, paradoxically, "while stressing the Catholic nature of the Church of England, were especially horrified when any of their number went over to Rome" (56). We have no record of Rossetti's response to Dodsworth's conversion, but the defection of a respected spiritual leader to Rome must have been disheartening for her, at best. Rossetti herself remained a staunch Anglican; the strength of this conviction was demonstrated some years earlier when she broke her engagement with the painter James Collinson because of *his* conversion to Romanism.[19] Rossetti, in her writings on the Eucharist and the role of the saints, always distances

---

18. For a detailed discussion of the influence of Anglo-Catholicism upon Rossetti, see Jan Marsh's *Christina Rossetti* (1994). See also the biography by Georgiana Battiscombe, *Christina Rossetti: A Divided Life* (1981). Diane D'Amico's *Christina Rossetti: Faith, Gender, and Time* (1997) is the first critical study to focus exclusively on intersections between Rossetti's religious and poetic identities, and thus provides valuable religious context for a more thorough understanding of Rossetti's writings.

19. "I have often thought that Christina's proper place was in the Roman Catholic Church," wrote her brother William, who suggested that she remained an Anglican out of filial devotion to her mother (qtd. in Battiscombe 33). As her volumes of prose writing amply demonstrate, Rossetti's Anglican identity had a far more substantial foundation than mere daughterly affection, but William's comment is interesting nonetheless.

herself from the least association with Romish error. Rossetti placed great importance on the sacrament of the Eucharist and believed in the Real Presence, but her frequent use of the terms "Flesh" and "Blood" seems to have been purely metaphorical.[20] In *Face of the Deep*, she states, "Already we eat of 'the true bread from heaven' in the Blessed Sacrament of Christ's Body and Blood. Eating thereof we receive strength to overcome; and truly it is 'hidden Manna' of virtue *indiscernible by fleshly eyes and carnal hearts* (71; emphasis added). Likewise, Rossetti upholds an Anglican position on the respect due to the Virgin Mary, emphasizing in *Called to Be Saints* that it is Christ, not Mary, who brings the sinner to God. Noting that Scripture tells us little of the Virgin Mary, Rossetti, in common with many Protestant preachers, suggests that this omission is perhaps for the best, as we might otherwise be more inclined to worship her in Christ's stead. "[F]or truly," explains Rossetti, "even as it is, one of her eyes and one chain of her neck have sufficed as it were to ravish the world" (137).[21]

Rossetti's awestruck description of the Virgin's allure seems to betray a yearning for a visible, concrete manifestation of divinity, even as the pursuit of such, in *this* life, is condemned as idolatrous. In *Time Flies* (1885), Rossetti reflects upon the privilege accorded to the Magi, who were able to see Christ in the flesh. Although we cannot share the Magi's happiness, says Rossetti, she provides her reader the consolation that "as those Wise Men offered their treasures to the Visible Presence, so can we offer ours to the Invisible" (10). In the *Face of the Deep* (1892), Rossetti reflects intensely on just one part of the Savior's body—his feet—as they might have been on earth:

> These are they which went about doing good, and grew weary along the paths of Palestine, and climbed Calvary, and were nailed to a cross. These are they which a penitent sinner and an accepted saint washed with tears, kissed, anointed with precious ointment, dried with tresses of hair. These are they which in infancy a Virgin Mother swaddled, and which after the Resurrection holy women were permitted to touch. (33)

Although Rossetti's description seems to indulge in fetishism, she continually reminds us that despite our desire to see, taste, and touch the Savior,

---

20. Diane D'Amico correctly points out that "[a]s a devout Anglican, Rossetti would not have accepted the Roman Catholic doctrine of transubstantiation; however, she would have viewed Holy Communion as far more than a commemoration of the Last Supper" (77).

21. The "chain of her neck" is a puzzling reference, but perhaps Rossetti is describing a necklace? At least one famous nineteenth-century apparition of the Virgin Mary—that at La Salette in 1846—represented the Virgin with multiple chains around her neck from which hung the instruments of Christ's Passion (see chap. 5).

he is no longer physically present. We cannot, Rossetti declares, give in to our desire to create material substitutes for him:

> Man burdened by the unbearable burden of self [...] stoops to sensible encouragements and has recourse to vivid symbols, oftentimes at the outset being fully convinced "that an idol is nothing in the world, and that there is none other God but One." Yet sooner or later the symbol supersedes that which it symbolizes [...]. [The] Word is spiritual. Man [...] is carnal; his unaided meditations debase their object, and his grasp defiles. (*Seek and Find* [1879] 72)

Rossetti's concern that the symbol might "supersede that which it symbolizes" echoes what Mary Arseneau describes as Rossetti's "fear that in loving the world too much a person can become blind to spiritual realities" (83). In matters of religious worship, however, the problem is even more vexing; the desire to see and know God in the flesh, although actuated by pious motives, might actually lead one *further away* from heaven. In Rossetti's world, this alluring yet dangerous paradox seems to have generated no small amount of spiritual anxiety. Rossetti's Anglo-Catholic contemporary, Elizabeth Missing Sewell, describes Catholic "material" worship as an almost irresistible temptation to the earnest young heroine of her 1847 novel, *Margaret Percival*. Throughout the novel, Margaret, an Anglican, agonizes over whether to convert to the Church of Rome:

> It was all very well to look at Romanism at a distance, and admire it; but there were grievous errors which never could be received. She could not worship the Virgin, and pray to the saints, and put faith in relics: all these were absurdities, and therefore safe-guards. *She might go as near as she liked to the forbidden fruit: she might look at, examine, touch; but she had been told that the taste was bitter, and therefore she need not dread the temptation of plucking it.* [...] If the trial had come in another form, if it had been an open sin which thus assailed her with its lures, she would have said at once that she could not trust herself [...] *and she would have shut her eyes and closed her ears* in distrust, not of the power of truth and holiness, but of her own inherent weakness. But the present temptation came to her in another shape, as an angel of light rather than of darkness. It appealed to her longing after perfection, to her belief of what the worship of God might and ought to be; and it did not invite her to find rest in another communion, it only opened her eyes to the glaring defects of her own. (313–14; emphasis added)

Considering Sewell's popularity as an Anglo-Catholic novelist, it's highly likely that Rossetti read *Margaret Percival*. But even if she had not, the parallel between the fruits of Romanism, as described in Sewell's novel, and Rossetti's goblin fruits is striking indeed. The fruit is so tempting because the sin at its core is so cleverly disguised; what reason to shut one's eyes and ears (as Lizzie does) when the fruit seems not merely harmless, but actively good, an "angel of light"? When placed alongside Sewell's novel and Rossetti's devotional writings—which are permeated with anxieties about the sin of idolatry—*Goblin Market*'s fruits all begin to resemble "Citrons from the South" (29)—the error of material worship as practiced in the Church of Rome. Such an interpretation, however, does not rule out the sexual nature of the fruit or of Lizzie's fall. In nineteenth-century anti-Catholic literature, after all, the doctrine of transubstantiation is derided as base, repulsive, and carnal—the same terms many Victorians would have used to describe acts of physical lust.[22] Although much modern criticism of the poem seems polarized into either "religious" or "sexual" interpretations of the goblin fruit, this uncannily Victorian view obscures one of the most radical dimensions of Rossetti's poem: its efforts to define a way of apprehending the divine in a way that is at once intensely physical yet nonidolatrous.

Critics frequently point out the Eucharistic connotations of Laura's rescue by Lizzie ("Eat me, drink me, love me; / Laura, make much of me" [471–72]); indeed, this is probably the most blatant and most famous Eucharistic metaphor in the entire Victorian literary canon. Somewhat less obvious, however, is that the poem in fact sets up a binary between *two* communions: the sisters' spiritually and physically redemptive Eucharist has its foil in the material, idolatrous, and arguably Romish communion the goblins offer Laura. For alongside all the other entities the goblins might symbolize (male sexuality, market capitalism, the public sphere), the leering, bestial "brothers" (93, 95) also beg a strong likeness to Protestant representations of the Roman Catholic priesthood. In the *Merchandize of Souls* (1845), Rev. H. J. Powell presents the whole sacrifice of the Mass as a profit-making venture: "Surely Mammon must rejoice," he exclaims, "in this merchandize of souls!! and Satan must glory in the manoeuvrings [sic] of those who, *for their own profit*, thus pretend to crucify the Son of God afresh, and put him to open shame!!" (16; emphasis in original). Here Powell refers not only to plenary indulgences and of Masses for the dead, but the Catholic teaching that Christ newly sacrifices himself for humanity every time the priest consecrates a host. And just as Catholic priests

---

22. Frederick Roden points out the erotic implications of the Catholic Eucharist—"the carnality of the sacrament" (18)—as represented in both Newman's writings on communion (18) and in Rossetti's *Goblin Market* (44).

presumably awed the laity out of their savings by pulling Christ from a jeweled chalice like a rabbit from a hat, the goblin "priests" elevate before Laura's dazed eyes their own profane sacrifice. "One reared his plate; / [...] One heaved the golden weight / Of dish and fruit to offer her" (98, 102–3). This ritual is repeated ("Stretched up their dishes, / Panniers, and plates" [351–52]) when Lizzie makes her visit to the goblins.

The goblins' trickery resides not just in the sensual hocus-pocus they employ to seduce Laura, but in the spurious nature of their "product" itself. Rebecca Stern argues that *Goblin Market* reflects Victorian consumers' anxiety about the widespread food adulteration and corruption, a problem which justified "the most paranoid attitudes toward market culture" (489). A similar distrust of market culture seems evident in Protestant suspicions of the Romish "product," the transubstantiated host. Anti-Catholic sermons and tracts repeatedly warned that the Romish host was, if not merely bread, an unknown quantity. In *The Mass in Bayswater* (1859), J. Aldwell Nicholson repeats one of the most popular arguments against transubstantiation, pointing to rules in the Roman Missal that outlined possible obstacles to consecration, such as the intention of the priest and the physical integrity of the elements. "Until the Romanist be sure that no adulteration of the flour of which the wafer was made has taken place," insists the writer of *Transubstantiation, Host-Worship, Mass-Sacrifice, and Half-Communion* (1842), "and that no adulteration of the wine has taken place, he cannot be certain that he is not, after all, worshipping an idol of bread and wine" (8). Similarly, Nicholson queries, "[W]hat security does the Church of Rome give you that she has duly and properly changed *your* wafer into God, before you adored it and swallowed it? I answer, she gives you no security. She only makes a sport and mockery of you" (42; emphasis in original). *Caveat emptor.* Just as Protestant authors portrayed the Romish host as a foreign, unknowable substance, so also does goblin fruit elicit anxieties about its mysterious origin: "Who knows upon what soil they fed / Their hungry thirsty roots?" (44–45). Of course the fruit poisons Laura, but its immediate effect is utter confusion and an inability to discern reality through the senses: "And knew not was it night or day / As she turned home alone" (139–40). This seems to echo popular accusations that transubstantiation "destroys the evidence of our senses, [and] [...] contradicts their testimony altogether" (Nolan 188).

Given Rossetti's anxieties about idolatry, and the fact that Catholic transubstantiation was widely condemned as one of the most egregious demonstrations of it, it is hardly surprising that Laura's supper with the goblins takes on Romish overtones. However, what do we make of the fact that the "good" communion, Laura's "sucking" of Lizzie and her juices, summons up just as "carnal" an image as Laura's original gorging on goblin fruit?

> Hug me, kiss me, suck my juices
> Squeezed from goblin fruits for you,
> Goblin pulp and goblin dew,
> Eat me, drink me, love me;
> Laura, make much of me [. . .] (468–72)

The most substantial difference between the two communions is the presence of Lizzie, who by her loving sacrifice, it seems, *literally* becomes Christ. I say "literally" here because what renders Romish communion problematic for Rossetti is not so much its physical nature, but that signs, symbols, and other substitutes for the divine are unstable, addictive, and dangerous. Through her direct physical contact with Lizzie, Laura enjoys *unmediated* access to what she learns to desire *in place of* the goblin fruit—the divine love of her sister. And the presence of Christ makes all things good: postincarnation and postredemption, nothing is too lowly or too sensual to be employed in the worship of God. Diane D'Amico, in her study of the influence of Rossetti's faith on her poetry, overlooks this important dimension of the poem's theology. "[T]he Eucharistic scene between Lizzie and Laura," she states, "though certainly a scene of love, does not appear as an affirmation of female sensuality or sexuality but rather as an affirmation of the power of the spiritual over the sensual." D'Amico suggests that because of Rossetti's reverence for Holy Communion, "it is hard to believe that she ever would have used Eucharistic language to represent the power of sensual desires or appetites" (78). Yet as Linda Marshall points out, the use of the body as a site of religious experience has a long and distinguished tradition in the lives and writings of female mystics. Referring to Caroline Walker Bynum's study, *Holy Feast and Holy Fast: The Religious Significance of Food to Medieval Women*, Marshall states:

> At the devotional center of the women's practices and language Bynum elucidates is the imitatio Christi, and it is an *imitatio*, like Lizzie's in "Goblin Market," singularly fleshly and gustatory. The humanity, the physicality of Christ in this *imitatio* was assumed in its full bodiness, and "imitation meant union—fusion—with that ultimate body which is the body of Christ." If God's becoming flesh in order to save humanity—humanity being precisely that flesh—is the very foundation of the Christian faith, then the body thereby becomes the ground of divinity. And since in the binary system of medieval theology women were identified with the flesh (as opposed to the spirit, male), the "goal of religious women," writes

Bynum, "was thus to realize the *opportunity* of physicality," which gave them a special, even literal, relationship to Christ. (438; emphasis in original)

Marshall's reading seems to concur with D. M. R. Bentley's observation that "a sacramental vision of reality such as Lizzie's involves not a rejection but an elevation of sensuality" (80). Yet it seems that in *Goblin Market*, at least, Lizzie goes even beyond *imitatio* to *becoming* Christ herself. Unless Lizzie's Christ-like love has erased the taint of Original Sin from her human flesh, Lizzie has been transfigured into Christ him/herself. How else can Laura commune in the flesh without committing idolatry? Either way, this Eucharistic encounter, as in *Aurora Leigh*, is a double transubstantiation involving the communion and transformation of two female bodies. Lizzie becomes Christ, and Laura (in a refreshing contrast to Marian's insistence that she has died) almost literally rises from of the grave:

Laura awoke as from a dream,
Laughed in the innocent old way,
Hugged Lizzie but not twice or thrice;
Her gleaming locks showed not one thread of gray,
Her breath was sweet as May,
And light danced in her eyes. (537–42)

Unlike *Aurora Leigh*, *Goblin Market* provides an ending in which everyone (except Jeanie) wins. Goblin fruits are unveiled as an unworthy object of human desire, and sisterly, Christ-like love demonstrates its power to transform both body and soul. While the idolatrous, Romish overtones of communion disappear along with the goblins, what *does* remain is a strong affirmation of the sacramentality of the human body, transfigured through Christ. As in *Aurora Leigh*, the poem asserts the value of women's agency in the world and their ability to participate in the work of Christian redemption, both in *and* out of the private, domestic sphere. *Goblin Market* seems almost euphoric in its conclusion, unsullied by the shadow of a fallen Marian. But does Rossetti's poem resolve the "problem" of the body in women's spiritual experience more completely and tidily than *Aurora Leigh*?

Modern readers and critics often describe *Goblin Market*, with its veneer of cheerful secularism, as a refreshing change from Rossetti's more earnest, overtly religious poetry. Yet when viewed in the context of Rossetti's devotional writings, the poem exudes a painful sense of unfulfilled yearning despite its happy ending. Rossetti's devotional prose is suffused with a longing for concrete encounters with the divine—what joy it would be, to see the infant Christ, admire the neck of the Virgin, and touch the Savior's feet. Rossetti describes her longing for these experiences and then resigns herself to their indefinite postponement—material divinity is not of this world. *Goblin Market* seems to deliver a similar message. Lizzie desires physical union with a desired object, but this object turns out to be poisonous and false. In the second half of the poem, Lizzie attains physical communion with her sister, but this redemption scene remains the stuff of fantasy—a fairy-tale ending. The transformation of the body into something worthy of heaven ultimately remains in the world of heaven. Rossetti, as a Victorian woman writer, could not have redeemed fallen Laura so completely or triumphantly in any other genre than the fairy tale. *Aurora Leigh*'s redemption story may present more immediate, obvious problems than that in *Goblin Market,* but Barrett Browning seized a more difficult challenge: to redeem the fallen women in *this* world, not the next.

Victorian controversies over the nature of the Eucharist were enormously complicated and might, to our perspective, seem like arcane theological hairsplitting. Nonetheless, the transubstantiated Eucharist, as a symbol of intersection between body and spirit, this world and the next, was an enormously meaningful and rich symbol to Victorian women writers such as Barrett Browning and Rossetti. In a culture that persisted in excluding the physical body from the feminine ideal, transubstantiation provided women writers with a symbolic vocabulary not only for sanctifying the female body, but also to legitimize women's spiritual agency beyond the hyperpurified domestic sphere. It helped women dismantle the culture's binary between sacred and profane that, among other things, restricted them to the home and forced them to repress fundamental aspects of human nature, such as appetite. In these poems, Eucharistic bread symbolizes multiple appetites: longings for food and drink, for sexual gratification, for creative outlets, for moral agency, for redemption. Through transubstantiation, what may be deemed an animalistic impulse (hunger and eating) is sanctified; hunger becomes elevated to spiritual striving, and the desired object also becomes sacred. Barrett Browning's and Rossetti's poems speak to Victorian women who felt starved from having to repress "profane" appetites for "profane" food. But the poems, along with the sermons and tracts on transubstantiation, also speak to an entire culture's anxiety, even despair, at the slippery, indeterminate nature of the very categories of "sacred" and "profane" and their waning relevance in modern society.

CHAPTER FIVE

The "Queen of Heaven" or a Very Confused Nun?

Our Lady of La Salette, George Eliot, and Victorian Anxieties about God

> The complete downfall of Evangelicalism,—which seems to have been effected in George Eliot's strong brain in a single fortnight of intercourse with Mr. and Mrs. Bray,—had taken in my case four long years of miserable mental conflict and unspeakable pain. It left me with something as nearly like a *Tabula rasa* of faith as can well be imagined. I definitely disbelieved in human immortality and in a supernatural revelation. The existence of God I neither denied nor affirmed. I felt I had no means of coming to any knowledge of Him. I was, in fact (long before the word was invented), precisely—an Agnostic.
> —*The Life of Frances Power Cobbe, by Herself* (1894)

IN 1854, Pope Pius IX declared the Immaculate Conception of Mary an essential component of Catholic dogma. This teaching, a binding article of belief for all Catholics, proclaimed that Christ's mother was free from Original Sin from the moment of her conception. Victorian Protestants, already rankled by Catholic absurdities such as auricular confession, celibate religious life, and transubstantiation, were newly outraged by what they perceived as Rome's virtual deification of a scripturally obscure woman. It was bad enough that Christ's mother, through the machinations of Pius IX, should usurp the redemptive role of Christ in Christian theology. To make matters worse, she was simultaneously demonstrating, in reported apparitions throughout Europe, an exasperating habit of stirring up the masses and deflecting public devotion away from her Son. Of the most prominent nineteenth-century Marian apparitions (from Paris in 1830 to Knock, Ireland, in 1879), the Virgin's purported 1846 apparition in La Salette, France, seems to have generated the most attention and public commentary in Victorian England. This apparition, according to Sandra Zimdars-Swartz, was "the first Marian apparition of modern times outside of a cloistered religious environment to attract widespread religious attention and to be officially 'recognized' by Roman Catholic authorities" (27). News of this unique "modern" apparition spread to England at the crux of anti-Catholic tensions. Victorian Protestant responses, both to the doctrine of the Immaculate Conception and to the apparition of La Salette, demonstrate how Mary, in John Singleton's phrase, "was a powerful and evocative figure around whom the competing religious parties of Victorian Britain arrayed their forces" (16). In addition to questions of religious identity, the seemingly omnipotent figure of the Virgin Mary raised concerns about the transgressive potential of female sanctity. As Carol Engelhardt Herringer argues, the Virgin Mary "was not a widely accepted figure [in Victorian England], because she was not seen as a quiescent woman" (21). In a book titled *Our Lady of Victorian Feminism,* Kimberly Van Esveld Adams also depicts the Virgin Mary as a "contested symbol" (5) as well as an "empowering ideal" (52) for Victorian female intellectuals.

As Adams acknowledges in her study, however, not all scholars would be comfortable applying the modern term "feminist" to Victorian concepts of the Virgin Mary. I myself wish to sidestep the question altogether; this chapter will not speculate whether the Virgin Mary—as represented in the Victorian era or at any other period—can or should be called a "feminist" figure. Issues of gender, of course, are inextricable from the centuries-old cult of the Virgin Mary, and from her manifold representations in religious practice, art, and literature. But in the Victorian period, the Virgin Mary elicited more anxiety as an emblem of secularism, not feminism. European Catholics embraced Mary as a potential Redemptress from the rising tides of unbelief. According to John Singleton, "Catholics hoped and prayed that the Virgin"—in addition to her powers to cure the sick—"would prove to be equally effective in the struggle against republicanism, atheism, socialism, liberalism, and nationalism" (17). From the perspective of British Protestants, however, the Catholic Virgin Mary was the dread harbinger of a secular, godless universe. This sentiment emerges repeatedly in Victorian sermons, tracts, and other theological literature. Whereas Protestants recognized the scriptural Mary as a devout mother and wife, they regarded the Catholic Virgin Mary as a false goddess who rivaled—and even eclipsed—God and His Son in Catholic theology. Many devout Catholics believed that devotion to Mary would only bring them closer to God; Protestants, however, regarded Marian devotion as the perfect embodiment of "masked atheism"—paganistic practices veiled in false piety. Hence Mary could be *either* the way to salvation or the way to perdition, just as the tran-

Figure 5.1. *Lithograph depicting the appearance of Our Lady at La Salette.* Rambler 10 (December 1852). Rare Books and Special Collections, The Catholic University of America

substantiated host could be either Christ himself or profane "cannibalism." The anxiety of discernment in these controversies was compounded by the fact that both demanded a suspension of the ordinary workings of the senses. Not only were Catholics to see God in an ordinary lump of bread, but they were also to believe that Mary could physically appear and disappear at will, in the middle of the nineteenth century.

Popular devotion to Mary and its effect on the gullible, uneducated masses is a central theme in George Eliot's *Romola* (1862), and its plot bears some striking parallels to British commentary on the 1846 apparition at La Salette. In December 1854, the *Times* published an article asserting that the "Virgin" of La Salette was none other than a mentally disturbed French nun who enjoyed playing dress-up:

> Arrived at Grenoble, Mademoiselle Lamerlière went to a merchant to obtain some lace of a peculiar quality. [. . .] Before the merchant and his family the lady opened her bandbox, and its trousseau was too remarkable to have been easily forgotten. One by one she drew out the white robe, the yellow apron, the cross, the pincers, the hammer. All were filled with amazement at so eccentric a costume [. . .]. This was about the beginning of September. On the 19th the children of Salette gave a description of a lady whom they saw on the mountain, and her dress and ornaments exactly correspond with those which had excited the astonishment of the worthy citizens of Grenoble some days before. A singular coincidence! Was it the nun or the Virgin that affrighted the little prophets? or did the Virgin, fascinated with their peculiar elegance, send from Heaven to borrow the contents of the bandbox? ("The Heroine of La Salette," *London Times*, 28 December 1854)

This assertion, of course, took for granted the stupidity of the young shepherds who saw her, as well as the craftiness of Catholic authorities who turned popular piety to their advantage. In *Romola*, whose heroine is at one point mistaken for the Virgin Mary by a simple peasant boy, devotion to the saints is also depicted as a way to manipulate and exploit others for selfish gain. As long as people persist in venerating the Madonna as a *Catholic* icon—in relation to God the Father and God the Son—they remain mentally enslaved by superstition and ignorance. The novel suggests, however, that the basis of Marian devotion—sensory observation and storytelling—can also serve to empower human beings as morally intelligent and self-sufficient agents. In *Romola,* this stage of human evolution is symbolized by the *secular* Madonna, the Madonna of anti-Catholic propaganda—the one whose very existence "kills" God.

Eliot's work, unlike the other texts in this study, portrays domesticity in a *consistently* negative light. Nearly all her heroines, whether Dorothea Brooke, Maggie Tulliver, Dinah Morris, or Romola de Bardi, quickly discover that domestic life exacts on women tremendous moral and spiritual sacrifices. Indeed, characters such as the stupid and shallow Mrs. Tulliver—a Madonna turned "a little sour" (62) who falls apart when creditors claim her china and monogrammed tablecloths—even portray domesticity as the bane of female potential. And while Eliot's novels champion female moral and spiritual integrity, these qualities are not dependent upon

Christianity. Conventional religious belief may provide Eliot heroines a temporary mode of self-assertion, but it is never a reliable or enduring one. Dorothea and Maggie turn away from religious reading and modes of expression ("I hardly ever pray anymore," says Dorothea), whereas Dinah Morris reluctantly complies with her church's ban on female preachers. *Romola*, Eliot's Comtean allegory of human development, goes even further, to suggest that Romola can only reach her full spiritual potential in a fatherless *and* godless universe. Whereas other Victorian women writers drew upon Catholic and anti-Catholic discourse to condemn secularism, Eliot's novel, infused with Catholic and anti-Catholic representations of the Madonna, alternately mourns and celebrates God's death.

The Immaculate Conception
Infallible Doctrine or Instrument of Satan?

In his 1855 reply to Cardinal Wiseman's Pastoral Letter on the Immaculate Conception, Protestant clergyman John Armstrong advises Catholic priests to take up Christian matrimony and fatherhood rather than "helping the poor old Pope to make a decree contrary to God's Word, on the subject of human 'conception,' a subject not at all right [for unmarried priests] to be dwelling upon; and God alone knows the amount of gross iniquity which will be introduced into the world by sensual minds being directed towards it" (7). Victorians could not mention pregnancy in polite society, but the urgency of refuting Popish "HUMBUG" (10) sparked earnest public debate over how babies (Baby Mary, at least) were made. Whereas Protestants complained of the degree of power the Immaculate Conception conferred upon Mary, they were primarily motivated by fears of idolatry and atheism. If this dogma had concerned a male saint (Saint Peter, for example), Protestants would have been no less outraged; at issue was the establishment of a potential rival to the Holy Trinity, and implications that God and his Son were somehow lacking, in need of the supplementary grace and mercy of Mary. While Mary's sex was not the primary issue in these debates, Protestant critics did find it useful when putting her back in her place. At one end of the spectrum, the historical Mary was portrayed as an ordinary woman given to meddling in her son's affairs; at the other end, the Catholic, deified Mary was a demonic imposter and a female Lucifer.

The Doctrine of the Immaculate Conception reinforced popular fears that Mary, not Christ, was the real focal point of worship for Catholics.

Three years before the pope's proclamation, Rev. J. B. Lowe had argued that "the Romish system of religion ought assuredly not so much to be called by the name of *Christianity* as by that of *Marianity*" (*The Worship of the Virgin Mary* 6). The Pope's new doctrine, then, seemed to be a frank admission of what Protestants had already suspected: Mary herself was a goddess. Now sermonizing in response to Pius IX, in 1855, Lowe argues that "this doctrine makes the Virgin independent of Christ. [. . .] from the very moment of her existence she is perfectly free from all sin, original and actual: she was never charged with any sin, and therefore never stood in need of forgiveness, or required a Saviour" (*The Immaculate Conception* 14). Indeed, why would the Virgin Mary, if already freed from Original Sin, need to bear the Christ Child at all? "Had she never been the mother of the Saviour," argued Rev. T. Butler, "she was divine; she was, in fact, the author of Christianity—the first divine being that was born in human nature" (27). Lowe's and Butler's concerns are echoed in an 1855 sermon by Bishop Samuel Wilberforce, who argued that an immaculate Mary plays too prominent a role in the redemption of sinful humanity. This idea "directly shake[s] the great doctrine of the incarnation" (21), he insists, and "place[s] on the Mediator's throne the Virgin mother instead of the incarnate Son" (22).

Protestant condemnations of the Immaculate Conception resonate with fear at the ease and frequency with which human beings create gods for themselves. These concerns gesture toward an even larger anxiety, that the Christian God might be similarly manmade. Rev. John Evans, in an 1852 sermon, describes Mariolatry as a symptom of "that innate depravity of the human heart" and adds that pagan mythology evinces "a strong predilection in favour of *female* deities" (14). A number of writers and preachers suggested that the authors of Scripture, anticipating human tendencies toward idol worship, *deliberately* withheld substantial information about Christ's mother. Elizabeth Rundle Charles, in *Mary, the Handmaid of the Lord* (1854), states that "whilst we may affectionately gather and string together the few [scriptural] notices given us of Mary the mother of Jesus, it must not be forgotten that their very scarcity is among their most significant lessons" (iii). An uneasy awareness of the human capacity for idol worship, moreover, encouraged reflection upon the limited, human constructions of Christian theology. The oft-repeated concern—that a powerful Mary competed with or diminished God the Father—betrays a serious lack of confidence in how the latter was depicted and perceived in Scripture and Church tradition. Rev. Carus W. Wilson (the "black pillar" of *Jane Eyre*) observes how easily and arbitrarily the supernatural properties of Almighty God can be displaced elsewhere: "[I]f the Virgin can hear those prayers [of Catholics], and still more, has the power to extend any beneficial consequences [. . .] on behalf of the supplicants, she must be omnipresent, omniscient, omnipotent, ubiquitous—in fact, invested with the attributes of Deity" (1). Even worse, Mary-as-deity seemed far more attractive and accessible than orthodox Christian constructions of God the father. An anonymous tract of 1846, *What Is Romanism?* argues that Mariolatry,

> [M]ake[s] the Almighty Himself an object of fear, and the Virgin an object of love; to invest Him, who is the Father of mercy and God of all comfort, with unapproachable majesty and awe, and with the terrors of eternal justice; and then, in direct and striking contrast, to array Mary with mercy, and benignity, and compassionate tenderness, and omnipotence in her love. (4)

In response to Mariolatry, Protestant writers such as Elizabeth Rundle Charles reminded readers of Mary's "real" life as recorded in Scripture, as "the surest antidote to the adoration of Mary, Queen of heaven" (iii). Not content, however, to emphasize Mary's simple life and her relatively small role in Christ's ministry, some Protestants constructed Mary as a clingy, overinvolved mother who prompted Christ to demonstrate, repeatedly, that "He does not allow her to meddle" (*Some Observations* 12). As Charles Bird Smith argues in an 1849 sermon:

> [. . .] Scripture reveals defects in Mary, as in all who partake of our fallen nature. In almost every case in which our Lord is introduced as speaking to her, there is a tone of *rebuke*,—intended, doubtless, to teach her and others, that the notion of *maternal right* (which has since been attached to her relation to him) was utterly inapplicable in her case. [. . .] Suffice it to say, that from the occasion, when, *at twelve years of age*, he rebuked her for venturing to remonstrate with him, on account of his staying behind in Jerusalem, up to the hour when he addressed her as he hung on the cross, he never once called her "*mother*." This should be kept in mind as we proceed. (emphasis in original)

Smith, Charles, and other writers argue that Christ dissolved his filial attachment and obligations to his mother at the commencement of his ministry, an act that Mary, as Charles suggests, stoically accepted: "I suppose most of us have felt something of a chill, in spite of all the explanations of commentators, at the words, 'Woman, what have I to do with thee?'—severing with so keen an edge the ties of years. It is difficult not to imagine they must have fallen bitterly on the mother's heart. Yet it does not seem that they did" (123). This defense (by a female author, no less) of Christ's dismissal of his mother is extraordinary, considering Victorians' veneration for motherhood in general. At least some Catholics found it shocking; Catholic priest Michael Tormey, in an 1855 essay on the Immaculate Conception, attacked Protestants' "revolting proposition that the Son of God absolutely hated, or at least was indifferent about, His Mother" (227), "as if the filial duties ranked with the lowest class of relations known to mere animal life" (230).

Tormey labels this rhetorical strategy "unintelligible and unnatural" (230); surely, he would have been even more incensed by some Protestant inferences that Catholic representations of Mary had satanic dimensions. Walter Farquhar Hook accuses Catholics of translating "the most humble and holy Virgin into an idol of pride and vanity [. . .] a vainglorious and aspiring creature like Lucifer" (qting. Bishop Bull in *Mother of Our Lord* 13). Bishop Christopher Wordsworth argues that through the decree of the Immaculate Conception, "Satan endeavours to use one of the most beautiful and blessed of all Creatures—the Virgin Mary—as an instrument to work our woe" (24). Even when not directly discussing the figure of Mary herself, anti-Mariolatry essays and sermons are especially likely to employ demonic female imagery to personify the Roman Catholic Church and its abuses. In an essay on *The Origin and Progress of Mariolatry* (1852), clergyman John Evans recounts Bishop Heber's 1824 description of Catholic missionaries in India competing with Protestant evangelicals. Although the Roman Catholic party presents itself as a "spectre" of goodness and piety: "outstrip her in the race, but press her a little too closely, and she turns around on us with all the hideous features of envy and rage. Her hallowed taper blazes into a sulphurous torch, her hair bristles into serpents [. . .] and her words are words of blasphemy" (37). In an 1855 sermon on the Immaculate Conception, Bishop Samuel Wilberforce also compares Roman Catholicism to a fair female illusion, "with all her grossness veiled from you, and she herself transformed into an angel of light, [come] to work your downfall [. . .] read and weigh the warning graven by the finger of God upon her forehead [. . .] THE MOTHER OF HARLOTS AND ABOMINATIONS OF THE EARTH" (32; caps in original). In these discussions, in which Mary as an arm of Satan easily shades into stereotypical representations of the Catholic Church as the Whore of Babylon, Victorian polarities of angelic mothers and demonic strumpets are eerily conflated. This frightening ambiguity echoes larger anxieties about successfully distinguishing between true Christian piety and secular profanity.

Apparition at La Salette

Call to Sanctity, or Argument for Atheism?

On 19 September 1846, Françoise Melanie Matthieu, aged fifteen, and Peter Maximin Giraud, aged eleven, were watering their cattle outside the remote village of La Salette in the French Alps when they encountered a weeping woman in a very distinctive costume. According to an 1849 account of the event, published in England,

> It was the Queen of Heaven; but the children had no idea that it was so: they wished to fix their gaze on her, but could scarcely endure the sight of her dazzling beauty. They remarked, however, the diadem which glittered on her forehead, and which was surmounted by a lofty Asiatic head-dress. [. . .] A chain of gold, three fingers in width, descended to her waist; another little chain of gold held a crucifix, about eight inches in length, on one side of which were seen a pair of pincers, half open, and hanging down; and on the other a hammer,—symbols of the Passion of our Saviour, which seemed suspended without any support. (Villecourt 9)

Unlike later apparitions at Lourdes and at Fatima, in which the young seers reported multiple visits from the Virgin Mary, Melanie and Maximin described only one visit, in which the Lady, weeping constantly, delivered a straightforward message: reform or suffer the consequences. The Lady, who claimed to be "hold[ing] back" the arm of her Son's wrath (10), complained of the neglect of religious observances: only elderly women attended Mass; people ate meat during Lent, neglected their prayers, and blasphemed freely. If people did not perform their religious duties, she warned, the crops would fail and young children would fall ill and die. After imparting to each child a "secret," the Lady vanished. The story of the "Weeping Virgin of the Alps" spread quickly; pilgrims arrived, miraculous cures were reported. In 1851, on the fifth anniversary of the Virgin's visit, the local Catholic bishop formally recognized the apparition, and La Salette continued to grow in popularity as a pilgrimage site.[1]

1. In the twenty-first century, the apparition at La Salette is believed to be genuine by some groups of Catholics in France, the United States, and elsewhere. Today the shine and Basilica at La Salette is considered a "minor place of pilgrimage" (Sacred Destinations Travel Guide, (http://www.sacred-destinations.com/france/la-salette-shrine-of-our-lady.htm), and at least

One reason that English Protestants felt so threatened by a French apparition is that it generated tremendous interest and excitement among English Roman Catholics. Despite the foreign locale and remoteness of La Salette, Birmingham priest Henry Formby exclaimed in an 1857 pamphlet on the apparition, "The voice of the heavenly turtle dove has, as we believe, been heard in our land. Accents falling from the sweet voice of her who stood by the Cross of Jesus [. . .] at length [. . .] have found their way to our ears" (4). In a skeptical age, here was (to believers at least) a clear manifestation of the divine, supernatural order of things, one documented by modern journalism. J. Spencer Northcote, a regular contributor to the Roman Catholic *Rambler,* exults that:

> The thing [establishment of La Salette as a place of pilgrimage] has grown up in our own times, we might almost say under our own eyes; even the newspapers of the day, both English and foreign, have given publicity to the main outlines of the history from the very first, so that we have an opportunity of studying this rare phenomenon, the creation of a new sanctuary or place of pilgrimage, with the most minute exactness. (*A Pilgrimage* 13)

Such a direct sign from God had, in Northcote's opinion, "a wonderful effect [. . .] on the moral and religious character of the people." Northcote contrasts the present state of religious devotion in France to the "deplorable condition" it was in before the apparition: "But now the face of things is entirely changed; the voice of the blasphemer is silenced; the Sunday, not profaned by labour; the churches are frequented [. . .], and the Sacraments approached with reverence" (67). Bishop Ullathorne, who made a pilgrimage to La Salette in 1854 and appears to have been the most prominent English advocate for the validity of the apparition, regards the Virgin's warning as a call to reverse the tide of secularism in England as well: "England is full of blasphemies, and what, before Heaven, is an English Sunday? What are the habits of our rude and ignorant poor? What their language? And what their life on Sundays? Does it stop here? Look at the late census and survey both town and country. The shops are closed and work ceases, but where are the great masses of people? Is it to God they give themselves? (*The Holy Mountain* 175).

While the apparition, for Ullathorne and other English Catholics, stood as a contradiction to modern secularism, Protestants complained that the absurd and unlikely nature of the apparition story was a mockery of

---

two shrines dedicated to La Salette have been built in the United States by the Missionaries of La Salette (established in 1852): one in Attleboro, MA, and another in Altamont, NY.

religion and a further inducement to atheism. In 1857, the *Edinburgh Review* published a review essay on books discussing the apparition, and joined the *Times* in insisting that the sham apparition was the contrivance of a deluded former nun, one Mlle Constance Lamerlière de St. Ferréol. The writer of the review also concurred with the *Times* in attributing the success and popularity of the apparition to the work of corrupt priests: "Can there be a greater offence in the eyes of God and man than a deliberate conspiracy to covert the vagaries of a half-witted nun into a divine revelation, to render this unfortunate wretch an object of worship, and to erect a temple to her on the scene of her performance?" (23). The writer implies that the incident has become so publicized and so far-fetched that it is now an embarrassment to Catholic authorities: "[T]hey found, like Frankenstein, they had given a shape to a monster which was too strong for them" (23). In the writer's opinion, the apparition story will only encourage, not counteract, the spread of atheism: "Can there be a more formidable weapon in the hands of scepticism than this living contemporary proof of the avidity of people to swallow the grossest inventions?" (25). The debate, carried out in the British media between Protestants and Catholics over the validity of La Salette, reached absurd dimensions. Bishop Ullathorne, in his 1858 rebuttal to the *Edinburgh Review* essay, went so far as to insist that the ex-nun in question was too elderly and too obese to convincingly impersonate the Virgin Mary. He reports the impressions of a man who interviewed Mlle Constance: "Any one more unlikely to act with success the part of a celestial being I could not readily imagine" (*Letters* 33).

One might be struck by the fact that Ullathorne found the possibility of an elderly or overweight Virgin Mary more difficult to believe than the mere fact of her appearance in the French Alps in 1846. More to the point, however, the bizarre tone of the British debate over La Salette underscores the desperation many (Protestants and Catholics alike) felt in the face of seemingly irreversible trends toward secularism. As the apparition texts—along with documents on the Immaculate Conception—amply demonstrate, the figure of the Virgin Mary was a powerful emblem for the crisis of Victorian secularism, and this provides a better understanding of how and why George Eliot continually invokes the Virgin's image in *Romola*. To consider Eliot's Virgin solely as an image of female power only scratches the surface of so complex a symbol. An attention to British reports of the apparition at La Salette also highlights the fact that Eliot's readers were familiar with the conventions of the Marian apparition narrative—recurrent themes in apparition stories that appear to be, in Zimdars-Swartz's words, central in attempts "to build comprehensive structures of meaning around apparitions and apparition messages" (251). *Romola* draws upon multiple narrative traditions, superimposing the form of a novel upon the older conventions of classical myth, epic, Christian hagiography, and more recently, nineteenth-century Marian apparition narrative. Through its combination of pagan and Christian narrative conventions, Eliot's novel tells a history of human moral development that culminates, full circle, in a sober embrace of secularism.

Romola as Hagiography

In the *Triptych and the Cross*, Felicia Bonaparte speculates that Eliot chose to set *Romola* in the pre-Reformation era because "it was Roman Catholicism [rather than Protestantism] that engaged her imagination [. . .] she understood that Roman Catholicism offered what no Protestant faith could—authority and coherence—and what few Protestant faiths do—mystery" (178). Based on her letters and journals, however, Eliot's attitude toward Roman Catholicism seems to have been no less ambivalent or conflicted than those of the other writers in this study. Like Brontë and Barrett Browning, Eliot enjoyed the vicarious thrill of passing for Catholic abroad, but was also outspoken in her criticisms of Romish superstition. At the beginning of George Eliot's visit to Rome in 1860, she reports "being taken up with seeing ceremonies, or rather with waiting for them":

> I knelt down to receive the Pope's blessing, remembering what Pius VII. said to the soldier—that he would never be the worse for the blessing of an old man. But altogether, these ceremonies are a melancholy, hollow business, and we regret bitterly that the Holy Week has taken our time from better things. I have a cold and headache this morning, and in other ways am not conscious of improvement from the Pope's blessing. (*Letters* III: 288, 4–6 April 1860)

Of course, Eliot had even more reasons than Brontë and Barrett Browning to condemn Catholicism. In a letter to Barbara Bodichon, Eliot explains that while "I enjoy [religious forms and ceremonies] myself [. . .] I have faith in the working-out of higher possibilities than the Catholic or any other church has presented [. . .]. The highest "calling and election" is to *do without opium* and live through all our pain with conscious, clear-eyed endurance" (*Letters* III: 366, 26 December 1860; emphasis in original). But Eliot's vision of a humanistic rather than religious worldview perhaps rendered her all the more receptive to the Virgin Mary's potential as an emblem of virtuous secularism. In *Romola,* moreover, Eliot demonstrates a fascination not only with the Madonna, but with the entire Catholic cult of the saints and the unique kind of narrative—hagiography—that evolved to educate and inspire the laity in regard to saints' lives. In their respective works, Brontë and Barrett Browning each appropriate an element of Catholicism deemed morally objectionable by most Protestants (auricular confession and transubstantiation) and "reforms" it to suit their artistic goals. Eliot employs a similar tactic in *Romola.* As the novel depicts Romola's evolution from a relative, dependent creature into a morally autonomous agent freed from the constraints of both fatherly and religious authority, it also sets up a binary between "sham" saints and manipulative hagiography, and "true" saints and ethically responsible storytelling.

In different ways in their respective works, Brontë, Barrett Browning, and Eliot all construct a fantasy of female moral agency unleashed from domestic confinement. Jane Eyre seems genuinely attracted to the idea of overseas missionary work *apart* from marriage to St. John Rivers; Aurora Leigh initially resists marriage to Romney, confident she can reform society solely through her role as artist; and in the sixty-seventh chapter of *Romola,* "Romola's Waking," the childless heroine finds herself cut off from both father and husband, free to risk her own life in caring for survivors of the plague. One might argue that the burgeoning agency of all three heroines is curtailed significantly by the conclusion of each narrative, whether through marriage (Jane and Aurora) or the adoption of children and other dependents (Romola). A major difference, however, is that while Jane and Aurora achieve both romantic *and* religious fulfillment by the ends of their stories, Romola's *bildungsroman* terminates in a double-edged loss—she must survive without the "opium" of love, whether from a human father or lover, or that of an omnipotent, benevolent God.

Critics have complained of Romola's passive, relatively powerless position in the novel's epilogue, but my reading suggests that Eliot, by leaving her heroine in a state of emotional and theological deprivation, also places her in the best position to take up her highest moral calling: that of a hagiographer. Ironically, while Brontë and Barrett Browning's works attempt to strike a balance between desire and duty for their heroines, it is the agnostic, Eliot, who in *Romola* resembles more overtly didactic writers (Fullerton and Sewell) in her fascination for morally enabling deprivation.[2] Grieving the loss of father, husband, godfather, and spiritual director in the

---

2. Victorian diarist Henry Crabb Robinson made an explicit comparison between Eliot and Sewell after reading Eliot's *Scenes of Clerical Life* (1857). Disappointed by the book's didactic tone, he declared that it would have given him more pleasure had it been written by "a regular Evangelical or pious High Church—Miss Sewell" (789–90).

final scene of the novel, Romola sustains their memory through performing ritual observances and, most important, weaving tales of their lives for the moral instruction of the next generation. While Romola's hagiographic practices mimic those of the ignorant Catholic masses, they are intended to represent a more evolved and morally responsible use of storytelling.

Despite the fact that Eliot considered *Romola* to be the best thing she ever wrote, it has long puzzled and frustrated modern readers. This is not only because the novel, as Susan Greenstein quips, was "researched to death in the womb" (496), but because the novel seems to violate Eliot's commitment to realism both in its characterization and its plot. The novel is set in fifteenth-century Florence and its heroine, Romola, is the beautiful young daughter of a blind old classical scholar. Romola, although intelligent, channels all her passion and energy into serving her father; eventually her husband, Tito, also claims a share of her love and devotion. Romola's emotional world begins to disintegrate when her father dies. Shortly after Bardo's death, Tito, a charming but selfish social climber who has betrayed his own adoptive father, sells Bardo's cherished library for personal profit. With Romola's father dead and her faith and love in her husband extinguished by his treacherous act, she turns to the religious reformer Savonarola to provide her life with meaning, purpose, and moral guidance. Although Romola's association with Savonarola leads her to perform numerous acts of public charity, she seems motivated more by idolatry for her spiritual director than by disinterested love for others. It is Romola's loss of faith even in Savonarola that precipitates her true moral transformation. When Savonarola refuses to save Romola's godfather from execution through his political influence, Romola breaks with Savonarola and flees Florence, without any clear direction or plan of action.

Up to this point in the novel, the plot (aside from its many erudite tangents on the history and culture of fifteenth-century Florence) seems fairly straightforward and believable. But then Eliot's novel lapses into a kind of dream sequence in which Romola sets herself adrift in a small boat and falls asleep. She awakes to find herself on the banks of a strange village and takes charge of a hungry Jewish baby orphaned by a recent outbreak of the plague. The surviving villagers, awestruck at the sudden manifestation of a beautiful woman with a baby on her arm, assume that she is the Madonna come to rescue them. At this point, Romola no longer requires a motive to do good: "the reasons for living, enduring labouring, never took the form of an argument" (527). Not only does Romola nurse the sick back to health, but the other villagers are shamed and inspired by her example into disregarding their fears of the pestilence and helping out as well. After this transfiguration of Romola into what J. B. Bullen describes as "a depressing paragon of virtue" (425), she carries her newfound moral outlook back to Florence, where she takes into her home the two illegitimate children of her now-dead husband, along with their mother, Tessa, an unlettered and simple-minded peasant. Romola is presented in the final scene of the novel as the head of an unconventional, female-dominated household, the keeper of the memories of all the important men in her life, and the moral educator of Tito's son Lillo.

In its plot and narrative conventions, *Romola* appears at first glance so distinct from Eliot's other works that a 1998 anthology devoted to criticism on *Romola* "invites readers to refuse the apparent fixity of the body of George Eliot the author—her biography, her intentions, her 'complete' works—in order to allow the single text [that of *Romola*] to become multiple and rich" (Levine and Turner 4). As interesting as such readings may be, I contend that *Romola* is often considered a failure precisely *because* we do not well enough understand its authorial and cultural contexts, in particular, the theological issues plaguing Eliot and other Victorian intellectuals. So far, the most convincing and successful readings of *Romola* are those, such as Carole Robinson's and Felicia Bonaparte's, which address the novel's obsession with the collapse of meaning and the death of God. Robinson remarks *Romola*'s potential as "a manifesto of a Victorian existentialism" (213) and draws attention to the book's "proliferation of father-figures" who die (often violently) in the course of the narrative, associating them with "the absent ultimate authority, the banished God of Victorian agnosticism" (219). Bonaparte suggests that in *Romola*, Eliot "anticipated Nietzsche in predicting that the death of God threatened to usher in the age of nihilism. For what indeed is there to believe in?" (141).

The successful closure of the typical nineteenth-century novel relies upon fulfillment, whether theological, material, erotic, psychological, or a combination thereof; *Romola* is a story of loss. This may explain, in part, why Eliot felt compelled to experiment so drastically with readerly expectation and novelistic convention. Bonaparte, along with J. B. Bullen and other critics, explains how *Romola* could be considered a symbolic story of human moral development—heavily influenced by Comtean Positivism—tracing humankind's development from egoism to altruism. Bonaparte regards *Romola*'s structure predominantly as modern myth, with "Romola as the traditional epic hero whose character and fate encompass the life of a people" (20)

Indeed, the story of Romola is steeped in classical allusion. But *Romola*'s structure is as much indebted to pre-Reformation Christian (and later, Roman Catholic) narratives as it is to pagan ones. Romola is initially figured both as Antigone, the loyal daughter of blind old Oedipus, and as

Ariadne, joined with Bacchus (Tito) in an exclusively pleasurable union that denies the fact of human suffering. As Romola comes to accept Christianity's narrative of the Suffering Servant, however, she "outgrows" classical narratives, and the novel becomes even more of a narrative hybrid. The novel's Proem, after all, describes a former Florentine who, though steeped in classical learning, "had not [. . .] neglected to hang up a waxen image or double of himself under the protection of the Madonna Annunziata, or to do penance for his sins in large gifts to the shrines of saints *whose lives had not been modeled on the study of the classics*" (7; emphasis added). Although Romola's narrative—like her life itself—appropriates elements of pagan myth, not until she embraces a distinctively Christian narrative can she evolve into a secular Madonna, and the narrative itself culminate as hagiography.

A few critics have considered hagiography in *Romola* as a uniquely appropriate form for a female *bildungsroman*. "It is though the only discourse George Eliot can trust when she seeks to express the vision of woman coming to authority," states Gillian Beer of *Romola*, "is that of the saint's legend." Beer points out Anna Jameson's influence on Eliot, including Jameson's suggestion that Catholic hagiography "should be seen as offering an alternative set of symbolic insights [. . .] for women" who did not have a classical education (123). Although Romola's reincarnation as a saint, an emblem of moral power, attracts some feminist critics, theories of hagiography reveal some inconsistencies between notions of sainthood as defined by various religious traditions, and modern ideals of female self-assertion. Kimberly Van Esveld Adams argues that Romola-as-Madonna is:

> Eliot's symbol of a woman who has developed her intellectual and emotional capacities, who lives for herself but also for others, as a wife and mother; a woman who is independent yet also materially grounded in her own body and connected to the social body. [. . .] The Madonna in Eliot thus represents that state woman should but cannot yet achieve. (161)

As attractive as this description is, sharing a cup of milk with a baby exposed to the plague, as Romola does (524), and devoting one's life to the care of one's husband's mistress and her children seem beyond the pale of living "for [one]self."

Madonna Romola's actions seem to conform more closely to Edith Wyschogorod's definition of a saint in *Saints and Postmodernism*. Drawing upon narratives of devout, altruistic men and women from all major world religions, Wyschogorod describes a saint as "[. . .] one whose adult life in its entirety is devoted to the alleviation of sorrow (the psychological suffering) and pain (the physical suffering) that afflicts other persons without distinction to rank or group or, alternatively, that affects sentient beings, whatever the cost to the saint in pain or sorrow" (34). What renders traditional constructions of sainthood contradictory to modern constructions of an empowered female self is that the practice of saintly action seems to negate the notion of "self" altogether. William James, who considered sainthood a legitimate psychological condition, described it in *Varieties of Religious Experience* as a permanent, paradigmatic shift in which the soul reaches a "genuinely heroic" state (211), one characterized by a shedding of all inhibitions and reservations in regard to the Other. Exhibiting the virtues of asceticism, moral fearlessness, purity, and charity, the saint is compelled "by organic consequence" of this "natural psychic complex" (225) to perform even unpleasant and arduous tasks of love and service for the Other. What James describes as the dropping of all inhibitions is, according to Wyschogorod's theory, the actual erasure of boundaries between Self and Other: "The Other is swallowed up by the self as an object of utility, desire, or representation and becomes part of the self's conative, affective, or cognitive structure" (33). To describe self-renunciation in terms of desire, as Wyschogorod does, may seem paradoxical, yet asceticism, as Geoffrey Harpham explains, "is essentially a meditation on, even an enactment of, desire. [. . .] [I]t proposes gratifications which are represented both as 'anti-desire'" and yet (for this reason) more desirable than desire because they do not insult the conscience" (45–46).

Another potential difficulty (or possibility) in using hagiography as a model of female empowerment is that hagiography attempts to transcend sex and gender, as barriers that separate Self from Other. "The hagiographic body," states Wyschogorod, "is neuter. No sexual identity can be inscribed on its surface because the saintly body accommodates all sexual identities [. . .]" (116). Of course, the heroine of *Romola*, on her progress toward secular, "neuter" sainthood, paradoxically must confront a succession of obstacles that faced all Victorian women concerned with issues of personal faith, spiritual integrity, and ethical agency. But the chapter of "Romola's Waking," which so many readers find unrealistic and even "depressing," attempts to represent a human subject transcending the shackles of self-interest and—to some extent—gendered roles. Even as Madonna Romola comes across as an essentialist vision of sacred womanhood, it is a vision of womanhood that eclipses male authority. Madonna Romola's status as "mother" does not rely upon any man, and her moral power—for the first time in the book—is not informed by father, godfather, or spiritual director. Madonna Romola possesses the authority to act as confessor to the village priest who withheld aid from the sick (525); on an allegorical level, she also wields supreme moral authority in place of God. In this manner, Romola demonstrates the lethal potential of sainthood. Sainthood is in fact "deadly" because it kills not only the self, but all self-projections that only serve to gratify the ego. In *Romola*, the most ambitious and most limiting of these self-projections is the anthropomorphic image of God, and God's death is essential for Romola's apotheosis, ending the chain of male deaths in the novel: father, brother, husband, godfather, and spiritual director.

Carnival Saints vs. "Real" Saints in *Romola*

In an article entitled "The Other Side of Carnival: Romola and Bakhtin," Hilda Hollis points out that "carnival is a natural element in Eliot's novel [. . .] [it] opens in the marketplace, and festivals and carnivals permeate it. All is brought into the realm of carnival" (233). The carnival, as a melding of pagan lore and superstition to orthodox church observances, represents both pre- and post-Reformation Catholicism as Protestants viewed it: a rich Christian tradition hopelessly corrupted by its own eagerness to pander to the basest aspects of human nature. The "logic" (or more accurately, illogic) of carnival also speaks to the position of the nineteenth-century intellectual—acutely aware (as she observes the religious procession) of the material, sham nature of carnival saints or "idols." Peter Stallybrass and Allon White, following the lead of Mikhail Bakhtin, discuss how carnival celebrates the lower-class body. "Fundamental to the corporeal, collective nature of carnival laughter is what Bakhtin terms 'grotesque realism.' Grotesque realism uses the material body—flesh conceptualized as corpulent excess—to represent cosmic, social, topographical and linguistic elements of the world" (9). Eliot's narrator, witnessing the Florentine carnival, vividly describes "grotesque" representations of celestial saints that are no more than the sum of dust, tinsel, and sturdy peasant bodies:

> [. . .] more wonderful still, saints of gigantic size, with attendant angels, might be seen, not seated, but moving in a slow, mysterious manner along the streets, like a procession of colossal figures come down from the high domes and tribunes of the churches. The clouds were made of good woven stuff, the saints and cherubs were unglorified mortals supported by firm bars, and those mysterious giants were really men of very steady brain, balancing themselves on stilts, and enlarged, like Greek tragedians, by huge masks and stuffed shoulders; but he was a miserably unimaginative Florentine who thought only of that—nay, somewhat impious, for in the

image of sacred things was there not some virtue of sacred things themselves? (80)

In this passage, Eliot emphasizes the carnival saints' size and their solidity, highlighting the paradox of seeking the immaterial sacred through an accretion of objects and an enlargement of human bodies. According to Stallybrass and White, carnivalesque, "[g]rotesque realism images the human body as multiple, bulging, over- or under-sized, protuberant or incomplete" (9). The novel demonstrates a real repugnance—what Stallybrass and White term "bourgeois hysteria"—for the lower-class body and its insatiable appetite. The task of representing St. John the Baptist, for example, "not among the prizes of high life," is compensated by a collection of delicacies including "a cake weighing fourteen pounds" (87). The novel shows us St. John the Baptist—who, according to Scripture, subsisted on locusts and honey—receiving his prize: "whereupon the eidolon of the austere saint at once invigorated himself with a reasonable share of the sweets and wine, threw the remnants to the crowd, and embraced the mighty cake securely with his right arm through the remainder of the passage" (87). These carnival figures ultimately speak to the absurdity of anthropomorphism, which Matthew Arnold described in *Literature and Dogma* (1873) as the mainstay of popular religion. U. C. Knopfelmacher suggests that George Eliot's humanism "finds its most immediate counterpart in the religious thought of Matthew Arnold"(62), and Eliot surely would have agreed with Arnold's assertion that "[p]opular theology rests on the eternal hypothesis of a magnified and non-natural man at the head of mankind's and the world's affairs" (120).

In *Literature and Dogma*, Arnold promotes a "revised" Christian worldview freed from *Auberglaube*, or "extra-belief": unnecessary and false doctrine. Along with the notion of an anthropomorphized God, Arnold carefully prunes away all other doctrines that render the human body a basis for religious belief: incarnation, redemption through Christ's physical death and resurrection, Christ's healing of the sick. According to Arnold, the body has no place in religion, and Eliot seems to concur. For Eliot, the difficulty with anthropomorphism is less that it is an empty signifier, but that it encourages a piety that is entirely self-focused. The religious devotion that most clearly illustrates this phenomenon is the Florentines' attitude toward the Virgin Mary, venerated especially "by hardy, scant-feeding peasant women [. . .] [holding] in their hearts that meager hope of good and that wide dim fear of harm, which were somehow to be cared for the Blessed Virgin" (133). As befits a people who "had a Madonna who would do as they pleased" (351), popular piety increases according to need when devotion to the Virgin might deliver Florence from its enemies.

Even worse, so attached are the Madonna's devotees to her visible bodily representations that Church authorities can control the masses by manipulating their cherished paintings and statues. Two of the images of the Virgin Mary mentioned in *Romola* are often or always concealed; on the Feast of the Virgin's Nativity the peasant women flock to see a "miraculous image, painted by the angels, [which] was to have the curtain drawn away from it on this Eve of her Nativity, that its potency might stream forth without obstruction" (133). In a later public religious observance, the "nucleus of the procession" is the Unseen Madonna:

> [...] the mysterious hidden Image—hidden first by rich curtains of brocade enclosing an outer painted tabernacle, but within this, by the more ancient tabernacle which had never been opened in the memory of living men, or the fathers of living men. In that inner shrine was the image of the Pitying Mother, found ages ago in the soil of L'Impruneta, uttering a cry as the spade struck it. (359)

Absence is a powerful motivator. When the cherished object disappears, the imagination runs riot and desire intensifies. The Church's strategy of hiding its saints is echoed in the novel by a merchant who rouses the interest of his female buyers by concealing his merchandise:

> Tito recognized his acquaintance Bratti, who stood with his back against a pillar and his mouth pursed up in a disdainful silence, eyeing everyone who approached him with a cold glance of superiority, and keeping his hand fast on a serge covering, which concealed the contents of the basket slung before him. Rather surprised at a deportment so unnatural in an anxious trader, Tito went nearer and saw two women go up to Bratti's basket with a look of curiosity, whereupon the pedlar drew the covering tighter, and looked another way. It was quite too provoking, and one of the women was fain to ask what there was in the basket? (134)

So skilled is Bratti at his game of concealment that the women agree to buy, and negotiate a price, even before he exhibits the talismans for sale: "two clumsy iron rings [...] the entirely hidden character of their potency [in warding off pestilence] [...] so satisfactory, that the grossi were paid without grumbling [...]" (135). Interestingly, Tito plays a hiding "game" with Romola later in the story when he conceals her dead brother's crucifix in a gaily painted triptych he commissioned as a betrothal gift. As he hides the crucifix, Tito attempts to convince Romola that he has buried death and human suffering "in a tomb of joy" (191). Romola, not fooled by such a maneuver, remains tantalized by the thought of Dino's crucifix and what it represents, to the point where she finally opens the triptych and wears the cross on her flight from Florence.

Tito has far more success in fooling Tessa, who seems to embody all the weaknesses and religious superstitions of her class. Tessa craves love, safety, food, and sleep. Her desires, centered on the most basic of human appetites, marks her state of eternal childhood, and to the end of the novel, she remains wrapped up in the pleasures of her *confetti* and cakes, her children (their actual upbringing confined to the care of Monna Lisa and Romola), her fine contadina dresses (in increasingly larger sizes [545]), and her sleep: "an amiable practice in everybody, and one that Tessa liked for herself" (546). While Tito has great success pandering to Tessa's bodily appetites (he is, for example, continually bringing her things to eat), he also exploits her primitive religious beliefs. Not surprisingly, all Tessa's religious observances are dictated by her childish desires, and she seems to equate spiritual virtue with the ability to get results. "I set myself Aves to say," she tells Tito, "to see if they would bring you back, but I left off, because they didn't" (141).

Tito and Tessa's relationship, in fact, seems to represent the Catholic Church's manipulation of the deluded lower-class Florentines throughout the entire novel. Tito, so beautiful of countenance that his barber tells the artist Piero to make "a Saint Sebastian of him that will draw troops of devout women" (40), controls Tessa through what she sees and does not see. Tessa seems incapable of abstract thought, for when Tito disappears, she cannot imagine "his whereabouts or his doings when she did not see him [. . .], her thought, instead of following him, had stayed in the same spot where he was with her" (146). Tessa bases her entire theology on what she sees, and makes impressively confident—if mistaken—judgments about good and evil based on appearance alone. "[H]e was the devil—I know he was" (101), pronounces Tessa of her abusive stepfather, and tells Tito, soon after she meets him, that she trusts him "[b]ecause you are so beautiful—like the people going into Paradise—they are all good" (102). Tessa also bases her faith in the Madonna on what her images and statues look like: "I think the Holy Madonna will take care of me; she looks as if she would; and perhaps if I wasn't idle, she wouldn't let me be beaten" (105). Tito is also able to fool Tessa into thinking their mock wedding ceremony is genuine, since "[t]he altar-like table, with its gorgeous cloth, the row of tapers, the sham episcopal costume, the surpliced attendant [. . .] were a sufficiently near parody of sacred things to rouse poor little Tessa's veneration; and there was some additional awe produced by the mystery of their apparition on the spot" (143).

Tito takes advantage of Tessa's inclination to deify every beautiful person she sets her eyes on (including Romola), and his visits to her echo the apparition tales of La Salette. Even believers' accounts of the apparition remark upon the ignorance of the "dull, unheeding shepherd children" (Villecourt 19); the *Times* insisted that the "dirty little peasants" "had been imposed upon by a simulated appearance," since "nothing could be easier than to deceive peasant children of that tender age" (November 1854). Tessa, whose mental capacity clearly lags behind her years, quickly assumes that Tito "was something come from Paradise into a world where most things seemed hard and angry" (103). The mysterious, unpredictable nature of Tito's visits also lends to his air of divine authority. On the day of his betrothal to Romola, he extracts from Tessa a promise "to be good and wait for me" and gives her a promise in return: "But I must go now. And remember what I told you, Tessa. Nobody must know that you ever see me, else you will lose me for ever. And now, when I have left you, go straight home, and never follow me again. Wait till I come to you. Good-by, my little Tessa: I *will* come" (189; emphasis in original). Tito, like the Virgin Mary in the stories of La Salette and of later apparitions, requests good behavior and threatens the withdrawal of divine favor if this request is not heeded. He also confers a sense of power on Tessa (and of course protects himself) by imparting to her a "secret"—in this case, the fact of the visits themselves.

In the Protestant view of apparition narratives, the Virgin's visits confer a significant but false sense of empowerment. Some Catholics insisted that transformations in Melanie's and Maximin's character were one proof of the apparition's veracity; Melanie, for example, was formerly "idle, disobedient, and inclined to pout" whereas after the Virgin's visit she became "active and obedient; and she said her prayers better." Her role was transformed from that of a slovenly shepherd girl (Ullathorne, *Holy Mountain*, 27) to "Sister Mary of the Cross," whose "demeanor [was] singularly modest and recollected, and her manner simple and religious" (Ullathorne, *Holy Mountain* 16). Maximin was less successful in maintaining an aura of piety, but what is remarkable is the confidence and consistency with which the two uneducated children described the events of the apparition.[3] They

---

3. Zimdars-Swartz writes that Maximin eventually "attempted several careers, ranging from liquor dealer to priest, only to find himself unsuited for any of them" (42). At one point he joined the Papal Zouaves (in defense of the Papal States against the Italian *Risorgimento*) only to be expelled for drunkenness (Harrison 300 n.106). Melanie became a nun, but her life was "unsettled and unhappy" (Zimdars-Swartz 42), and she butted heads with Church authorities

took the Virgin's request for secrecy so seriously that they would not disclose the entirety of her message until they were allowed to send their "secrets" in a letter to the pope himself. In *Romola*, Tessa undergoes a marked transformation of her own. In her own eyes, she has been elevated from a helpless peasant girl to a well-off, respectable wife and mother. More significant, however, she recounts her own apparition narrative to Baldassarre (Tito's cast-off father) with the air of a theologian capable of understanding ineffable mysteries. When Baldassarre inquires as to the identity of her "husband," she replies:

> "[. . .] [H]e is more beautiful and good than anybody else in the world. I say prayers to him when he's away. You couldn't think what he is!"
>
> She looked at Baldassarre with a wide glance of mysterious meaning, taking the baby from him again, and almost wishing he would question her as if he wanted very much to know more.
>
> "Yes, I could," said Baldassarre, rather bitterly.
>
> "No, I'm sure you never could," said Tessa, earnestly. "You thought he might be Norfri [Tessa's stepfather]," she added with a triumphant air of conclusiveness. "But never mind; you couldn't know. What is your name?" (284)

Tessa's assumption of religious and theological authority, based entirely on the evidence of her senses, is just one of many carnival inversions in the novel. The cult of the Virgin Mary has, in the history of the Catholic Church, been driven and shaped by popular religious practices and the desires of the masses.[4] Typically, ordinary men and women assert the validity of an apparition long before the Church does; in the case of La Salette, official sanction of the site as a place of pilgrimage did not occur until 1851, five years after the actual event. Had not an estimated "sixty thousand pilgrims" flocked to La Salette on the first anniversary of the apparition (Fortier 31), the Church might conceivably have delayed or withheld its sanction altogether. Similar to the seers at La Salette (and the pilgrims that initially followed), Tessa does not require orthodox approval or outside guidance to anthropomorphize God through the comely person of Tito.

---

over matters pertaining to her accounts of the Apparition.

4. In the nineteenth century, for example, "The Church was often reluctant to accept popular visions because they threatened the hierarchy and doctrine of the male-dominated faith. However, persistent displays of popular piety, combined with favorable outcomes of ecclesiastical investigations, sometimes led the Church to incorporate these visions into mainstream Catholic thought" (Kaufman 207 n.2).

While Tito's "apparitions" appear to have given Tessa voice and authority, she is of course merely exploited. In her first meeting with Baldassarre, she is depicted as a fallen Madonna, "a pretty loving apparition" (282), who, although ignorant of her real social status as an unwed mother, immediately conveys it to Baldassarre when she produces her "bimbo." She is, to Baldassarre, an image which inspires pity rather than reverence: "'Poor thing! poor thing!' he said [. . .]. It did not seem to him as if this guileless loving little woman could reconcile him to the world at all, but rather that she was with him against the world, that she was a creature who would need to be avenged" (284). When Tessa takes leave of Baldassarre, she, too, makes a promise, but one she cannot enforce, given her subordinate status in the household, beneath Tito and even the servant Monna Lisa: "You will come here and rest when you like; Monna Lisa says you may. And don't you be unhappy, for we'll be good to you" (284). "Poor thing!" repeats Baldassarre in reply, knowing that Tito, when he returns, will not be "good" to him.

Although Tessa, in her newfound prosperity, demonstrates sensitivity to the pain of others who once suffered like herself, her exploited position hinders her from the full exercise of her moral agency. Tessa's interactions with her "saint," therefore, are notable only in the immediate—if superficial—gratifications they provide her, as well as the extent to which they limit her power even as they improve her material circumstances. She can speak about her holy patron with the air of authority, but Baldassarre, knowing the truth, will never be persuaded to adopt Tessa's view of his traitorous son. Tessa's situation, which represents the false empowerment and exploitation perpetuated by the Florentine cult of the Madonna, sets the stage for *Romola*'s depiction of "true" sainthood, visible apparitions which, while still relying on the evidence of the viewer's/hearer's senses, prompt in them *genuine* moral transformations and *effective* altruistic behavior. Wyschogorod defines hagiography in part by its effect on its hearers; significantly, these effects have nothing to do with self-gratification:

> The [saint's tale's] chronological strands and textual voices may appear to the reader to convey information and, as such, to reflect an attitude of factuality toward what is recounted [. . .]. But even if what occurs is brought to light in the indicative mood, the hagiographic material is united and framed by the imperative mood. [. . .] [T]he imperative mood of the tale solicits others to transform their lives. [. . .] The story's success is not measured in aesthetic or cognitive terms but rather in regard to whether the addressees experience the saint's spiritual rebirth as an existential demand. (10)

Although hearing the story of a saint's life does not possess the immediacy of witnessing a saint's appearance (whether naturally or supernaturally) firsthand, hagiography is, according to Wyschogorod, an attempt to replicate the "flesh and blood existent" (3) that inspires people to perform moral acts in turn. The successful saint's tale—like the successful apparition in *Romola*—has an "imperative" quality, in that it prompts people not toward self-love but toward self-sacrifice and unconditional love for the Other (the "existential demand").

For Romola to perform saintly action, and for her narrative to take on a hagiographic quality, two conditions must be met. First, Romola must act, not out of love or reverence for any authority or father figure, but out of spontaneous love (*agape*) for the Other in need. To wean Romola off her chronic dependence on human authority, the novel literally kills off all the men in her life. Although Savonarola and Tito do not die until the end of the novel, they are already emotionally severed from Romola by the time she climbs into her boat. Romola's terrifying trip downriver illustrates the depth of her bereavement:

> Romola felt orphaned in those wide spaces of sea and sky. She read no message of love for her in that far-off symbolic writing of the heavens, and with a great sob she wished that she might be gliding into death.
>
> She drew the cowl over her head again and covered her face, choosing darkness rather than the light of the stars, which seemed to her like the hard light of eyes that looked at her without seeing her. (475)

Romola, as she drifts downriver, feels that she is in her grave, "touching the hands of the beloved dead beside her, trying to wake them" (475). This scene evokes the agonies of religious skepticism and the one underlying, horrible question which so haunted thoughtful men and women throughout the nineteenth century: Could there be any meaning or purpose in life without a God? Ambitiously, Eliot attempts to provide an answer in the very next chapter: the way out of secularism's existential dilemma is a complete and radical "shift of emotional center towards love and compassion—toward a 'yes, yes,' rather than a 'no, no'" (James 4) in respect to the Other. This kind of moral heroism, traditionally modeled by the Catholic Church as a state of being which best emulates the life of Christ, is only attainable in Romola once "the likenesses and analogies of God" have been erased. While the Suffering Christ on Dino's crucifix represents for Romola the only true and worthwhile route to human happiness, all motives for her altruism ultimately must emanate from within. Romola's transfiguration into the Virgin Mary suggests that true moral heroism depends upon *becoming God* ourselves, so that perfect benevolence becomes an inherently human (rather than divine) attribute.

The second condition for Romola's "sainthood" is that her benevolent actions carry with them a moral imperative for others. Although Romola, upon awakening in her little village, feeds the hungry and nurses the sick, her most significant contribution is her ability to inspire altruism in others. As Wyschogorod argues, "exemplary lives in which saintly power and its renunciation figure teach moral practice by way of practice" (52). When Romola first manifests herself at the village well, the case of mistaken identity that ensues closely resembles the incident at La Salette. Relying on the evidence of his senses alone, a young man mistakes the imposing, mysterious visitor for the Virgin Mary:

> Romola certainly presented a sight which, at that moment and in that place, could hardly be seen without some pausing and palpitation. With her gaze fixed intently on the distant slope, the long lines of her thick grey garment giving a gliding character to her rapid walk, her hair rolling backward and illuminated on the left side by sun-rays, the little olive baby on her right arm now looking out with jet-black eyes, she might well startle that youth of fifteen, accustomed to swing the censer in the presence of a Madonna less fair and marvelous than this.
>
> "She carries a pitcher in her hand—to fetch water for the sick. It is the Holy Mother, come to take care of the people who have the pestilence."
>
> It was a sight of awe: she would perhaps, be angry with those who fetched water for themselves only. The youth flung down his vessel in terror [. . .]. (522)

The youth's first reaction to this vision is a sense of shame for neglecting the sick. This presents an interesting contrast to the Virgin at La Salette, who scolded her people *only* for a lack of reverence and devotion to herself and her Son: blaspheming God's name, missing Sunday Mass, eating meat during Lent. Madonna Romola is not so selfish and evokes a sense of shame for the neglect of other flesh-and-blood human beings. This shame also fills the village priest as soon as he hears about the apparition from his young altar boy: "[H]e trembled at the pestilence, but he also trembled at the thought of the mild-faced Mother, conscious that the Invisible Mercy might demand something more of him than prayers and 'Hails'" (524). When the priest does encounter Romola shortly afterward, she holds him morally accountable for the neglect of his office and demands a change in his behavior: "And now tell me father, how this pestilence came, and why you let your people die without the Sacraments, and lie unburied. For I am come over the sea to help those who are left alive—and you, too, will help them now" (525). Romola enlists both the priest and the youth to aid her in caring for the sick: "That was a dreadful proposal to Jacopo, and to the priest also; but they were both under a peculiar influence forcing them to obey. The suspicion that Romola was a supernatural form was dissipated, but their minds were filled instead with the more effective sense that she was a human being whom God had sent over the sea to command them" (526). The priest's and the youth's motivation to altruism is "more effective" once they realize that Romola is an ordinary human being, because it is rooted less in fear now than in an admiration for Romola's selfless love.

The villagers persist in regarding Romola as one sent by God, and they reverence her as a saint. But yet again, this is not for any supernatural quality she demonstrates, but for the extraordinary power of her benevolence toward others:

> Every day the Padre and Jacopo and the small flock of surviving villagers paid their visit to this cottage to see the Blessed Lady, and to bring her of their best as an offering—honey, fresh cakes, eggs, and polenta. It was a sight which none of them could forget, a sight they all told of in their old age—how the sweet and sainted Lady with her fair face, her golden hair, and her brown eyes that had a blessing in them, lay weary with her labours after she had been sent over the sea to help them in their extremity [. . .]. [S]he told them if they loved her they must be good to Benedetto [the Jewish orphan baby]. (526–27)

Romola's moral influence does not fade after she returns to Florence. Indeed, the legend of her benevolence and her command to "be good" flourishes in her absence, to the point where storytelling functions as a means to fill the void left by the Madonna's departure. The reader is left to presume that this story will be different from those told about the "Hidden Madonna" of the Florentines, however, for it depicts the Madonna actively working for others—to the point of exhaustion—in a way that ordinary men and women can and must imitate: "Yes, yes," cry the villagers in response to Romola's command, "we will be good to the little Benedetto!" (530).

Some critics have expressed disappointment with the seemingly anticlimactic nature of *Romola*'s epilogue: After tearing herself away (or being torn away) from all ties that constrain her, Romola heroically rescues a plague-stricken village, only to return to Florence and a small domestic enclosure where she watches over Tito's children and "the feeble women in her domestic circle" (Booth 126). Certainly the epilogue seems less fantastic and more realistic than the altruistic utopia of the village, where Romola can exercise saintly action untrammeled by "all the special ties of marriage, the State, and religious discipleship" (527) in Florence. Unlike the village, Florence as yet has no use for a "Visible Madonna," so Romola must accommodate herself to one of the few female roles sanctioned by her society, that of a widowed matriarch. Nonetheless, Romola still retains an aura of sainthood through her motivations and actions. Her decision to adopt Tito's children emanates not from a sense of duty, but from pure desire: "She never for a moment told herself that it was heroism or exalted charity in her to seek these beings; she needed something that she was bound specially to care for; she yearned to clasp the children and to make them love her" (532). And once again, the very strength of Romola's altruistic example compels others to follow suit. Romola's cousin Monna Brigida, who could not be deterred from her self-indulgent ways even by Savonarola's hell-and-brimstone rhetoric, now readily agrees to help Romola care for Lillo and Ninna—despite her contempt for their Tessa as a "puss-faced minx" (534). Fittingly, Romola returns to Tessa in the form of an apparition, clasping a favorite lost necklace round Tessa's neck, declaring that "God has sent me to you again" (534).

Another surprising aspect of the novel's epilogue is that Romola, whose multiple bereavements helped to transform her into a saint, is finally shown paying wistful homage to the memories of Savonarola, her father, and Tito. Romola's powerful moral agency seems downplayed, as the reader's attention is pulled toward Savonarola's altar, which young Ninna is decorating in commemoration of his death. Romola's final words in the novel are delivered to Lillo, whom she hopes to make into a scholar, like her father, who "had the greatness that belongs to integrity" and "chose poverty and obscurity rather than falsehood," and praises Savonarola for his "struggle against powerful wrong" and his attempt "to raise men to the highest deeds they are capable of" (547). Most surprising, however, are Romola's remembrances of the treacherous Tito, who, she insisted, "never thought of doing anything cruel or base" when she first met him. But the novel's conclusion suggests that Lillo—who already demonstrates some of his father's less admirable characteristics, such as a love for pleasure—may well gain more moral instruction from an honest account of Tito's shortcomings than from glowing tales of Bardo's or Savonarola's virtue. Romola promises to tell Lillo, one day, about a man "who denied his father, and left him to misery" and "betrayed every trust reposed in him, that he might keep himself safe and get rich and prosperous" (548).

Inspired by midcentury controversy over the Roman Catholic cult of the saints, controversies over the Immaculate Conception, and published tales of the apparition at La Salette, Eliot reforms hagiography in *Romola* in several distinct ways. Eliot's Madonna, as she is in Protestant-authored texts, remains a symbol of secularism, but a secularism, paradoxically, that frees both women and men to develop their highest moral potential. Father Louis De Montfort, a seventeenth-century French priest whose book, *True Devotion to Mary*, was translated and published in England by Frederick Faber in the 1860s, proclaimed that Mary "will consequently produce the greatest saints that there will be in the end of time" (21). De Montfort regards Mary as the primary assailant against evil in the world's final age and argues that her saints "shall be singularly devout to our Blessed Lady, illumined by her light, strengthened by her nourishment, led by her spirit, supported by her arm and sheltered under her protection" (27). In Eliot's novel, Romola-as-Madonna does represent an apocalyptic age of fulfilled moral potential, but how differently than De Montfort pictured: an age made possible by the absence of God. Without God as a mirror of the self, secular saints are free to direct their love toward the suffering Other.

This moral ideal presented in *Romola*, however, refers to a future age, and Romola's final tales of Savonarola and Tito—highly gifted but flawed men—suggests that in the interim, hagiography does not require morally perfect subjects. One of the insights Romola receives on her return to Florence is that high moral ideals can and must hold steady in spite of human weakness. Recalling how both Tito's and Savonarola's behavior had assaulted her faith in goodness, she reflects: "Was she then, something higher, that she should shake the dust from off her feet, and say, 'This world is not good enough for me'? If she had been really higher she would not so easily have lost all her trust" (529). By picking and choosing the material of others' lives to create a morally edifying tale, Romola is depicted, in the book's epilogue, as both hagiographer and artist. Margaret Homans has pointed out that Romola, who passes the days in her father's household reading aloud to him, "submissively bear[s] the word of women's exclusion from and silencing within literature" (201) and is represented "not touching, and being untouched by, the texts she transmits" (202). But Romola as hagiographer—the keeper of a largely oral tradition for the moral guidance of the uneducated—represents a literary form far more useful, powerful, and long-lived than the classical treatises Bardo so cherished, represented in Dino's nightmare as dry parchments disintegrating into blood and consumed by fire (152–53). As hagiographer, Romola no longer possesses the heroic stature of a life-giving Madonna. By encouraging others toward moral action through her stories, however, she can remain a Madonna by proxy—a role, perhaps, that Eliot (who encouraged various friends and admirers to call her "Madonna") envisioned for herself.

In the twenty-first century, the Virgin Mary and her apparitions continue to serve as an emblem of the clash between secularism and traditional religious beliefs. As Sandra Zimdars-Scwartz has noted, La Salette was only the beginning of a series of modern apparitions that have attracted international attention. Today, people from all over the world flock to Medjugorje in the former Yugoslavia (Herzegovina), which believers claim as the site of ongoing apparitions and messages from Mary since 1981. This is the best known of recent apparitions, but far from the only one. "The considerable public attention that has been given to some of the apparitions of the past several decades," states Zimdars-Scwartz, "has created the impression that apparitions are proliferating—an impression that inspires different responses from different quarters" (18). Just as the accounts of the Virgin of La Salette provoked both Catholics and Protestants (albeit in different ways) anxious about secularism, the messages from Medjugorje appeal to modern believers' anxieties about loss of faith and the impending Day of Judgment. Many believers (akin to Louis De Montfort) interpret Mary's messages as a call to join her in an apocalyptic "battle between good and evil," a notion that has "very frequently led to a militant Marian ideology united with conservative political forces" (19). Skeptics, on the other hand, simply identify secularism as the key pressure fueling apparition claims.

In the United States, the Virgin Mary has come to represent the clash between (or perhaps the merging of) the sacred and the profane in quite different ways. The news media is quick to report stories of weeping statues and incidents of religious pareidolia—that phenomenon where individuals discern familiar, religious images in a field of ambiguous stimuli. "Apparitions" such as the Virgin Mary's image on the side of a Florida bank building in 1996, or more recently, her face on the surface of a grilled cheese sandwich, provide opportunities not only for secular news media to poke fun at religious beliefs, but also for good old-fashioned American entrepreneurship (the grilled cheese sandwich fetched $28,000 on eBay). Is there any element of religious belief, longing, or reverence in popular enthusiasm for such phenomena? That is a question for another study.

| CHAPTER SIX |

"Seven years a tiny Paradise a making"

Michael Field's Domestic Piety

ACCORDING to scholars of nineteenth-century anti-Catholicism, the Victorian preoccupation with Rome was a rather neatly contained phenomenon. E. R. Norman and D. G. Paz argue that anti-Catholic politics and sentiment declined dramatically after the 1870s due to a "waning of all religious feeling in English society" (Norman 20) and the "rise of alternative sources of entertainment" (Paz 300). In a similar vein, Susan Griffin interprets the relative scarcity of anti-Catholic themes in late-nineteenth-century fiction as a symptom of secularism, as well as a shared cultural sense that "[Catholicism's] threat has so far weakened that that it offers neither such deep gratifications nor such decided terrors" (214). With the fade of anti-Catholic sentiment, one might be left with the impression that Catholicism itself didn't matter anymore. This study argues that secularism, rather than emerging at the end of the century to quell Victorians' obsession with Catholicism, functioned as a powerful ingredient in popular responses to the Church of Rome throughout the entire century. In this final chapter of *Masked Atheism*, I wish to emphasize, moreover, the continuing importance and relevance of Catholicism for fin de siècle writers and aesthetes. As Emma Donoghue has suggested, Catholicism continued to provide writers with a vantage point well removed from the social status quo: "Being Catholic in [early-twentieth-century] England meant becoming slightly foreign, aloof from the establishment; as a church it was associated with the rich and the poor, but definitely not with the bourgeoisie" (124).

Ellis Hanson's *Decadence and Catholicism* adroitly demonstrates how "Roman Catholicism is central to both the stylistic peculiarities and the thematic preoccupations of the decadents" (5), emphasizing, in particular, their exploration of "the powerful historical relationship between homoeroticism and Roman Catholicism" (24). Far less attention, however, has been given to female aesthetes and their engagements with Roman Catholicism.[1] While this topic can (and ought to) inspire the writing of a future book, my purpose here will be to consider how the Catholicism of fin de siècle writers Michael Field (Katherine Bradley and Edith Cooper) might situate them within the larger group of Victorian women writers discussed in this book.

Michael Field presents a special challenge because they seem, at first glance, so resistant to being "Victorianized." Field critics demonstrate a curious inclination to discuss Katherine Bradley and Edith Cooper as completely severed from a Victorian context and/or exclusively within the context of male decadent writers.[2] Indeed, one might puzzle at length over any similarity between the novels of conventionally pious Lady Georgiana Fullerton—the only other Catholic convert discussed at length in this study—and the "bacchic," pagan, homoerotically charged works of the Fields. When one turns to the Fields' largely unpublished journal, *Works and Days*, however, two overlapping threads tie it to conventional preoccupations of earlier female authors: spirituality and the home.[3] But Fields'

---

1. Although Michael Field is a good place to begin, as recent analyses of the Fields' Catholicism by Frederick Roden and Marion Thain demonstrate. See chapter 7 of Roden's *Same-Sex Desire in Victorian Religious Culture* (2002), and Thain's chapter on the Fields, "'Damnable Aestheticism' and the Turn to Rome" (in *The Fin-de-Siècle Poem* edited by Joseph Bristow [2005]). Martha Vicinus, in *Intimate Friends: Women Who Loved Women: 1778-1928*, also discusses the Fields' conversion, but implies that it had a deleterious effect on their poetry.
2. Michael Field, argues Angela Leighton, in *Victorian Women Poets*, "belongs altogether outside the tradition of Victorian women's verse" (204); "It is as if [their] poems exist in an atmosphere altogether outside the moral and ideological structures of the age" (225). Julia Saville, in "The Poetic Imaging of Michael Field" (in *The Fin-de-Siècle Poem*), highlights the Fields' "determination to engage shoulder to shoulder in debate with leading male intellectuals" (178) of their time, while Thain discusses the Fields' conversion to Rome within the context of their friendship and correspondence with priest and former Decadent poet John Gray.
3. *Works and Days* is the handwritten, twenty-eight-volume diary chronicling the Fields' life together from 1888 to their deaths in 1914. (This refers to volumes 2 through 29 of the thirty volumes of Field diary material, now held in the British Library. Volume 1 is authored by Bradley alone, and records her trip to Paris in 1868-69. Volume 30 contains miscellaneous material removed from earlier volumes. Following the Fields' instructions, executor Tommy Sturge Moore opened the journals fifteen years after their deaths and published, in 1933, selected entries and letters to form "a connected biography" (qtd. in Donoghue 143). Moore's compila-

FIGURE 6.1. *Katherine Bradley (Michael Field) with Whym Chow.*
Reprinted with permission of the English Province of the Order of Preachers

treatment of such themes is, naturally, far from conventional. An analysis of selected portions of *Works and Days* suggests that, while the Fields were surprisingly reliant on the Victorian notion of sacred domesticity, their embrace of Catholicism helped them to preserve their sense of home as sacred space, even as they confronted loss, chaos, and meaninglessness in the death of their adored dog, Whym Chow.

A brief glance at one of the Fields' fellow writers and Catholic contemporaries, Alice Meynell, throws into relief the variety of ways Catholicism might have related to authorial identity at the fin de siècle. Recent scholarship on both Alice Meynell and Michael Field includes considerations of

---

tion, titled *Works and Days: From the Journals of Michael Field*, reproduces only a very small portion of the diaries. In this section (unless indicated otherwise) I quote from *Works and Days* itself, the original handwritten journals.

the influence of Catholicism on their poetry.[4] For both Meynell and the Fields, however, authorial identity was as carefully crafted as anything they wrote and published. For each author, this act of creation was particularly vexed in a period when traditional ideals of the Angel in the House coexisted uneasily with the iconoclastic New Woman. Talia Schaeffer suggests that Meynell's "most successful act of literary creation" was "her own angelic reputation" (162). In her book *The Forgotten Female Aesthetes*, Schaeffer discusses how Meynell, to whom Coventry Patmore entrusted his original manuscript of the "Angel in the House" (Schaeffer 169), in fact struggled to negotiate a delicate compromise between the two dominant female models of the fin-de-siècle, apparently proving to her admirers that "New Womanism and traditional femininity could merge seamlessly" (161). In an interpretation of Patmore's poem published in 1921, Meynell, as Schaeffer argues, "revises the Angel into a strong, vengeful, prophetic male. Here we see Meynell taking charge of her own idealized role, superintending its transformation into something more relevant for the modern world" (169).[5]

There appears a general consensus among critics that Meynell's Catholic identity helped to soften her modern edge and contributed—either directly or indirectly—to her image as a living, breathing Household Angel. Schaeffer, for example, suggests that the Angel in the House "conveys Meynell's Catholic piety" (163), whereas Vanessa Furse Jackson ties the poet's Catholicism to her creative qualities of "restraint, intellection, and detachment," qualities rendering her popular as "a poet who reassured and reinforced cherished, threatened values" (460). Given Catholicism's association at midcentury with all things irreligious and antidomestic, however, the notion of Catholicism as a bolster to Meynell's angelic image is somewhat surprising. It could be, perhaps, that Meynell's admirers apotheosized her *despite* her Catholicism, just as they overlooked her chaotic housekeeping and her abstracted, unsentimental attitude toward her seven children.[6] Or, perhaps Meynell's case supports Susan Griffin's argument

---

4. Many scholars, such as Angela Leighton, Talia Schaeffer, Vanessa Furse Jackson, and Ana Parejo Vadillo at least mention Catholicism as significant to Meynell's poetry and value system; more sustained discussions of Catholicism and Meynell's poetry include those by John S. Anson (1986) and F. Elizabeth Gray (2003). Thain's and Roden's reassessments of the Fields' religious writings (as texts evincing "a dynamic as exhilarating as that found in their earlier work" [Thain 313]) include close readings of selected "postconversion" poems.

5. Schaeffer quotes Meynell's review directly: "[I]t is possible that this early poem [Patmore's "Angel in the House"] is contemned because the reader takes the 'Angel' to be the woman, and an angel obviously feminine is a kind of sentimentality. But I prefer to take the 'Angel' to be Love" (169).

6 Schaeffer observes that "Meynell's abstraction from household affairs never interfered with her status as the incarnation of housewifery. Instead, admirers transmuted Meynell's

that Catholicism, by the end of the nineteenth century, comes to signify (in fiction, at least) a "relic" of religion, or religious nostalgia, rather than a threat to religion itself. "The Church of Rome that earlier narratives warn the Protestant faithful against," she argues, "is now recast as attraction to a limited and limiting comfort that the modern culture of disbelief cannot offer" (214). Part of the appeal of Meynell's public persona was a shared sense that the Household Angel was itself a "relic" of bygone times, so Griffin's observation about Catholicism in late-nineteenth-century novels might be usefully applied to Meynell's act of self-construction as well.

Meynell's careful cultivation of her public persona indicates how important a feminine aura was, even at the dawn of the Modern era, for the woman writer. While the creation of this palatable angelic identity was difficult for Meynell, for the Fields it was downright impossible. The Fields' adoption of a single, male pseudonym and their strenuous attempts to conceal their true identities were, on one hand, a straightforward attempt to bracket sex as a factor in the public reception of their writings. One might also consider, however, how much more difficult it would be for the Fields, two aging spinsters, to play the role(s) of Household Angel. And, of course, that wasn't all. While Bradley and Cooper's sexual relationship may have escaped close public scrutiny at the turn of the century, the modern reader of *Works and Days* finds a chronicle of a domestic life that would have utterly scandalized Victorians had they been able to read it. Even in 1922, in the first biography of the Fields, author Mary Sturgeon glosses over unconventional aspects of Bradley and Cooper's relationship, implying, finally, that their bond most closely resembled that of mother and child.[7] She does not, of course, include diary passages such as the following:

> As for the Love + me—we are tenfold more to each other [. . .]. We are re-united in our desire to publish, we are much more united in our walk + all airy pleasures. We are each more of a bodily sweetness together as

---

housewifely incompetence into proof that her mind was above gross materialism" (164). In *Alice Meynell*, the poet's daughter Viola Meynell quotes her brother Everard's recollection of their childhood: "Blandishments we had little of; we were taken to her arms, but briefly; exquisitely fondled, but with economy, as if there were work always to be resumed. We were at once the most befriended of children, yet the most slighted; we fitted into the literary life and the business of the household" (89).

7. "But of [Katherine's] devotion to [Edith], its passion, its depth, its tenacity and tenderness, it is quite impossible to speak adequately. From Henry's [Edith's] infancy to her death—literally, from her first day to her last—Michael [Katherine] shielded, tended, and nurtured her in body and spirit. Probably there never was another such case of one mind being formed by another" (45).

we breathe a close life together. I only want always to have my beloved beyond escape [. . .]. God keep us inseparable! (Edith on New Year's Eve, 1904, 202)[8]

Frequently in the journal volumes prior to Bradley's and Cooper's conversions to Roman Catholicism in 1907, the Fields describe themselves and their lives together as "bacchic" and "pagan." Earnest Victorians would have agreed; ultimately, the journals document a domestic existence that would have resembled, in the eyes of staunch Protestant Victorians, the interior of a debauched Catholic convent. Eschewing heterosexual marriage and motherhood for a committed homosexual relationship and the vocation of professional authorship, the Fields, as Ana Parejo Vadillo points out, occupied a space that conflated the categories of "work" and "home" (166). When not composing poetry and plays in their study room, Bradley and Cooper seem to have devoted large amounts of time, money, and energy to the cultivation of aesthetic wardrobes (they were especially fond of hats) and luxurious home décor. Strikingly absent from the journals are Victorian preoccupations with female virtue and "duty." "On one occasion," writes Emma Donoghue, quoting the journals, "they were driving to Shoreditch in London to collect the perfect sofa, they passed hordes of 'sad, mis-shaped, mis-featured work-people'; the tone was that of travelers on safari" (59).

Throughout the journals, however, there are surprising echoes of Victorian domestic fiction—most notably, Hannah More's *Coelebs in Search of a Wife*—in the Fields' sustained construction of the home as a sacred space, a material stage on which poets and lovers enacted lives permeated with spiritual, creative, and intellectual transcendence, in defiance (or denial) of a world that was, quite simply, going to hell in a handbasket. On New Year's Eve, 1906, Edith writes,

> The whole of life and government now, is for the brute mass—as if Athens had laid out her life for the satisfaction of her Slaves. To give these brute-masses satisfaction food must be adulterated, all objects vulgarised, books entirely written for them, manners lost, the capital of the land squandered, the sea-coast betrayed, motor-buses raging, smelling [. . .]. Speed is the one God + motors are his angels. (235)

---

8. In most cases, the diary volumes are divided by year; each year and volume has its own separate pagination. For future reference, the 1904 journal is volume 18 (Add Ms 46793), the 1906 journal is volume 20 (Add Ms 26795), the 1912 journal is volume 27 (Add Ms 46802), the 1913 journal is volume 28 (Add Ms 46803), and the 1914 journal is volume 29 (Add Ms 46804 A).

For Bradley and Cooper (at least prior to their conversion), the real menace to civilization is not atheism, but other consequences of modern life: processed food, bad books, noise, and traffic—and, one suspects, a reading public largely indifferent to the poetic genius of Michael Field.

One reason that the Fields turned to Catholicism after Whym Chow's death is that their joyful paganism could not sustain them in the face of suffering and loss. Yet even before their conversion, it is clear that the Fields relied upon a Victorian religion of the home (with some significant revisions) to validate and celebrate their most unconventional domestic arrangement, a "marriage" and a working partnership between two women. This is especially evident in the Fields' representations of Paragon, the first and only home the poets had all to themselves. Heeding a longing for "a wedded life with my Love in our own home" (Edith qtd. in Donoghue 100), the Fields moved from Durdans in Reigate, which they had initially shared with both Edith's father, James, and sister Amy, to 1, The Paragon, a small Georgian house on the Thames, in Richmond, in 1900.[9] In *We are Michael Field*, Emma Donoghue describes at length "their temple of love and beauty" (103), a domestic interior filled with artwork, masses of fresh flowers, potpourri, curios, luxurious textiles, and jewels: "Every sense was meant to be delighted" (106). The Fields shared the interior of their home with a pair of dogs and a pair of doves;[10] outside, they enjoyed the beauties of their well-tended garden, which included an altar to Dionysus.

Home as paradise provided the Fields with a comfortable and familiar conceptual framework on which to graft their shared life together, but perhaps it also served a more public purpose as well. The Fields kept their diary private in their own lifetimes, but arranged for its eventual, partial publication fifteen years after their deaths in 1914. As Edith and Katherine penned their diary entries, surely they knew that the details of their lives together would eventually be consumed and evaluated by the public. And the Fields seemed aware that they had some explaining to do. While the Fields' domestic piety would, on one hand, make their lives more familiar and understandable to outsiders, other aspects of it were somewhat baffling. Even the Fields' most intimate friends failed to comprehend the dynamics of their household; this fact was made glaringly evident to the Fields upon the death of Whym Chow, when friends assumed that they

---

9. In *Women Poets and Urban Aestheticism*, Ana Parejo Vadillo discusses the Fields' residence at Durdans in Reigate, including in her analysis a description of the home's décor and the Fields' "aestheticisation of the domestic [. . .] in which paintings, photographs, drawings and texts create a space for poetry and writings" (166).

10. According to the diaries, Whym Chow was considered Katherine's dog, while a basset hound, Music, belonged to Edith.

had merely lost a favorite pet.[11] Whym Chow, however, was no mere pet—he was the figurehead of the Fields' domestic religion. This religion might seem a parody of Christianity, except that the Fields, in their journal entries, were so utterly sincere in describing it. Nearly a year after Whym Chow's death, on the brink of her conversion to Roman Catholicism, Edith explains that "[f]or years I have worshipped the Holy Trinity, ever since I prayed, + Michael [Katherine] used to pray for the little Earthly Trinity Whym Chow + Hennie [Edith] + Michael to the ineffable Divine Trinity—that symbol all creatures must adore who attain to its fastness of life. Closer than ever was this worship when Whymmie died [. . .]" (29 December 1906, 231). The Chow formed one person of the Fields' domestic Trinity, a union of *three* lovers—two human, one canine. "Michael and I love Chow as we have loved no other human being," writes Edith, "for central + to us is his Love—our Flame of Love" (January 1906, 26). To Edith, at least (who writes far more than Katherine in *Works and Days* about the significance of Chow upon his death), Chow's devotion was somehow the model and inspiration of the perfect love that the Fields themselves strove to attain. "And my love for Whym-Chow is the very core + living of my whole heart," Edith writes later. Even Michael in herself alone *is not* quite at that origin of all that is profoundest in my love—her dog just reaches it first + waits for her impatiently to come into her mightier possession than his" (July 1906, 126; emphasis in original).

The manner in which Edith and Katherine regarded their Chow, for all Edith's attempts at explaining it, remains—perhaps appropriately, as befits all divine mysteries—something of a cipher.[12] What is clear, however, is that within the mystical little Trinity, *Chow* was the Household Angel, the "golden flame" at Paragon—or, as Edith dubs their home in one entry, "The Palace of our Golden Chow" (12 May 1906, 85). This becomes especially evident in January 1906, when the entire concept of "home" perishes along with Chow. After the veterinarian puts the dog down, on 28 January, Katherine breaks the news to Edith:

> When she [Katherine] enters our desolated Paragon, home no more forever—she says "my little dog is at rest—at rest—you hear it—he is at rest." It is like the sound of icebergs that grow + laugh+ then break up. It

---

11. In May 1906, Edith writes to a Mrs. Turnbull that she and Katherine have spent the past four months living in "complete solitude," since "[o]ur friends have failed to understand we are in any grief at all" (1906, 90). The Fields' outraged comments regarding lukewarm or insensitive responses to Whym Chow's death are scattered throughout the 1906 journal.

12. Both Roden and Thain discuss Whym's figuration as Holy Spirit and the nature of the Fields "Trinity" at greater length.

is hideously + greatly tragic. Our grief is blind, is potent . . . we scarcely touch food but bring back to order the rooms, now grown so hateful that we realise we must go. "Yes," I say to Michael, "we must let Paragon + get a little flat in town." (28 January 1906, 18)

Katherine and Edith prepare to flee the now odious Paragon, even as they prepare an elaborate burial ceremony for Chow. They go to town to make the requisite arrangements and are confronted, upon their return home, with the great yawning void of the front hall:

And in the afternoon a cab—our manuscripts + jewels, that we only remember had value, taken to Bank, money taken out . . . flowers, bunches of flame-tulips and wreaths of similax with which to receive our Beauty next day . . . the sense as we approach Paragon of the nothingness of it—the entrance into a silent hall, where has been a whirl-storm of the most golden welcome—a dance as if the sun had come down carrying love instead of his light. [. . .] Oh the bitter tears for that silent hall the symbol of a silent World where for us there is no welcome. Whym Chow, Whym Chow—O my little love! [Edith, 29? January 1906, 19][13]

Four months after this entry, Edith still refers to the front door of Paragon as "an entrance into the cave of death" (12 May 1906, 84). In mourning Whym Chow, the Fields seem to grieve not only the loss of a beloved pet, but also the light of their home: now empty, desolate, and, as Katherine describes it in a later entry, a "Charnel-House" (6 March 1906, 51).[14] The Fields' depictions of home, at this point in the journal, appear oddly similar to Dickens's representations of domestic spaces bereft of ministering angels, such as the households of Paul Dombey and Ebeneezer Scrooge.

But Whym's passing symbolized for the Fields even more beyond the loss of home. Marion Thain suggests that Whym Chow, who "had represented many aspects of pagan desire for the two women [. . .] died at a time when that desire was being 'defined' by a new normative category of sexuality" (312). It is very possible that Whym Chow's death foreshadowed to the poets a new direction for their "pagan desire," what Thain describes as "their shift away from sensual abandon to spiritual devotion" (312). But on a more fundamental level, the Fields had, quite simply, lost their reli-

---

13. This long entry appears to have been started on the date of Chow's death (28 January) and continued into the following day.

14. "We return to Paragon—March 6th. And it is as if Romeo went down to Juliet's Charnel-House not meaning to die there—to be there a little while, and then pass out [. . .]" (1906, 50).

gion and their conviction of a perfect, benevolent, and loving force active in their lives. "[I]n this bare world," wrote Edith to her friend Marie Sturge Moore, "we went to him as our brazier of love, the flames + the incence [sic], the motion + thrill we found perfect alone in the passion Chow had for Michael—a love that has consumed his life in 8 years, when he should have lived 8 years more" (29? January 1906, 20). Accordingly, Chow receives a burial fit for deceased royalty—or deity. According to Edith's journal entry of January 30, Katherine tenderly prepared Whym for burial, wreathing the little body with "Bacchic ivy" and tucking "wine-coloured Christmas roses" beneath his chin. Edith entrusts Chow with "the best lock of my hair from its roots," and Katherine places a fire-opal between his paws. "We each touched a wine-cup over the little Chow, + Michael spilt the wine of the Sacrament on the tan fur of his flank—blood on his brow [from the vet's bullet], wine on his side!—what should not grow up to us from the sacred stains!" (23).

Even before their conversion to Catholicism, the Fields' domestic religion fused significant Christian symbols with pagan allusions. They would not, however, recover a sense of pride or love for Paragon until the balance of their beliefs shifted toward Christianity and a fascination with the Church of Rome toward the end of 1906. From February until December of 1906, the diary entries chart the evolution of a revised domestic religion for the Fields, alongside increasingly frequent mentions of their growing friendship with Father John Gray.[15] But this transformation was long in coming. For months after Whym Chow's death, the Fields spent a considerable amount of time away from Paragon, which they were determined to vacate for good. For some reason, however, they were unsuccessful in finding a new tenant for the house. "We should have to live in street poverty, if Paragon does not let," writes Edith on 24 March (58), "+ tho for life's sake we will do it unhesitatingly." Confounding the Fields' dilemma was the fact that Paragon still held a strong fascination for them. Edith, in a letter to a friend, writes:

> These walls sometimes shriek like mandrakes when we threaten to remove their shelves + appurtenances. But whether we let or not we *vacate* in May. We go forth simply for our souls' health: here we live only a memorial life + Michael, stomping an archangelic foot, vows he will not lead a memorial life [. . .]. (March 1906, 60; emphasis in original)

15. Interestingly, Katherine is introduced to John Gray for the first time just days before Whym's death, in January 1906. Edith does not meet Gray in person until the Fields' trip to Edinburgh in August of that year. For more information on Gray's considerable influence on the Fields, see Thain's essay.

Despite Katherine's determination not to "lead a memorial life," by May her diary entries reveal considerable ambivalence about leaving Paragon. She describes it as a biblical Eden, watched over by a conventional, Christian-sounding God. "And the old garden blooms new flowers: Seven years a tiny Paradise a making. And God has flourished it out of His heaven" (May 1906, 89). Two pages later, she writes, "I believe we are being kept at Paragon that we may overcome the terror of the little grave [Whym was buried in the rose garden], + wholly dissociate this from the spirit of Flame that is our sure possession of God" (91). The following month, in an entry dated "Trinity Sunday," Katherine writes,

> Little Paragon shines in great beauty. Our little house is like Paradise—the Angel at the gate sits smiling his sword across his knees—And we know not whether it is the will of the lord of the garden that we should depart—or remain to dress + tend the garden. If the angel should draw his sword,+ forbid us to depart? (97)

One might surmise that the Fields' gradual reconciliation with life at Paragon was inevitable once their grieving for Chow had run its course. What is clear, however, is that Catholicism, in some way, helped the Fields to make sense of Chow's death and to incorporate it into their sense of a larger, divine plan for their salvation. These moments of recognition are interspersed in the diary alongside revelations of their changing attitude toward home.

In August, the Fields made a brief stop at Paragon before a trip to Ireland and Scotland (during which they visited Father Gray in Edinburgh), and to their delight, "for the first time a return [to Paragon] has not been all pain—we have caught the sense of what our home is" (Edith, 3 August, 144). (The beginning of this entry is headed, in Katherine's handwriting, "to our Home—the Paragon," the word "Paragon" topped with a sketch of a royal crown.) In the entry penned immediately after their trip, Katherine notes triumphantly, "And we have just resolved to settle down merrily in Paragon—to warm + to embellish it—and to be happy within it" (23 September, 179). A page later, Edith describes her love for Chow, using a phrase from the Latin Mass. "O Salutaris Hostia—I only know worship when I hear that—Love lifted up—the same sort of love I give to Chow, lifted up to God whole as a world" (180). As the Fields embraced Catholic theology and worship, they began to describe Whym not as irretrievably lost (as they do earlier in 1906), but as eternally present. Interestingly, the dog's metaphysical and mystic significance did not seem to diminish for the Fields. This entry, written by Edith when she was attending Mass regularly, just months before her formal conversion in April 1907, evinces no sense of incongruity between adoration of Chow and adoration of a (presumably) more orthodox, Catholic conception of the Holy Trinity:

> Oh Truth—*Vera Veritas!* My Love + I + Chow are together+ garner what this year 1906 has brought of marvel + immediacy of life. Though our Whym was taken at once from our mortal sight + touch+ the [dear?] habit of being in the flesh—let me say rather in his golden Fleece—at our side, we are closer to him now, more instant to the marvellous love of his heart + soul than when he lay on our couch. And ever is he living by our hearts + thoughts + conception one with us both + with each, prayed for, dwelt on adored forever + in the might of the Divine Majesty—Sancta Trinitas. (New Year's Eve, 1906, 234)

With a newly revised understanding of Chow as living and present among them in spirit, the Fields were able to do something that would have been unthinkable in January 1906: spend Christmas at Paragon. In October, Katherine writes, "Deep in my heart I ask if we may not—mastering our sorrows—spend our Christmas *here*—we three together delivered from memory—winged +serene? O little Paragon where [. . .] we are conquering Death—God prolong our home to us!" (192; emphasis in original).

On 25 December 1906, the Fields spend a triumphant Christmas Day, interspersed between the homey comforts of Paragon and the sublime interior of a Catholic sanctuary. They first attend Low Mass, where Katherine marvels over the "Bacchic" quality of the carol at the service (220). "Then," writes Edith, "resting and refreshing ourselves at Paragon" (224), the women pass the time until Benediction decorating a Christmas tree. At Benediction, it is Edith's turn to marvel at the "Bacchic sight" of the lights joined with song. Returning once more to Paragon, the Fields indulge in turkey and plum pudding—taking a walk afterward to overcome "the grossness of both"—then it is time for the exchange of presents. Katherine gives Edith a copy of *The Garden of the Soul,* and both women receive gifts of Catholic missals from Edith's sister Amy (225).[16]

Juxtaposing domestic and sacred spaces, Catholic and "bacchic" worship, spiritual contemplation with the decking of halls and consuming of pudding, Edith's description of Christmas Day 1906 suggests that for the Fields, at least, religious conversion is not a radical departure from the

---

16. Edith's sister Amy married a Catholic, John Ryan, in 1900. Edith, Amy, and Katherine all converted to Rome in the same period, between 19 April and 8 May of 1907.

past, but a continued dialogue with it.[17] Perhaps the strongest evidence of this, however, is Edith's belief that Chow spends the holiday with them, not so differently as he did the previous year:

> A beautiful Christmas day of paramount blessing + responsive gratitude—always with us that darling Whym, lighter of our Torch, our greatest lover. I remember last Christmas he had a bow of rosy heliotrope suddenly got by his "Minnie"—I did not like it,—it detracted from his fur—Whym was not gay I am sure. (225–26)

Whym's ghostly presence in 1906 also suggests how difficult it was for the Fields to dispense with the concept of a Household Angel. Rejecting for themselves such a role, the Fields displace it onto the family pet.[18] But when the dog dies, domestic felicity does not seem possible for the Fields until they can find a way to envision Whym still alive and present in their midst. "I have always disowned the Church of my childhood," writes Edith on 29 December 1906, "because it was destitute of the real centre of all true religion—an altar with its present Deity + because the Dead had no portion in its services" (231). In Catholicism, a religion that emphasizes both sacrifice and the sacramental presence of Deity alive and at work in the world, the Fields seem to have found a workable vocabulary, both for "resurrecting" Whym and recovering a sense of coherence and transcendence in their domestic life together.

If the Fields' "revised" domestic piety helped them to retain the notion of home as a sacred space in spite of death, it also fortified them against other threats in later years, such as the growing urbanization of their formerly peaceful suburb of Richmond. In May of 1912, Edith, already stricken with cancer, describes a distressing afternoon, ruined by street traffic:

> Motor-buses, rivalling each other in their constant + noisome traffic, had overcome our patience during the afternoon when I tried a little drive. The

---

17. Thain argues that "Michael Field ultimately chose to transform rather than destroy—to write over rather than 'erase' completely. [. . .] [W]e discover [in the Fields' religious poetry] the fluidity of a poetic identity that interlaces past and present, as well as self and lover, to create a personal mythology that is not only governed by its own logic but also strives for a coherent interface with the cultural concerns of the age" (332).

18. This arrangement perhaps accommodated the Fields' sexual identity in a more traditional Christian sense as well. Roden suggests that for the Fields, "love of and devotion to an animal enabled the two women to avoid the standard heterosexual trope of bridal mysticism. [. . .] Thus the two women could come to God not as brides of Christ but as mothers and lovers of their dog" (194).

air was heavy—the stench of the oil was all the freshness I got. We tried to turn away—+ got a tiny space of relief in a pilgrimage to the river through by-ways. But the sadness of this ruined world of Richmond + the personal misery suggested that we might have to leave the beloved Paragon for the sake of health and sanity. (57)

Tortured both by the motor buses and the loud music of a German family living next door, the Fields, as in 1906, regard the decision to retain or quit Paragon as a question of God's will—but how to discern his wishes? In August, on the Catholic feast of Our Lady of the Snow (commemorating a miracle, by which the Virgin Mary left instructions for the location of her chapel by a snowfall), Edith writes,

> How I pray that as [the Virgin] clearly showed where she would have her home by the wonder of white snow in summer, she will as clearly show us about our home + throw a whiteness over Paragon if we are to remain or a whiteness of direction as to where we are to go if it is God's will we should leave our Paragon. (92)

The Fields finally decide to remain at Paragon, but not before consulting their priest, Fr. Vincent McNabb, about the morality of the issue, and making a novena (a series of prayers said over nine days). In the course of the deliberations, both Katherine and Edith consider whether the "Paradise Lost" (58) of Richmond and the resulting domestic inconveniences might actually bring them *closer* to God. In August 1912, Edith writes: "It may be that God is calling me to this meritorious mortification of the senses by sending motorbuses with their horse + smell + Germans with their music at late hours to haunt Paragon. It may be He wishes me by victory over the senses—even the humblest—*smell*—it has been remarked that the Hill of Skulls may well have mortified God's own nostrils" (100; emphasis in original). "[M]ortification of" and "victory over" the senses seems a stark contradiction to the Fields' aesthetic approach to life, in which experiences of transcendence depended so heavily on external, mostly material, conditions: solitude, tasteful decorating schemes, flowers, jewels. Catholicism's emphasis on mortification, however, allowed the Fields to convert external distractions into spiritual opportunities and provided a pair of aging and ill women a sense of power over forces beyond their control. Six years prior, the Fields' Catholicism helped preserve Paragon in the face of death; now, despite encroaching noise and smells, it could help retain for them Paragon's sacramental significance—that is, as a sign of God's presence in their lives.

Despite the Fields' belief in the spiritual value of sensory mortification, they remained devoted to their luxurious surroundings. Edith's interpretation of the motor buses and Germans as God's instruments does, however, betray a guilty suspicion that perhaps the sensual life of an aesthete was incompatible with that of a devoted Catholic. A month later, in September, Edith remarks that Paragon's bedrooms, which she had expensively redecorated, are "a little provoking to the conscience" (28 September, 119). In October, she consults McNabb about her spending, "as from time to time poets spend in their fine frenzy to rebuild their world" (2 October, 131). McNabb puts her scruples to rest, saying—as he views the pricey new curtains in the bedroom Edith describes as "my gift, my gilded cage for the loved Michael" (128)—that "the Thames is worthy to be framed in silk" (131).

Perhaps one of the most surprising things about *Works and Days* is the marked contrast between the 1906 entries—the year of Whym Chow's death—and the entries Katherine pens in the wake of Edith's death in December 1913. While the dog's death utterly prostrated the Fields, Katherine's reaction to the loss of her life partner is, as recorded in the journals, resigned and peaceful in comparison. Whym Chow's death sent the Fields flying from their beloved home, but Edith's death compelled Katherine to embrace Paragon all the more. Paragon seems to have provided Katherine with enormous comfort, and her reflections on it suggest that she continued to feel Edith's presence there. Her description of Christmas 1913—written just weeks after Edith's death—contains some interesting parallels to the Fields' entry from Christmas Day 1906, when Whym seemed present in spirit, if not in body. By this time, Katherine's own cancer (which she never disclosed to Edith) is at an advanced stage. Katherine spends part of her holiday with her nurse, an Irish nun whose blue veil, as the diary records, Edith would have liked, as it is "so harmonious in the lovely rooms of Paragon" (24 December 1913, 98). Even better, the nun expresses intense admiration for the Fields' beautiful home:

And of Christmas Day!

And then Nursie comes. I walk with afterwards in the fresh terrace-gardens. It is sweet. Then I return + read Matins. I just turn a little sick at the turkey, and wisely betake myself after dinner at once to writing letters. Asleep—the Blue Light returns—she is full of the dancing of the Novices—the White Doves—with their exquisite step-dancing. I order her tea in the Sun-Room. And then, Hennie My Beloved, she kindles to all the beauty thou has built for us in Paragon—[. . .] the flowers, the soft colouring the charm. [. . .] our rooms—the sun-room, the river-room, the gold room, the little gold-room. And thus, tho' she is come to dress a deadly wound I have given her delight, +, coupled with the dancing novices, she has had a gay Christmas Day. (99)

Katherine does not go so far as to say that *she* enjoyed Christmas day; the nun's enjoyment seems enough, especially as it is due, in part, to Edith's tasteful decorating. The nun's admiration of Paragon seems a further confirmation, for Katherine, that Edith's devotion to beauty still bears living fruit; one wonders whether the nun even reminds Katherine a little of Edith (although according to Donoghue, this nun got overly attached to Katherine and had to be discharged [139]). Throughout this period, she writes to Edith as if she were still reading her journals, and—as with Whym Chow later in 1906—implies that Edith is continually present in Paragon. A few weeks after Christmas, she writes: "I cannot tonight suffer the little Blue—my beloved and I must be alone—I will go into the sun room + read with her" (12 January 1914, 6).

One of Katherine's regrets in her final months, in summer 1914, was that she would not have the comfort of dying at Paragon. Emma Donoghue describes how Katherine, having moved to a small cottage in Staffordshire to be near Father Mc Nabb, railed about the ugliness of her surroundings: "Like Oscar Wilde, she was troubled by the décor: 'I am suddenly asked to die in a stuffy Drawing room with a grand piano, & lusters & every form of vulgar & horrible details.' But outside her window was an overgrown lawn, at least, so she made the best of things and named the place 'Paragon Cottage'" (140). Donoghue also mentions how Katherine, in a theological discussion with Fr. John Gray, expressed her difficulty with the notion of Purgatory, and especially the thought that Edith might have to linger there; not knowing Edith's precise fate, she explained, was the difference between "Henry landing in Australia & enjoying the kangaroos, & Henry still tossed on unknown seas" (143). As amusing as this picture is, it seems surprising that Katherine's metaphor for heaven relies on an exotic, outdoor location rather than a comfortable domestic interior. This picture of heaven sharply contrasts with the Fields' representation of it in their many years of journaling. As *Works and Days* indicates, Paragon was their heaven on earth, a paradise presided over by Dionysus, Whym Chow, Jesus, the Virgin Mary, and finally, Edith's beauty-loving spirit.

The fact that Paragon remained sacred to two personalities who might, without exaggeration, be described as fickle and unpredictable is less a testament to the Fields' creativity in decorating or color schemes than it is to another kind of "home renovation." The Fields' attitudes toward, and representations of, Paragon proved highly adaptable, varying in response to the sea changes of death, religious conversion, and urbanization. On one hand, the Fields' flexible attitude toward home highlights their aesthetic creed and their determination to live in love and beauty. But it was also meant to dignify, even sanctify, a domestic situation that many Victorians would have labeled as profane and associated much more readily with hellfire than with heavenly bliss. And in the ever-evolving construction of home, Catholicism was, for the Fields, a vital discursive tool. We have seen, throughout this book, how women writers appropriated Catholic imagery and symbolism to represent *both* the terrifying spectacle of godless homes *and* homes that stand as fortresses (like Wemmick's castle) against the raging forces of secularism, atheism, consumerism, and Modernism. But as the Fields' writings demonstrate particularly well, Catholicism, as the century progresses, does not speak only to those writers wishing to condemn or to deny change. Even though the Fields, in moving from a secular to a religious worldview, seem, at first glance, to reverse the trajectory of their society as a whole, this change had potentially dire implications for both their relationship and their art.[19] Rather than erase their identities and pagan past, however, the Fields found in Catholicism—a religion of paradoxes and contradictions—a means for reconciling past and present, and for enabling personal change while sustaining cherished values and commitments.

---

19. A number of scholars (including Leighton and Vicinus) have suggested that the Fields' religious conversion was bad for their poetry. Perhaps the Fields themselves shared this apprehension (of both creative and personal transformations) in the years leading up to their conversion. In 1904, Katherine, after reading the new biography of Christina Rossetti, writes that "[a]pparently religion was a deteriorating influence on her [. . .] + on her art. [. . .] Woe to the gods that ruined her" (3 February 1904, 26–27). In the same year, Edith presents a rather sinister sketch of her friend, Catholic convert Alice Trusted: "Her face under Catholic direction looked strained and harder—the excitement plays like ignus fatuus round the fatal and cruel conditions of soul" (154).

CONCLUSION

THIS book opened with a discussion of Catholic convert Lady Georgiana Fullerton and closed with a discussion of Catholic converts Katherine Bradley and Edith Cooper. I have already remarked how amusing it might be to see these three writers together at a dinner party. Being denied that opportunity, I have been able, at least, to compare my experiences presenting Fullerton's work in a conference venue, to those I had a few years later, in presenting material from the chapter on Michael Field. When I prepared my conference paper on the Fields, I was a little apprehensive. Even though we now consider homosexual relationships and same-sex domestic partnerships completely normal and unremarkable, I still worried whether or not my conference audience would take the Fields seriously. Even through our twenty-first-century lenses, the Fields can appear undeniably—well, odd. What would my audience make of the fact that Katherine and Edith, in addition to their sexual relationship, were close blood relations? That they were often cloyingly self-absorbed in their insular little home? That their love for their dog, as recorded in their diaries, betrayed some unnervingly erotic undertones? That they mourned for Whym Chow as they would for a departed god or head of state?

My fears were groundless, however; my conference audience, so kind and generous, did *not* laugh when I described Whym's funeral, and they nodded very earnestly when I explained that Edith's love for Chow was "the very core + living of [her] whole heart." What did make me uneasy, though, was a sudden memory of an earlier conference, at which I presented to my audience Lady Georgiana Fullerton's *Lady-Bird*. My audience, although similarly kind and generous, could not resist laughing at the notion that *Lady-Bird*'s heroine, Gertrude, could conquer her adulterous love for Adrien d'Arberg simply by praying about it, or that Fullerton could be so grim and humorless as to keep Gertrude and Adrien from marrying at the end, simply to convey a moral lesson. To many, I suspect, Fullerton's habit of confessing her sins to a priest twice a week would appear more bizarre than the Fields' worship of Whym Chow. And this dramatic difference in the receptions of Lady Georgiana Fullerton and Michael Field reminded me, as I finished up this manuscript, why I had to write this book.

Well over a decade ago, Jenny Franchot—frustrated and deeply disturbed at the lack of serious engagement with religious belief and culture among Americanist literary scholars—queried, "[W]here is religion? Why so invisible?" (834). Franchot argued that in contrast to American culture at large, in which so many public debates were framed "within religious discourses" (833), literary studies treated religion as an "invisible domain." "[R]eligious voices, like certain kinds of shame," she argued, "have become unmentionable. In its place, we talk volubly about conditions of being that [...] have been deemed safer: those of gender, race, and to a significantly lesser extent, class" (837). Much has changed. Since 1995, many fine literary studies—both American and British—have emerged which treat religious experience as a category no less important than race, class, or gender in the creation of literary texts and the representation of individual and group identities. But all too often, our work still betrays our inability, or perhaps our unwillingness, to engage with something that has grown so radically foreign to us.

One reason why today's readers may relate to Michael Field more easily than, say, Lady Georgiana Fullerton or Elizabeth Sewell, is because the Fields had no qualms about customizing their religious beliefs to suit their unique private circumstances. "I'm not religious, but I am spiritual," many of my students say, and this comment seems to imply a distancing from any communal, orthodox worldview, and a simultaneous embrace of self-identity and self-governance. In many ways, the Fields also seem more "spiritual" than "religious," in that Catholicism became, in a sense, one more shade of ink the Fields used to write the poetry of their lives together. What do we do, however, when faced with religious beliefs, such as Fullerton's, Sewell's, or even Charlotte Brontë's, that seem oriented more toward self-constraint and cultural conformity than self-assertion? As this study suggests, such religious beliefs, when examined closely, are often not as limiting as we might expect. And when they are, it is reductive and dishonest to present them otherwise, as if Charlotte Brontë or

Christina Rossetti were just forerunners of radical feminist theologians like Mary Daly. One must accept, finally, that orthodox religious beliefs do not negate the possibility that the writer might still have something worthwhile to say.

The Fields represent the Victorians' worst nightmare in more ways than one. Not just because they embraced homosexuality and rejected conventional marriage and motherhood, but because their highly personalized attitude toward religion was a dramatic departure from earlier understandings of it. I do not wish to make the error of overstating the Fields' individuality in religious matters here, as they subjected themselves to the judgment and moral advice of their confessors, attended Mass regularly, and followed—in letter, if not in spirit—the Catholic Church's teachings on celibacy outside of heterosexual marriage. But their religious sensibilities do provide evidence of a widespread cultural shift over the course of the nineteenth century, a shift from a shared worldview—a tacit public agreement that "God [was] in his heaven and all [was] right with the world"—to the notion of religion as a private and highly personal matter. This attitude, of course, did not emerge in the fin de siècle. Religion had begun its retreat into the private sphere even before the early nineteenth century, when Hannah More depicted Charles and Lucilla's domestic paradise in *Coelebs in Search of a Wife*. Unlike Lucilla, however, Katherine and Edith did not promulgate their beliefs among younger siblings and the community at large—their faith, rather, might be considered a Gnostic creed: available and comprehensible only to a privileged few, namely, two poets and their dog.

This notion of religion as a personal matter may seem liberating, but to many Victorians it was an isolating, solipsistic, chaotic, and untenable state of affairs. Of course, these fears may be difficult for us to relate to today, especially in the United States, where the separation of church and state, and the civic values of freedom and religious tolerance reinforce assumptions that people get along best when religion remains private. But to witness, in our own times, the cultural panic generated by impending secularism (whether defined as the disappearance of all religious belief, or merely religion's retreat into arbitrary and invisible private realms) one need only pick up a current newspaper or turn on the television. In the United States, of course, we have witnessed a late-twentieth-century Evangelical Protestant revival; for years, the religious right has wielded tremendous political and social influence, often at the expense of strict distinctions between church and state. Europe, in the meantime, has become the backdrop for a "complicated wrestling match involving secularism,

Christianity and Islam" (Shorto 63). Islam is now "the fastest-growing religion in Europe" (Shorto 45) and Pope Benedict XVI, according to Russell Shorto in the 8 April 2007 edition of the *New York Times Magazine*, regards the re-Christianization of Europe as the only corrective to the spread of Islamic radicalism. "Benedict's goal [is to bring] Europe back into the fold and [to make the Church] a mediator between godless secularism and the fervent Islam of many of the Continent's newest residents" (63). In Benedict's view, Muslims are not threatened by Christianity per se, "but by the cynicism of a secularized culture that denies its own foundations" (Ratzinger qtd. in Shorto 44).

A remarkable facet of this contemporary religious/secular "wrestling match" is the emphasis placed on women and gender roles. In Victorian England, the figure of the middle-class woman was co-opted by both Protestants and Catholics anxious about the erosion of traditional religious worldviews. In the twenty-first century, women remain central to debates about secularism and belief. Shorto notes that Benedict's call for Europeans to turn back to Catholicism may be thwarted by his lack of "interest in reforming some of the basic policies affecting the lives of ordinary Catholics" (63), in particular, policies relating to sexuality and reproduction. Most feminists, of course, are hardly pleased with traditional Catholic teachings on birth control and abortion. The Church's continued refusal to ordain women, moreover, further alienates feminists, and it also exacerbates the dire shortage of Catholic clergy worldwide. In Islam, even more so than in Catholicism, women's roles are also fraught with controversy. Just as the Catholic nun elicited different responses from different religious groups in England, the Islamic woman—and in particular, the Islamic woman in hijab—represents very different things to different cultures. Jane Freedman, in her analysis of contemporary European efforts to ban public wearing of the hijab, points out that "the discourse surrounding these policies and legislation is often framed in terms of a defence of the rights of Muslim women against the patriarchal order which requires them to cover their heads" (29). But more than a threat to Western notions of gender equality, traditionally dressed Muslim women have also been represented as "agents of 'fundamentalism' or 'terrorism,' and as indicators of the inassimilable nature of Muslims in Europe" (30). For Muslim communities, and Muslim women who choose to wear headscarves, however, this item of dress is not "a symbol of religious fundamentalism, but [. . .] something with many more varied meanings" (41), such as an affirmation of cultural identity, or even a source of "empowerment," in that it allows women to move freely through the public sphere (42).

There are, of course, many differences between the respective situations of Catholics and Protestants in England in the nineteenth century, and Catholics, Protestants, secularists, and Muslims in the West today. But it is striking to observe how, in both eras, debates about women's roles and rights become symptomatic of larger anxieties about national security and competing worldviews. Without forcing the comparison too far, it may be safe to suggest that many involved in today's culture wars could relate to the view expressed by John Henry Newman in his *Apologia Pro Vita Sua* (1864), on why he clung to his own worldview:

> I look out of myself into the world of men, and there I see a sight which fills me with unspeakable distress. [. . .] If I looked into a mirror, and did not see my face, I should have the sort of feeling which actually comes upon me, when I look into this living busy world, and see no reflexion of its Creator. [. . .] Were it not for this voice, speaking so clearly in my conscience and my heart, I should be an atheist, or a pantheist, or a polytheist when I looked into the world. [. . .] The sight of the world is nothing else than the prophet's scroll, full of "lamentations, and mourning, and woe."
>
> To consider the world in its length and breadth [. . .] the tokens so faint and broken of a superintending design [. . .] the greatness and littleness of man, his far-reaching aims, his short duration, the curtain hung over his futurity, the disappointments of life, the defeat of good, the success of evil, physical pain, mental anguish, the prevalence and intensity of sin, the pervading idolatries, the corruptions, the dreary hopeless irreligion, that condition of the whole race, so fearfully yet exactly described in the Apostle's words, "having no hope and without God in the world,"—all this is a vision to dizzy and appal [sic]; and inflicts upon the mind the sense of a profound mystery, which is absolutely beyond human solution.
>
> What shall be said to this heart-piercing, reason-bewildering fact? I can only answer, that either there is no Creator, or this living society of men is in a true sense discarded from His presence. [. . .] And so I argue about the world;—*if* there be a God, *since* there is a God, the human race is implicated in some terrible aboriginal calamity. It is out of joint with the purposes of its Creator. (186–87; emphasis in original)

In this passage, Newman paints a sobering picture of his world and hints that it could have led him to abandon religious faith just as easily as it compelled him to embrace it. Newman's words, like this book itself, suggest that religious quests and controversies are far more than arguments for or against the existence of God. They are, on a larger level, reactions to the "unspeakable distress" and the "heart-piercing, bewildering" experience of looking out into a world which contradicts one's cherished perceptions of self, society, and the meaning of human life. In Victorian England, as in many cultures today, one of the most rapid and threatening areas of change has been women's roles and the structure of home and family. It is no accident, therefore, that discourses about social change, religion, and women's roles were—and still are—completely inextricable from each other.

WORKS CITED

Adams, James Eli. *Dandies and Desert Saints: Styles of Victorian Masculinity*. Ithaca, NY: Cornell University Press, 1995.
Adams, Kimberly Van Esveld. *Our Lady of Victorian Feminism*. Athens: Ohio University Press, 2001.
Address to Every Lady in Britain; by a Protestant. London, 1835.
Allchin, A. M. *The Silent Rebellion: Anglican Religious Communities 1845–1900*. London: SCM Press, 1958.
Anson, John S. "The Wind Is Blind: Power and Constraint in the Poetry of Alice Meynell." *Studia Mystica* 9, no. 1 (1986): 37–50.
Anson, Peter F. *The Call of the Cloister: Religious Communities and Kindred Bodies in the Anglican Communion*. London: SPCK, 1955.
Armstrong, John E. *Armstrong's Reply to Wiseman's Pastoral Letter on the Immaculate Conception*. London: Wertheim and Macintosh, 1855.
Arnold, Matthew. *Literature and Dogma*. 1873. London: Ballantyne Press, 1924.
Arnstein, Walter L. *Protestant versus Catholic in Mid-Victorian England: Mr. Newdegate and the Nuns*. Columbia and London: University of Missouri Press, 1982.
Arseneau, Mary. "Incarnation and Interpretation: Christina Rossetti, the Oxford Movement, and *Goblin Market*." *Victorian Poetry* 31, no. 1 (Spring 1993): 79–93.
Auerbach, Nina. *Woman and the Demon: The Life of a Victorian Myth*. Cambridge, MA: Harvard University Press, 1982.
Baker, Joseph Ellis. *The Novel and the Oxford Movement*. 1932. New York: Russell & Russell, 1965.
Barlow, Luke. *Marriage Commended, and Adultery Condemned: A Sermon*. Market Drayton: D. Procter, 1816.
Barrett Browning, Elizabeth. *Aurora Leigh*. Ed. Margaret Reynolds. New York and London: W. W. Norton and Co., 1996.
———. *The Brownings' Correspondence*. Ed. Philip Kelley and Ronald Hudson. 15 vols. Winfield, KS: Wedgestone Press, 1984.
———. *Elizabeth Barrett Browning: Letters to Her Sister, 1846–59*. Ed. Leonard Huxley, LLD. London: John Murray, 1929.

Battiscombe, Georgiana. *Christina Rossetti: A Divided Life.* London: Constable, 1981.

Beer, Gillian. *George Eliot.* Bloomington: Indiana University Press, 1986.

Belaney, Robert. *A Letter to the Lord Bishop of Chichester, Assigning His Reasons for Leaving the Church of England.* London: C. Dolman, 1852.

Bentley, D. M. R. "The Meretricious and the Meritorious in *Goblin Market*: A Conjecture and an Analysis." In *The Achievement of Christina Rossetti*. Ed. David A. Kent. Ithaca, NY and London: Cornell University Press, 1987.

Bernstein, Susan: *Confessional Subjects: Revelations of Gender and Power in Victorian Literature.* Chapel Hill and London: University of North Carolina Press, 1997.

Besant, Annie. *An Autobiography.* 2nd ed. London: T. Fisher Unwin, 1893.

Best, G. F. A. "Popular Protestantism in Victorian Britain." In *Ideas and Institutions of Victorian Britain: Essays in Honour of George Kitson Clark.* Ed. Robert Robson. London: G. Bell & Sons, Ltd., 1967: 115–42.

Bonaparte, Felicia. *The Triptych and the Cross: The Central Myths of George Eliot's Poetic Imagination.* New York: New York University Press, 1979.

The Book of Common Prayer and Administration of the Sacraments & Other Rites and Ceremonies of the Church according to the Use of the Church of England. London: William Pickering, 1844.

Booth, Alison. *Famous Last Words: Changes in Gender and Narrative Closure.* Charlottesville and London: University Press of Virginia, 1993.

Bowles, Emily. "Memorials of John Henry Newman, Cardinal Deacon." Unpublished manuscript, 1883–84. John Henry Newman Papers, St. Philip's Oratory, Birmingham, England.

Bradley, Ian. *The Call to Seriousness: The Evangelical Impact on the Victorians.* London: Jonathan Cape, 1976.

Brockman, H. J. *Letter to the Women of England on the Confessional.* London: Protestant Electoral Union, 1867.

Brontë, Charlotte. *Jane Eyre.* 1847. Ed. Michael Manson. New York and London: Penguin Books, 1996.

——. *Shirley.* 1839. New York: Penguin Classics, 2006.

——. *Villette.* 1853. Ed. Mark Lilly. New York: Penguin Books, 1979.

Bullen, J. B. "George Eliot's *Romola* as a Positivist Allegory." *Review of English Studies,* n.s., 26, No. 104 (November 1975): 425–35. Rpt. in *George Eliot: Critical Assessments.* Vol. 3. Ed. Stuart Hutchinson. Mountfield: Helm Information Ltd., 1996.

Burstein, Miriam Elizabeth. "Protestants against the Jewish and Catholic Family, c. 1829–1860. *Victorian Literature and Culture* (2003): 333–57.

Butler, T. *The Immaculate Conception.* London: J. Miller, 1855.

Bynum, Caroline Walker. *Holy Feast and Holy Fast: The Religious Significance of Food to Medieval Women.* Berkeley: University of California Press, 1987.

Carpenter, Mary Wilson. "'Eat me, drink me, love me': The Consumable Female Body in Christina Rossetti's *Goblin Market*." *Victorian Poetry* 29, no. 4 (Winter 1991): 415–34.

Carson, Alexander. *The Doctrine of Transubstantiation Subversive of the Foundations of Human Belief.* Dublin: Richard More, 1827.

Ceraldi, Gabrielle. "'Popish Legends and Bible Truths': English Protestant Identity in Catherine Sinclair's *Beatrice.*" *Victorian Literature and Culture* 31, no. 1 (March 2003): 359–72.

Chadwick, Owen. *The Victorian Church*. Vol. 2. New York: Oxford University Press, 1970.
Charles, Elizabeth Rundle. *Mary, the Handmaid of the Lord*. London: James Nisbet and Co., 1854.
Christ, Carol. "Victorian Masculinity and the Angel in the House." In *A Widening Sphere: Changing Roles of Victorian Women*. Ed. Martha Vicinus. Bloomington: Indiana University Press, 1977: 146–62.
Clark-Beattie, Rosemary. "Fables of Rebellion: Anti-Catholicism and the Structure of *Villette*." *ELH* 53, no. 4 (Winter 1986): 821–47.
Clowes, John. *The Golden Wedding-Ring; or, Thoughts on Marriage, in a Conversation between a Father and His Two Children*. Manchester: J. Gleaye, 1813.
Cobbe, Frances Power. *Life of Frances Power Cobbe, by herself*. London: Richard Bentley and Son, 1894.
Cohen, Monica. *Professional Domesticity in the Victorian Novel: Women, Work, and Home*. Cambridge and New York: Cambridge University Press, 1998.
Colby, Vineta. *Yesterday's Woman: Domestic Realism in the English Novel*. Princeton, NJ: Princeton University Press, 1974.
Coleridge, Christabel. *Charlotte Mary Yonge: Her Life and Letters*. London: Macmillan and Co., 1903.
Coleridge, Henry James., trans. *Life of Lady Georgiana Fullerton*. 2nd ed. By Mrs. Augustus Craven. London: Richard Bentley & Son, 1888.
"The Confraternity of La Salette." *Edinburgh Review* 106 (1857): 1–26.
Considerations on Marriage, Addressed to Christian Professors. London: Wright and Albright, 1840.
Cooper, Helen. *Elizabeth Barrett Browning, Woman and Artist*. Chapel Hill and London: University of North Carolina Press, 1988.
Cusack, Margaret Frances. *Five Years in a Protestant Sisterhood and Ten Years in a Roman Catholic Convent*. London: Longmans, Green, & Co., 1869.
D'Amico, Diane. *Christina Rossetti: Faith, Gender, and Time*. Baton Rouge: Louisiana State University Press, 1999.
Dammast, Jeanie Selina. *St. Mary's Convent; or, Chapters in the Life of a Nun*. London: S. W. Partridge, 1866.
Davidoff, Leonore, and Catherine Hall. *Family Fortunes: Men and Women of the English Middle Class: 1750–1850*. Chicago: University of Chicago Press, 1987.
De Montfort, Louis. *True Devotion to Mary*. Trans. Frederick Faber, 1862. Rockford, IL: Tan Books and Publishers, 1941.
Dick, Alexander. *Reasons for Embracing the Catholic Faith. By a Convert*. Edinburgh: James Marshall; London: Doman, Jones, and Burns, 1848.
Dickens, Charles. *Our Mutual Friend*. London: Chapman & Hall, 1865.
Doctrine of Transubstantiation Refuted, And Proved by Scripture and Reason to be Anti-Scriptural, Irrational, and of Human Invention. By a Layman. London: T. C. Savill, 1838.
Dodsworth, William. *Discourses on the Lord's Supper. Preached in Margaret Chapel, St. Marylebone*. 2nd ed. London: James Burns, 1836.
Dolan, Frances. *Whores of Babylon: Catholicism, Gender and Seventeenth-Century Print Culture*. Ithaca, NY: Cornell University Press, 1999.
Donoghue, Emma. *We Are Michael Field*. Bath, Somerset: Absolute Press, 1998.

Eliot, George. *Adam Bede*. 1859. Ed. Stephen Gill. New York: Penguin Classics, 1980.

———. "GE to Mme Eugène Bodichon." 26 December 1860. In *The George Eliot Letters*. Vol. 3. Ed. Gordon S. Haight. New Haven, CT: Yale University Press, 1954.

———. "GE to Mrs. Richard Congreve." 4–6 April 1860. In *The George Eliot Letters*, vol. 3.

———. *Middlemarch*. 1871–72. Ed. Bert G. Hornbeck. New York and London: W. W. Norton, 2000.

———. *Mill on the Floss*. 1860. Ed. Gordon S. Haight. Oxford: Clarendon Press, 1980.

———. *Romola*. 1862–63. Ed. Andrew Brown. New York and Oxford: Oxford University Press, 1998.

———. "Silly Novels by Lady Novelists." *Westminster Review* 66 (October 1856): 442–61.

Ellis, Sarah Stickney. *The Daughters of England, Their Society, Character, and Responsibilities*. 1842. New York, 1843.

Endell, Tyler J. *Image-Worship in the Church of Rome Proved to Be Contrary to Holy Scripture*. London: Francis and John Rivington, 1847.

Evans, John. *The Origin and Progress of Mariolatry*. London: William Edward Painter, 1852.

Field, Michael. "Works and Days." Unpublished manuscript volumes, 1968–1914. Microfilm access under *Michael Field and Fin-de-Siècle Culture and Society: The Journals, 1868–1914, and the Correspondence of Katherine Bradley and Edith Cooper from the British Library, London*. Add Mss. 46776–46804, 45851–45856, and 46866–46897.

———. *Works and Days: From the Journal of Michael Field*. Ed. T. and D. C. Sturge Moore. London: John Murray, 1933.

Fordyce, James. *Sermons to Young Women*. 1766. Third American from the Twelfth London edition. Philadelphia: M. Carey, 1809.

Formby, Henry. *Our Lady of La Salette*. London: Burns and Lambert, 1857.

Fortier, Wolfgang J. *Our Lady of La Salette*. London: Burns Oates & Washbourne Ltd., 1931.

Foster, Shirley. "Two against Rome: A Family Contribution to Victorian Anti-Catholic Fiction." *Durham University Journal* 44 (1977): 255–62.

———. *Victorian Women's Fiction: Marriage, Freedom, and the Individual*. London and Sydney: Croom Helm, 1985.

Foucault, Michel. *The History of Sexuality*. Trans. Robert Hurley. New York: Pantheon Books, 1978.

Franchot, Jenny. "Invisible Domain: Religion and American Literary Studies." *American Literature* 67 (December 1995): 833–42.

———. *Roads to Rome: The Antebellum Protestant Encounter with Catholicism*. Berkeley and London: University of California Press, 1994.

Freedman, Jane. "Women, Islam and Rights in Europe: Beyond a Universalist/Culturalist Dichotomy." *Review of International Studies* 33 (January 2007): 29–44.

Fullerton, Lady Georgiana. *Ellen Middleton. A Tale*. 3 vols. London: Moxon, 1844.

———. *Lady-Bird. A Tale*. 3 vols. London: Edward Moxon, 1852.

Gaskell, Elizabeth. *Cranford*. 1853. Ed. Patricia Ingham. New York: Penguin Classics, 2006.

———. *The Life of Charlotte Bronte*. 1857. Ed. and intro. Winifred Gérin. London: Folio Society, 1971.

Gilbert, Sandra, and Susan Gubar. *The Madwoman in the Attic: The Woman Writer and the Nineteenth-Century Literary Imagination*. 2nd ed. New Haven, CT: Yale University Press, 1979.
Gill, Gillian. *Nightingales: The Extraordinary Upbringing and Curious Life of Miss Florence Nightingale*. New York: Random House Trade Paperbacks, 2005.
Gladstone, William. Rev. of *Ellen Middleton*, by Lady Georgiana Fullerton. *English Review* 1 (1844): 336–61.
Gordon, John. *Reasons of My Conversion to the Catholic Church*. London: James Burns, 1849.
Gray, F. Elizabeth. "Making Christ: Alice Meynell, Poetry, and the Eucharist." *Christianity and Literature* 52, no. 2 (Winter 2003): 159–79.
Greenstein, Susan M. "The Question of Vocation: from *Romola* to *Middlemarch*." *Nineteenth Century Fiction* 35 (March 1984): 487–505.
Griffin, Susan M. *Anti-Catholicism and Nineteenth-Century Fiction*. Cambridge and New York: Cambridge University Press, 2004.
Hanson, Ellis. *Decadence and Catholicism*. Cambridge, MA: Harvard University Press, 1997.
Harpham, Geoffrey Galt. *The Ascetic Imperative in Culture and Criticism*. Chicago and London: University of Chicago Press, 1987.
Harrison, Carol E. "Zouave Stories: Gender, Catholic Spirituality and French Responses to the Roman Question." *Journal of Modern History* 79 (2007): 274–305.
Hawtrey, C. S. *The Mystery of Iniquity, or, A Warning to Protestants. A Sermon, preached on Sunday, November 5, 1826. At the Episcopal Jews' Chapel, Cambridge Heath*. London: L. B. Seeley and Son, 1827.
Heimann, Mary. *Catholic Devotion in Victorian England*. Oxford: Clarendon Press, 1995.
"The Heroine of La Salette." *The Times*, 28 December 1854, p. 8, col. d.
Herringer, Carol Engelhardt. *Victorians and the Virgin Mary: Religion and Gender in England 1830–1885*. Manchester: Manchester University Press, 2008.
Hogan, William. *Auricular Confession and Popish Nunneries*. 4th ed. London: Arthur Hall; Liverpool: Edward Howell, 1848.
Hollis, Hilda. "The Other Side of Carnival: Romola and Bakhtin." *Papers on Language and Literature* 37, no. 3 (2001): 227–54.
Homans, Margaret. *Bearing the Word: Language and Female Experience in Nineteenth-Century Women's Writing*. Chicago and London: University of Chicago Press, 1986.
Hook, Walter Farquhar. *Auricular Confession: A Sermon*. London: F. & J. Rivington, 1848.
———. *The Mother of Our Lord, and Mariolatry. A Sermon*. London: F. and J. Rivington, 1847.
———. *Peril of Idolatry: A Sermon*. London: J. G. F. & J. Rivington, 1842.
Horne, Rev. Melville. *The Great Mass Idol*. Manchester: Joseph Pratt, 1822.
Irons, Joseph. *Beware of Idolatry. A Sermon*. N.p., 1845.
Jackson, Thomas. *Marriage and Adultery Considered: A Sermon*. Chelsea: J. Tilling, 1810.
Jackson, Vanessa Furse. "'Tides of the Mind': Restraint and Renunciation in the Poetry of Alice Meynell." *Victorian Poetry* 36, no. 4 (1998): 443–74.
Jaeger, Kathleen. "Lady Georgiana Fullerton (1812–1885): A Reassessment." Diss. Halifax University, 1985.

James, John Angell. *Sermons to Young Women*. London, 1852.
James, William. *Varieties of Religious Experience*. 1902. Cambridge, MA and London: Harvard University Press, 1985.
Jay, Elisabeth. *The Religion of the Heart: Anglican Evangelicalism and the Nineteenth-Century Novel*. Oxford: Clarendon Press, 1979.
Jay, William. *The Mutual Duties of Husbands and Wives: A Sermon, Occasioned by the Marriage of Robert Spear, Esq*. 3rd ed. London: C. Whittingham, 1801.
Kaplan, Cora. "Aurora Leigh." In *Feminist Criticism and Social Change*. Ed. Judith Newton and Deborah Resenfelt. New York and London: Methuen, 1985: 134–64.
Kaufman, Suzanne K. *Consuming Visions: Mass Culture and the Lourdes Shrine*. Ithaca, NY and London: Cornell University Press, 2005.
Keane, W. *Romanism and Hinduism*. Dublin: George Herbert; London: Seeleys, 1852.
Keble, John. *The Christian Year: Thoughts in Verse for Sundays and Holydays throughout the Year*. 1827. London: Frederick Warne, 1880.
Kennedy, Grace. *Father Clement*. 1823. New York: Garland Publishers, 1976.
Kenyon, Frederick G., ed. *The Letters of Elizabeth Barrett Browning*. London: Smith, Elder and Co., 1898.
King, Rev. John. *The Real Presence of Christ in the Sacrament of the Lord's Supper. A Sermon Preached in Christ's Church, Hull, August 20th, 1843*. Seeley, Burnside and Seely, n.d.
Knopfelmacher, U. C. *George Eliot's Early Novels: The Limits of Realism*. Berkeley and Los Angeles: University of California Press, 1968.
Kreuger, Christine L. *The Reader's Repentance: Women Preachers, Women Writers, and Nineteenth-Century Social Discourse*. Chicago and London: University of Chicago Press, 1992.
LaMonaca, Maria. "'Her Director, Her Priest, . . . Her God': Victorian Women Writers on Confession." *Nineteenth Century Studies* 17 (2003): 73–90.
———. "Jane's Crown of Thorns: Feminism and Christianity in *Jane Eyre*." *Studies in the Novel* 34, no. 3 (Fall 2002): 245–63.
———. "Paradise Deferred: Religion, Domesticity, and Realism in the Victorian Novel." Diss. Indiana University, 1999.
———. "Virgins and Martyrs: Heroic Spinsterhood in Elizabeth Missing Sewell's *The Experience of Life*." *Victorians Institute Journal* 30 (2002): 67–89.
Article on La Salette. (Anonymous, untitled.) *The Times*, 22 November 1854, p. 6, col. d.
Lawson, Kate. "Reading Desire: *Villette* as Heretic Narrative." *English Studies in Canada* 17 (March 1991): 53–71.
Lecky, William Edward. *History of European Morals from Augustus to Charlemagne*. 1869. New York: George Braziller, 1955.
Leighton, Angela. *Elizabeth Barrett Browning*. Bloomington: Indiana University Press, 1986.
———. *Victorian Women Poets: Writing against the Heart*. Charlottesville and London: University Press of Virginia, 1992.
"Letters of Elizabeth Barrett Browning and Robert Browning on *Aurora Leigh*." In Elizabeth Barrett Browning, *Aurora Leigh*. Ed. Margaret Reynolds. New York and London: W. W. Norton and Co., 1996.
Levine, Caroline, and Mark W. Turner, eds. *From Author to Text: Re-Reading George Eliot's* Romola. Aldershot and Brookfield, VT: Ashgate, 1998.
Lewis, Agnes Smith. *Select Narratives of Holy Women*. London: C. J. Clay, 1900.

Lewis, Linda M. *Elizabeth Barrett Browning's Spiritual Progress: Face to Face with God.* Columbia and London: University of Missouri Press, 1998.
Linton, Eliza Lynn. *Under Which Lord?* London: Chatto & Windus, 1879.
Lowe, J. B. *The Immaculate Conception. A Lecture.* Liverpool: Adam Reid; London: James Nisbet & Co., 1855.
——. *The Worship of the Virgin Mary, as Held and Practised in the Church of Rome.* Liverpool: Arthur Newling; London: Thomas Hatchard, 1851.
Lowe, Thomas Hill. *Auricular Confession: A Sermon*, 2nd ed. Exeter: A Holden, 1852.
Lucas, Frederick. *Reasons for Becoming a Roman Catholic: Addressed to the Society of Friends.* London: Charles Dolman, 1839.
Lyons, Rev. John. "The Sacrifice of the Mass." In *A Course of Sermons on the Principal Errors of the Church of Rome; Preached in St. Andrew's Church, Liverpool, by Ten Clergymen of the Church of England.* London: J. Hatchard and Son; A Newling, Liverpool, 1838: 297–339.
Maison, Margaret. *Search Your Soul, Eustace: A Survey of the Religious Novel in the Victorian Age.* London: Sheed & Ward, 1961.
Maitland, Charles. *The Church in the Catacombs.* London: Longman & Co., 1846.
Marriott, Harvey. *Sermons on the Character and Duties of Women.* London: J. Hatchard and Son, 1832.
Marsh, Jan. *Christina Rossetti: A Literary Biography.* London: Pimlico, 1994.
Marshall, Linda E. "'Transfigured to His Likeness': Sensible Transcendentalism in Christina Rossetti's 'Goblin Market.'" *University of Toronto Quarterly* 63, no. 3 (Spring 1994): 429–50.
Maxwell, Catherine. "Tasting the 'Fruit Forbidden': Gender, Intertextuality, and Christina Rossetti's *Goblin Market.*" In *The Culture of Christina Rossetti: Female Poetics and Victorian Contexts.* Ed. Mary Arseneau, Antony H. Harrison, and Lorraine Janzen Kooistra. Athens: Ohio University Press, 1999: 75–102.
McDonnell, T. M. *Letters on the Confessional: Addressed to the Editor of the Plymouth Journal.* Plymouth: I. Latimer, 1851.
Mermin, Dorothy. *Elizabeth Barrett Browning: The Origins of a New Poetry.* Chicago and London: University of Chicago Press, 1989.
Meynell, Viola. *Alice Meynell: A Memoir.* London: Jonathan Cape, 1929.
Michelet, Jules. *The Confessional and the Conventual System: Extracted from Michelet's "Priests, Women, and Families"* [1845]. London: Seelys, 1850.
Millett, Kate. "Sexual Politics in *Villette.*" In *Villette.* Ed. Pauline Nestor. New York: St. Martin's Press, 1992.
M'Neile, Hugh. "The Characteristics of Romanism and Protestantism, as Developed in Their Respective Teachings and Worship." In *Lectures to Young Men, Delivered before the Young Men's Christian Association.* London: William Jones, 1849.
Moglen, Helene. *Charlotte Brontë: The Self Conceived.* New York: W. W. Norton, 1976.
More, Hannah. *Coelebs in Search of a Wife.* 1808. Ed. Mary Waldron. London: Thoemmes Press, 1995.
Morris, Kevin L. "John Bull and the Scarlet Woman: Charles Kingsley and Anti-Catholicism in Victorian Literature." *Recusant History* 23 (October 1996): 190–218.
Mumm, Susan. *Stolen Daughters, Virgin Mothers: Anglican Sisterhoods in Victorian Britain.* London and New York: Leicester University Press, 1999.
Newman, John Henry. *Apologia pro Vita Sua.* 1864. Ed. David DeLaura. New York: W. W. Norton, 1968.

———. *Callista: A Tale of the Third Century.* 1853. London, 1898.

———. "The History of a Conversion to the Catholic Faith, in the Years 1840–44, Exhibited in a Series of Letters." Unpublished manuscript. John Henry Newman Papers, St. Philip's Oratory, Birmingham, England.

———, ed. *The Lives of the English Saints.* Vols. 1–6. 1844–45. Whitefish, MT: Kessinger Publishing, 2006.

The New Testament, Revised Standard Version. New York: American Bible Society, 1980.

Nicholson, J. Aldwell. *The Mass in Bayswater. Lectures on the False Doctrines of the Romish Altar.* London: Judd & Glass, 1859.

Nightingale, Florence. *Suggestions for Thought.* Ed. Michael D. Calabria and Janet A. Macrae. Philadelphia: University of Pennsylvania Press, 1994.

Nockles, Peter Benedict. *The Oxford Movement in Context: Anglican High Churchmanship, 1760–1857.* Cambridge and New York: Cambridge University Press, 1994.

Nolan, Rev. Thomas. *Transubstantiation.* In *Protestant Lectures on the Errors and Abuses of Romanism.* London: A. M. Pigott, 1851: 177–220.

Norman, Edward. *The English Catholic Church in the Nineteenth Century.* New York: Clarendon Press, 1984.

Norman, Edward R. *Anti-Catholicism in Victorian England.* New York: Barnes and Noble, 1968.

Northcote, J. Spencer. *A Pilgrimage to La Salette.* London: Burns and Lambert, 1852.

O'Malley, Patrick R. *Catholicism, Sexual Deviance, and Victorian Gothic Culture.* Cambridge and New York: Cambridge University Press, 2006.

Paphnutius, Junior. *The Cannibal Church; or, Theo-Anthropophagan Religion.* London: Sold by William Alley, 1851.

Parkes, Bessie Rayner. Letter to Barbara Bodichon. August 1861. BRP 10 6/2. Papers of Bessie Rayner Parkes, Girton College Library, Cambridge University.

———. Letter [fragment]. June 1865. BRP X 31. Papers of Bessie Rayner Parkes.

Paz, D. G. *Popular Anti-Catholicism in Mid-Victorian England.* Stanford: Stanford University Press, 1992.

Penny, Anne Judith. *The Afternoon of Unmarried Life.* London: Longman & Co., 1858.

Peschier, Diana. *Nineteenth-Century Anti-Catholic Discourses: The Case of Charlotte Brontë.* Houndmills, Basingstoke, Hampshire; and New York: Palgrave Macmillan, 2005.

Poe, Edgar Allan. *Marginalia.* Vol. 17 of *The Complete Works of Edgar Allan Poe.* Ed. James A. Harrison. New York: AMS Press, 1965.

Polhemus, Robert M. *Erotic Faith: Being in Love from Jane Austen to D. H. Lawrence.* Chicago and London: University of Chicago Press, 1990.

Poovey, Mary. *The Proper Lady and the Victorian Woman Writer. Ideology as Style in the Works of Mary Wollstonecraft, Mary Shelley, and Jane Austen.* Chicago: Chicago University Press, 1984.

———. *Uneven Developments: The Ideological Work of Gender in Victorian England.* Chicago: Chicago University Press, 1988.

"Popery Like Paganism." In *Lectures to Young Men, Delivered before the Young Men's Christian Association.* London: William Jones, 1849.

Powell, H. T. *Merchandize of Souls: or the Money Method of Salvation in the Church of Rome.* London: Painter; Coventry: Charles A. N. Rollason, 1845.

Prescott, Joseph. "Jane Eyre: A Romantic Exemplum with a Difference." In *Twelve*

Original Essays on Great English Novels. Ed. Charles Shapiro. Detroit: Wayne State University Press, 1960.

The Priest and the Lady; or, Transubstantiation Exposed. London: Printed for the Protestant Evangelical Mission, n.d.

Procter, Adelaide. Undated letter to Bessie Rayner Parkes. BRP VIII 37. Bessie Rayner Parkes Papers, Girton College Library, Cambridge University.

"Protestant Authors and Publishers, and Catholic Readers." *The Rambler*, August 1853: 93–105.

Qualls, Barry V. *The Secular Pilgrims of Victorian Fiction: The Novel as Book of Life*. New York: Cambridge University Press, 1982.

Raverat, Gwen Darwin. *Period Piece: A Cambridge Childhood*. London: Faber, 1952.

Reed, John Shelton. *Glorious Battle: The Cultural Politics of Anglo-Catholicism*. Nashville, TN and London: Vanderbilt University Press, 1995.

Rev. of *Ivors*, and other Tales, by the Author of *Amy Herbert* [Elizabeth Missing Sewell]. *Christian Remembrancer* 33 (1857): 291–349.

Rev. of *Lady-Bird*, by Lady Georgiana Fullerton, and *Villette*, by Currer Bell. *Christian Remembrancer* 25 (1853): 401–43.

Rich, Adrienne. "Jane Eyre: The Temptations of a Motherless Woman." *Ms.*, October 1973: 89–106.

Richardson, Eliza Smith. *Five Years a Catholic: with incidents of foreign convent life*. London: Walsall, 1864.

———. *The Veil Lifted: The Romance and Reality of Convent Life*. London, 1865.

Ritchie, Anne. "Toilers and Spinsters." *Cornhill Magazine* 3 (1861): 318–31.

Richardson, Samuel. *Clarissa: Or the History of a Young Lady*. 1747–48. Ed. Angus Ross. New York: Penguin Classics, 1986.

Robinson, Carol. "*Romola*: A Reading of the Novel." *Victorian Studies* 6 (1962–63): 29–42. Rpt. in *George Eliot: Critical Assessments*. Vol. 3. Ed. Stuart Hutchinson. Mountfield: Helm Information Ltd., 1996.

Robinson, Henry Crabb. *Henry Crabb Robinson on Books and Their Writers*. Vol. 3. Ed. Edith J. Morley. London: J. M. Dent, 1938.

Robertson, Solveig C. "Lady Georgiana Charlotte Fullerton." In *Oxford Dictionary of National Biography*. Ed. H. C. G. Matthew and Brian Harrison. Vol. 21. New York: Oxford University Press, 2004: 172.

Roden, Frederick S. *Same-Sex Desire in Victorian Religious Culture*. Houndmills, Basingstoke; and New York: Palgrave Macmillan, 2002.

Rossetti, Christina. *Called to Be Saints: The Minor Festivals Devotionally Studied*. London: SPCK, 1881. Bristol, England: Thoemmes Press, and Tokyo, Japan: Edition Synapse, 2003.

———. *The Face of the Deep: A Devotional Commentary on the Apocalypse*. London: SPCK; New York: E. & J. B. Young and Co., 1892.

———. *Goblin Market*. 1862. In *Christina Rossetti: The Complete Poems*. Ed. R. W. Crump. London and New York: Penguin Books, 2001: 5–20.

———. *Seek and Find: A Double Series of Short Studies of the Benedicte*. London: SPCK, 1879.

———. *Time Flies: A Reading Diary*. London: SPCK, 1885.

———. "A Triad." 1862. In *Christina Rossetti: The Complete Poems*. Ed. R. W. Crump. London and New York: Penguin Books, 2001: 23.

Russell, C. W. Rev. of *Priests, Women, and Families*, by Jules Michelet. *Dublin Review*

19 (December 1845): 458–518.
Sandeman, Robert. *The Honour of Marriage Opposed to All Impurities: An Essay*. Edinburgh: G. Caw, 1800.
Saville, Julia F. "The Poetic Imaging of Michael Field." In *The Fin-de-Siècle Poem: English Literary Culture and the 1890s*. Ed. Joseph Bristow. Athens: Ohio University Press, 2005: 178–206.
Schaeffer, Talia. *The Forgotten Female Aesthetes: Literary Culture in Late-Victorian England*. Charlottesville and London: University Press of Virginia, 2000.
Schiefelbein, Michael. *The Lure of Babylon: Seven Protestant Novelists and Britain's Roman Catholic Revival*. Macon, GA: Mercer University Press, 2001.
Scott, Benjamin. *The Content and Teachings of the Catacombs at Rome*. London: Working Men's Educational Union, 1853.
Scott, Patrick. "Genre, Perspective and Opinion in the Study of Victorian Ideology: The Case of Elizabeth Missing Sewell." *Philological Association of the Carolinas* 1 (1983): 15–26.
Sewell, Elizabeth Missing. *The Autobiography of Elizabeth M. Sewell*. Ed. Eleanor L. Sewell. London: Longmans, Green and Co., 1907.
———. *The Experience of Life*. London: Longman, Brown, Green, and Longmans, 1853.
———. *Ivors*. 2 volumes. London: Longman, Brown, Green, Longmans, & Roberts, 1856.
———. *Margaret Percival*. London: Longman, Brown, Green, & Longmans, 1847.
———. *Ursula; A Tale of Country Life*. London and New York: D. Appleton, 1858.
Seymour, M. Hobart. *Nunneries. A Lecture*. Third Thousand. Bath and London, 1852.
Shelley, Mary. *Frankenstein*. 1818. Ed. J. Paul Hunter. New York and London: W. W. Norton, 1995.
Sherwood, Mary Martha. *The Nun*. London: RB Seeley & Burnside; and LB Seeley & Sons, 1833.
Shorter, Clement K. *The Brontës and Their Circle*. 1896. London: J. M. Dent, 1918.
Shorto, Russell. "Keeping the Faith." *New York Times Magazine* (8 April 2007): 39–63.
Sinclair, Catherine. *Beatrice, or, The Unknown Relatives*. 1852. New York and London: Garland Publishing, 1975.
———. Letter to J. G. Lockhart, 7 January 1852. MS 930, folio 120, National Library of Scotland.
Singleton, John. "The Virgin Mary and Religious Conflict in Victorian Britain." *Journal of Ecclesiastical History* 43, no. 1 (1992): 16–34.
Smith, Charles Bird.. *Mariolatry; or, The Romish Worship of Mary. A Lecture, Delivered before the Islington Protestant Institute, 1849*. London: J. H. Jackson; Seeleys; and Hatchards, n.d.
———. *Transubstantiation Tried by Scripture and Reason*. 2nd ed. London: Hatchards, Piccadilly; Nisbet, Berners-Street; Reading: Welch, Duke-Street, 1839.
Smith, Naomi Royde. *The State of Mind of Mrs. Sherwood*. London: Macmillan & Co. Ltd., 1946.
Some Observations on the Doctrine of the Immaculate Conception, Showing the Results of Its Being Admitted. Dublin: George Herbert, 1855.
Spencer, Rev. John Ward. *The Real Presence in the Heart, Not in the Elements*. London: John Crockford; Taunton, W. A. Woodley, 1853.
"The Spinster's Dream." London: W. Kent & Co., 1869.

Stallybrass, Peter, and Allon White. *The Politics and Poetics of Transgression.* Ithaca, NY: Cornell University Press, 1986.
Stephenson, Glennis. *Elizabeth Barrett Browning and the Poetry of Love.* Ann Arbor and London: UMI Research Press, 1989.
Stern, Rebecca F. "'Adulterations Detected': Food and Fraud in Christina Rossetti's 'Goblin Market.'" *Nineteenth-Century Literature* 54, no. 4 (Spring 2003): 477–511.
Stone, Marjorie. *Elizabeth Barrett Browning.* New York: St. Martin's Press, 1995.
Stothert, J. A. "Living Novelists." *Rambler* 1 (January 1854): 41–51.
Sturgeon, Mary. *Michael Field.* London: George G. Harrap & Co., 1922.
Sturrock, June. *"Heaven and Home": Charlotte M. Yonge's Domestic Fiction and the Victorian Debate over Women.* Victoria, B.C.: University of Victoria, English Literary Studies, 1995.
Sugg, Joyce. *Ever Yours Affly: John Henry Newman and His Female Circle.* Trowbridge, Wiltshire: Redwood Books, 1996.
Tatam, Rev. W. K. *Transubstantiation. A Sermon.* Preston: H. C. Barton, 1851.
Taylor, Fanny M. [Mother Mary Magdalen Taylor]. *The Inner Life of Lady Georgiana Fullerton, with Notes of Retreat and Diary.* London: Burns & Oates; New York and Cincinnati, OH: Benziger, 1899.
———. "Miss Sewell and Miss Yonge." Rev. of *The Experience of Life* and *Ursula* by Elizabeth Missing Sewell, and *The Heir of Redclyffe* by Charlotte Yonge. *Dublin Review* 45 (December 1858): 313–28.
Teodor, John. *Eliza Barry, the Child of a Cloister.* London: Houlston & Stoneman, James Paul; Derby, G. Wilkins and Son, 1850.
Thain, Maron. "'Damnable Aestheticism' and the Turn to Rome: John Gray, Michael Field, and a Poetics of Conversion." In *The Fin-de-Siècle Poem: English Literary Culture and the 1890s.* Ed. Joseph Bristow. Athens: Ohio University Press, 2005: 311–36.
Tonna, Charlotte Elizabeth. *Personal Recollections.* 4th ed. London: Seeleys, 1854.
Tonna, Charlotte Elizabeth, and L. H. J. Tonna. *Life of Charlotte Elizabeth, as Contained in Her Personal Recollections, with Explanatory Notes; and a Memoir, Embracing the Period from the Close of Personal Recollections to Her Death.* New York: W. W. Dodd, 1851.
Tormey, Michael. *The Immaculate Conception: An Essay.* Dublin: James Duffy, 1855.
Transubstantiation, Host-Worship, Mass-Sacrifice, and Half-Communion. London: British Society for Promoting the Religious Principles of the Reformation, 1842.
Ullathorne, William Bernard. *The Holy Mountain of La Salette: A Pilgrimage of the Year 1854.* London: Richardson and Sons, 1854.
———. *Letters on La Salette, in Reply to Articles in the* Edinburgh Review *and* Rambler. London: Burns and Lambert, 1858.
———. *A Plea for the Rights and Liberties of Religious Women, with Reference to the Bill Proposed by Mr. Lacy.* London: Derby printed, 1851.
Vadillo, Ana Parejo. *Women Poets and Urban Aestheticism: Passengers of Modernity.* Basingstoke, Hampshire; and New York: Palgrave Macmillan, 2005.
Vanita, Ruth. *Sappho and the Virgin Mary: Same-Sex Love and the English Literary Imagination.* New York: Columbia University Press, 1996.
Vejvoda, Kathleen M. "The Dialectic of Idolatry: Roman Catholicism and the Victorian Heroine." Diss. University of Texas at Austin, 2000.
———. "Idolatry in *Jane Eyre.*" *Victorian Literature and Culture* (2003): 241–61.

Vicinus, Martha. *Intimate Friends: Women Who Loved Women: 1778–1928.* Chicago and London: University of Chicago Press, 2004.

Villecourt, Clément. *The Apparition of the Blessed Virgin on the Mountains of the Alps.* London: James Burns, 1849.

Walsh, Walter. *The Secret History of the Oxford Movement.* London: Swan Sonnenschien, 1897.

What Is Romanism? No. IX. On the Worship of the Virgin. London: SPCK, 1846.

Whateley, Richard. *The Errors of Romanism Traced to Their Origin in Human Nature.* London: B. Fellowes, 1830.

Wheeler, Michael. *The Old Enemies: Catholic and Protestant in Nineteenth-Century English Culture.* New York and Cambridge: Cambridge University Press, 2006.

Wilberforce, Samuel. *Rome—Her New Dogma and Our Duties. A Sermon.* Oxford and London: John Henry Parket, 1855.

Wilson, Carus W. *Mariolatry: Correspondence with a Jesuit on the Subject of Mariolatry.* London: Seeley, Jackson, and Halliday, 1856.

Wiseman, Nicholas, Cardinal. *Fabiola; or the Church of the Catacombs.* 1854. Philadelphia: H. L. Kilner & Co., n.d.

———. *Pastoral Letter of His Eminence Cardinal Wiseman, Archbishop of Westminster, Announcing the Definition of the Immaculate Conception of the Blessed Virgin Mary.* London: T. Jones and Co., 1855.

———. *The Real Presence of the Body and Blood of Our Lord Jesus Christ in the Blessed Eucharist, Proved from Scripture.* In Eight Lectures. London: Joseph Brooker, 1836.

Wolff, Robert Lee. *Gains and Losses: Novels of Faith and Doubt in Victorian England.* New York and London, 1977.

Wordsworth, Christopher. *On "The Immaculate Conception."* N.p., 1857.

Wyschogorod, Edith. *Saints and Postmodernism: Revisioning Moral Philosophy.* Chicago and London: University of Chicago Press, 1990.

Yonge, Charlotte. *The Daisy Chain.* 1856. London: Macmillan, 1879.

Zimdars-Scwartz, Sandra L. *Encountering Mary: From La Salette to Medjugore.* Princeton, NJ: Princeton University Press, 1991.

Zonana, Joyce. "'The Embodied Muse': Elizabeth Barrett Browning's *Aurora Leigh* and Feminist Poetics." *Tulsa Studies in Women's Literature* 8, no. 2 (Fall 1989): 243–59. Rpt. in Elizabeth Barrett Browning, *Aurora Leigh.* Ed. Margaret Reynolds. New York and London: W. W. Norton and Co., 1996: 520–33.

INDEX

Adam Bede (George Eliot), 10, 106n10
aestheticism, 190–91, 196n9, 204
Afternoon of Unmarried Life (Anne Judith Penny), 123–24
agnosticism, 3, 172, 174
Angel in the House, 54
Anglicanism, 39, 98n3; Anglo-Catholic movement within, 9n7; in *Aurora Leigh* (Barrett Browning), 138; conflict with R. Catholicism, 38; Evangelicalism within, 12n11, 41; of G. Fullerton, 27; in *Margaret Percival* (Sewell), 24, 154; 38; practice of confession within, 70n2, 71n4, 74, 79; of C. Rossetti, 152n19, 153n20; sisterhoods and, 103n7; and views of the Eucharist, 128n3, 129. *See also* Church of England
anthropomorphism, 178
Apologia Pro Vita Sua (John Henry Newman), 211
Armstrong, John, 164
Arnold, Matthew: *Literature and Dogma*, 178
asceticism: in *Aurora Leigh* (Barrett Browning), 149–50; in Catholicism 14, 124; in description of J. H. Newman, 25; and domesticity, 10; in *Jane Eyre* (Brontë), 44–46, 52, 55, 106; in *Lady-Bird* (Fullerton), 61; practiced by G. Fullerton 36n3, 76; quality of sainthood, 176; as self-assertion, 117n19

Assumption, Catholic feast of, 91
atheism: Catholicism as, 1, 3; cultural anxieties about, 29, 98, 196, 206; domesticity as, 5; J. H. Newman and, 211; transubstantiation and, 131; Virgin Mary and, 161, 164, 168, 170
Aurora Leigh (Elizabeth Barrett Browning), 18, 20, 29, 126–27, 128n1, 133n7, 134, 136, 138, 139n12, 141, 144–47, 150, 151, 158

Bakhtin, Mikhail, 177
Baptism, 47. *See also* sacramentalism
Barlow, Luke, 40
Barrett Browning, Elizabeth, 23, 128n1; attitude towards Catholicism, 134n8, 135, 136n9, 171; *Aurora Leigh*, 3–4, 18, 20, 29, 126–27, 143–46, 150; contempt for R. Catholic converts, 148–49; description of E. M. Sewell in correspondence of, 114n7; and Eucharist 159; and female moral agency, 72; influence on C. Rossetti, 151n16; influenced by R. Catholicism, 133; influenced by *Villette* (Brontë), 139n12
Beatrice, or the Unknown Relatives (Catherine Sinclair), 6n4, 14, 17, 72, 98n2, 100, 102–3n6
Belaney, Robert, 22
Benedict XVI, Pope, 210

225

Besant, Annie, 111–12
Blessed Sacrament, 24, 131, 153. *See also* Eucharist
Bodichon, Barbara, 22, 171
Book of Common Prayer, 71n4, 129
bourgeois hysteria, 178
Bowles, Emily, 25–26
Bradley, Katherine, 21, 26, 30, 191n3, *192*, 194–96, 207. *See also* Field, Michael
British Empire, 102. *See also* imperialism
Brockman, H. J., 68, 70, 77
Brontë, Charlotte, 3, 4, 15n14,23, 26, 43n6, 110, 208; comparisons to G. Eliot, 171–72; condemnation of idolatry, 38, 77; criticism of marriage, 34; Evangelical background, 41, 47n9; influence on E. Barrett Browning, 139n12; interest in *Experience of Life*, 116n18; *Jane Eyre*, 18, 20, 27–28, 44, 49, 51; and novelistic convention, 65–66; representations of spinsters, 105–6, 124; as "sick soul," 75–76; similarities to Fullerton, 35–37; 55–56, 68; *Villette*, 69–70, 85–86n10, 92–94, 108, 138
Brontë, Emily, 76
Browning, Robert, 149
Butler, T., 165
Byron, George Gordon, Lord, 84

Called to Be Saints (Christina Rossetti), 153
Callista (John Henry Newman), 109n13, 111–13, 116
cannibalism, 1–2, 132, 162
Carson, Alexander, 131
Catholic Emancipation Act, 9, 14, 111n16
Cavendish, Lady Harriet, 27n18, 34n2
celibacy: Catholic tradition of, 18, 28, 105; as "culturally queer," 96; H. Darwin's and W. Wordsworth's opinions on, 95; in *Experience of Life* (Sewell), 124–25; M. Field's practice of, 209; in organized sisterhoods, 99; Protestant condemnation of, 1n1, 14, 26, 51, 160. *See also* chastity
Chambers, Thomas, 104n8
Charles, Elizabeth Rundle, 165
chastity, 15, 145. *See also* celibacy

Christian Year (John Keble), 109n13
Church of England, 9n6, 71, 111n15, 128–29, 152. *See also* Anglicanism
Clarissa (Samuel Richardson), 140n14
Clough, Arthur Hugh, 147
Clowes, John, 39
Cobbe, Frances Power, 74, 160
Coelebs in Search of a Wife (Hannah More), 40, 42, 195, 209
Collinson, James, 152
communion, 2, 22, 58, 128n1, 130, 133n7, 136–37, 140, 143–45, 153n2, 154, 155n22, 156–59. *See also* Eucharist
confession, 4, 14, 26, 28, 68, 94, 160, 172; among Anglo-Catholics, 9n7, 70n2, 71n4; in *Aurora Leigh* (Barrett Browning), 139–40, 145, 148; in *Ellen Middleton* (Fullerton), 78–81, 83–84, 93n14; and idolatry, 77; negative scholarly interpretations of, 69n1; and Protestant-Catholic controversy, 72n5; in *Romola* (Eliot), 176; and the "sick soul," 73–76; in *Villette* (Brontë), 85n10, 86n10, 86n11, 87, 89–92
convents, 9n6, 29, 107, 126, 195; anti-convent novels, 101–3, 105; in *Aurora Leigh* (Barrett Browning), 140; in *Jane Eyre* (Brontë), 46, 48, 51, 106; proposed legislation again, 104n8; Protestant condemnations of, 14–15, 96–99, 100n5; in *Villette* (Brontë), 87, 88n13, 148. *See also* nuns, sisterhoods
Cooper, Edith, 21, 26, 30, 191, 194–96, 207. *See also*, Field, Michael
courtship plot, 105, 108, 113–14, 120, 125. *See also* romance novels
Cranford (Elizabeth Gaskell), 106n10
creature worship, 28, 36, 43, 64, 68, 126, 141. *See also* idolatry
Cusack, Margaret Frances, 22, 104

Daisy Chain (Charlotte Yonge), 107
Daly, Mary, 209
Dammast, Jeanie Selina: *St. Mary's Convent*, 98n2, 100–104
Darwin, Charles, 95
Darwin, Henrietta, 95
De Montfort, Louis, 188

De Vere, Aubrey Thomas, 134n8
Decadence, 4n2, 191
Dick, Alexander, 126
Dickens, Charles, 24, 27, 66, 79, 198
Dickinson, Emily, 55, 70n3
Dodsworth, William, 152
Dombey and Son (Charles Dickens), 79
domesticity, 26, 33n1, 69n1, 126, 207, 209; in anticonvent novels, 98–101, 103–105; anxieties about, 3–6, 8–12; in *Aurora Leigh* (Barrett Browning), 150; Catholicism as threat to, 14; in *Coelebs in Search of a Wife* (More), 40–43; and confession, 71–73, 93–94; Eliot's representations of, 163, 172; in *Ellen Middleton* (Fullerton), 83–84, 93–94; in *Experience of Life* (Sewell), 120–21; M. Field's construction of, 192, 194–95, 196n9, 197–99, 201–6; in *Jane Eyre* (Brontë), 43–44, 47, 51–55; in *Lady-Bird* (Fullerton), 55–56, 59–60, 63–66; in *Romola* (Eliot), 186–87; spinsterhood as challenge to, 107, 110–12; women writers' attitudes toward, 15–18, 20, 28–30, 35, 96, 158–59. *See also* private sphere

Eliot, George, 3–4, 23, 26, 30; *Adam Bede*, 10, 106n10; comparison with E. M. Sewell, 172n2; *Middlemarch*, 10, 115; *Romola*, 160, 162–64, 170–71, 173–75, 177–78, 184, 188–89; "Silly Novels by Lady Novelists," 99
Ellen Middleton (Lady Georgiana Fullerton), 28, 34n2, 70n3, 75, 77–80, 83, 85–87, 89, 90, 92–94
Ellis, Sarah Stickney, 112
Endell, Tyler J., 16
erotic faith, 89, 124
Eucharist: in *Aurora Leigh* (Barrett Browning), 133n7, 137, 143, 151; as cannibalism, 1; "carnality" of, 155n22; Catholic doctrine of (transubstantiation),18; W. Dodsworth and Real Presence, 152; doubts about nature of (M. F. Cusack) 22; in poetry of E. Barrett Browning and C. Rossetti, 29, 127, 128n1; Protestant-Catholic controvery over, 128nn2–3, 159; C. Rossetti's view of, 153; in *Villette*, 90. *See also* Blessed Sacrament, Communion

Evangelicalism, 9, 12n11, 40, 46–47, 160
Evans, John, 165, 167
Eve (in Genesis and Milton's *Paradise Lost*), 27, 38, 39n5, 40, 42–43, 46, 50, 53–54, 59
Experience of Life (Elizabeth Missing Sewell), 15, 96, 108n12, 112, 114, 116n18, 123–24

Faber, Frederick, 188
Fabiola (John Henry Newman), 109n13
Face of the Deep (Christina Rossetti), 153
Father Clement (Grace Kennedy), 14, 76
Fatima, apparition at, 168
feminism, 18, 21, 22n16, 27, 69, 123, 161, 175, 209–10
Field, Michael, 3, 16, 21, 26, 30; 190, 191nn1–3, *192*n3, 193n4; twenty-first century attitudes toward, 207–9; *Works and Days*, 194–95, 196n9, 197nn11–12, 198, 199n15, 200–1, 202nn17–18, 203–5, 206n19. *See also* Bradley, Katherine, and Cooper, Edith
Fordyce, James, 39n5
Formby, Henry, 169
Foucault, Michel, 69
Foxe's *Book of Martyrs* (John Foxe), 111n16
Freud, Sigmund, 104
Fullerton, Lady Georgiana, 3, 15, 21, 26, 28, 30, 126–27; biographical information, 27n18; *34*n2, 35, 36n3; compared with G. Eliot, 172; contrasted with M. Field, 191, 207–8; and "creature worship," 37–38; *Ellen Middleton*, 68–69, 70n3, 75–77, 78n6, 79–80, 84–85, 92–94; *Lady-Bird*, 55n13, 56, 58–59, 63, 66; and F. M. Taylor, 108n11

Gaskell, Elizabeth, 76, 93, 106n10, 147
Giraud, Peter Maximin, 168, 181n3
Gladstone, William Ewart, 70n3, 78n6
Gordon, John, 22

Grantley Manor (Lady Georgiana Fullerton), 34n2
Granville, Countess, 35. *See also* Cavendish, Lady Harriet,
Gray, John, 191n2, 199n15, 200, 205
Great Expectations (Charles Dickens), 79

hagiography: martyrdom in, 111; narrative conventions of 120; Roman Catholic tradition of, 28; in *Romola* (Eliot), 171–72, 175–76, 183–84, 188. *See also* saints, cult of
Hawtrey, C. S., 20–21
Heir of Redclyffe (Charlotte Yonge), 108n11
Hinduism, 17, 103n6
History of the Fairchild Family (Elizabeth Rundle Charles), 98n6
Hogan, William, 72
Holiday House (Catherine Sinclair), 98n2
Holmes, Mary, 24–25
Hook, Walter Farquhar, 38, 72, 167
Horne, Melville, 131

idolatry: anxieties about, 11–12, 14–16; 26–28, 37, 38n4, 68, 97; and confession, 77; devotion to Mary viewed as, 144, 164–65, 167; in *Ellen Middleton* (Fullerton), 78, 81; in *Jane Eyre* (Brontë), 18, 20, 42, 43n6, 45–48, 50, 53–55; in *Lady-Bird* (Fullerton), 55–58, 61–66; in *Romola* (Eliot), 173; in Rossetti's devotional prose and *Goblin Market*, 151, 153–56, 158; transubstantiation viewed as, 131–32; in *Villette* (Brontë), 85–86, 89, 92–93. *See also* creature worship
Immaculate Conception, 160–61, 164–65, 167, 170, 188
imperialism, 98, *See also* British Empire
Incarnation, doctrine of, 131
infidel, 11, *See also* atheism
Irons, Joseph, 37
Islam, 210, *See also* Muslims
Italian (Ann Radcliffe), 99
Ivors (Elizabeth Missing Sewell), 108n12, 112–14, 123–24

Jackson, Thomas, 33, 38, 66
James, John Angell, 11
James, William, 68, 176
Jane Eyre (Charlotte Brontë), 18, 20, 27n19, 35–36, 38n4, 41–42, 43n6, 54, 55n13, 56–57, 59–61, 63–66, 68, 80, 93, 106, 126, 136, 139n12, 141, 145, 150, 165, 172
Jay, William, 39
Judaism, 17n15, 173, 186

Keane, W., 17
Keble, John, 109n13
Kennedy, Grace, 76
King, John, 128n3

La Salette, apparition at, 30, 153n21, 160–61, *162*, 163, 168–69n1, 170, 181–82, 185, 188–89
Lacy, Henry Charles, 104n8
Lady-Bird (Lady Georgiana Fullerton), 27, 34n2, 35–36, 55n13, 56–57, 59, 64–66, 68, 93, 207–8
Leveson-Gower, Lord Granville, 27n18, 34n2
Lewis, Agnes Smith, 112, 120
Linton, Eliza Lynn, 14
Lives of the English Saints (John Henry Newman, ed.), 109n13
Lockhart, J. G., 6–7
Lourdes, apparition at, 168
Lowe, Thomas Hill, 72, 165
Lucas, Frederick, 23
Lyons, John, 130

Maitland, Charles, 16
Manning, Cardinal Henry Edward, 25
Margaret Percival (Elizabeth Missing Sewell), 24, 108n12, 154–55
Martineau, Harriet, 78n6, 80
"A Martyr" (Christina Rossetti), 111
"The Martyr" (Christina Rossetti), 111
martyrdom: in Anglo and Roman Catholic tradition, 96, 109n13; in *Experience of Life* (Sewell), 15, 29, 116, 118–20, 123, 125; in *Ivors* (Sewell), 112–14; in *Lady-Bird* (Fullerton), 65; in Prot-

estant tradition (*Foxe's Book of Martyrs*), 111n16
"Martyr's Song" (Christina Rossetti), 111
Matthieu, Françoise Melanie, 168, 181n3
McDonnell, T. M., 72n5
McNabb, Vincent, 203–4
Medjugorje, apparitions at, 189
Meynell, Alice, 192, 193–94n6
Michelet, Jules, 72n5, 77, 94
Middlemarch (George Eliot), 10, 115, 118
Milton, John, 27, 38, 39n5, 40, 42–43, 50, 53–54, 59
Mitford, Mary Russell, 134n8
monasticism, 14, 40, 87, 138
Monk (Matthew Lewis), 99
More, Hannah, 40, 44, 195, 209
Muslims, 17, 210–211, See also Islam

Newman, John Henry: and Anglo-Catholic movement, 148n15, 152; anxieties about idolatry, 11; *Apologia pro Vita Sua*, 211; association with M. Holmes and E. Bowles, 24–25; *Callista* and *Lives of the English Saints*, 109n13, 111n15, 116; female correspondents of, 21n16; response to *Ellen Middleton* (Fullerton), 93n14; writings on communion, 155n22
Nicholson, J. Aldwell, 146, 156
Nightingale, Florence, 12n11, 41, 125
Northcote, J. Spencer, 169
Nun (Mary Martha Sherwood), 29, 101–2
nuns, 29, 48n10, 98n3, 100, 102, 104, 160–61 See also convents, sisterhoods

Our Mutual Friend (Charles Dickens), 13
Oxford Movement, 9n6, 27, 71, 108n2, 110

Papal Aggression, 9, 95, 98n2
Paphnutius, 1n1, 2–3, 132
pareidolia, 189
Parkes, Bessie Rayner, 22, 25
Patmore, Coventry, 193n5
Penny, Anne Judith, 124
Pius IX, Pope, 160, 165
Poe, Edgar Allan, 70n3, 78, 81

Poor Servants of the Mother of God, 34, 36n3, 108n11
Popish Legends and Bible Truths (Catherine Sinclair), 6n4, 101, 103n6
Positivism, 174
Powell, H. J., 155
private sphere, 209. See also domesticity
Procter, Adelaide, 22
profession ceremony (in sisterhoods), 48n10, 68, 103n7, 104
Protestantism, 3–4, 6, 126, 194–95; Anglo-Catholicism, 9nn6–7, 109n13, 111n15; attraction/repulsion toward Catholicism, 18–30; in *Aurora Leigh* (Barrett Browning), 137–38, 139n12, 144–46; E. Barrett Browning's attitude toward, 134n8; constructions of marriage in 33–35, 38, 40, 42; and domesticity, 14–15; Evangelicalism, 9, 209; *Foxe's Book of Martyrs*, 111n16; in *Jane Eyre* (Brontë), 42–46, 48, 50, 54, 55; *Lady-Bird* (Fullerton) as critique of, 65–66; opposition to confession, 69–73, 76–77; Protestant identity 7–8; representations of Judaism in, 17n15; and responses to apparition at La Salette, 169–70, 181, 189; and responses to Immaculate Conception, 164–67; in *Romola* (Eliot), 171–72, 177, 188; in C. Rossetti's devotional prose and *Goblin Market*, 151, 153, 155–56; teachings on the Eucharist and opposition to transubstantiation, 128n2, 129, 130nn4–5, 131n6, 132–33, 135; views of celibacy in, 96–97, 98n3, 99, 100n5, 103n6, 104–5; views of the Virgin Mary, 160–61; in *Villette* (Brontë), 86–89; 93; women's roles as defined by, 10–11, 12n11, 13n12, 210–11
Pusey, Edward, 70n2, 148n15

Rambler (periodical), 12–13, 78, *162*, 169
Real Presence, doctrine of, 152
Reformation, 9n7, 71, 111, 128, 171, 174, 177
Richardson, Eliza Smith, 15, 98n2, 100n5, 103–4, 140

Ritchie, Anne, 105n9
ritualism, 9
Robinson, Henry Crabb, 172n2
romance novels, 60, 65, 125. *See also* courtship plot
Romola (George Eliot), 30, 162–64, 170, 171–77, 179–88
Rossetti, Christina, 3, 23, 209; and Anglo-Catholicism, 152nn18–19, 153n20; anxieties about idolatry, 11; Barrett Browning's influence on, 151n16; K. Bradley's thoughts about, 206n19; *Called to Be Saints*, *Face of the Deep* and *Time Flies*, 153n21; *Goblin Market*, 21, 29, 127, 128n1, 133, 155n2, 156–59; "A Martyr," "The Martyr," and Martyr's Song," 111; possible influence of E. M. Sewell on, 155; practice of confession, 73, 75; *Seek and Find*, 154; "A Triad," 18
Rossetti, Dante Gabriel, 73
Rossetti, William, 152n19
Russell, Charles William, 72n5, 77

sacramentalism, 1; Barrett Browning influenced by, 18, 135; 151–53; Catholic sacrament of confession, 71, 76, 89; as concrete manifestation of the Divine (for M. Field) 202–3; Eucharist, 22, 128–29; 133n7, 136–37, 143, 149, 150; 151–53, 155n22, 158; in Tractarianism, 151–53
saints, cult of: in Anglo and Roman Catholicism,109n13; definitions/theories of sainthood, 175–77; *Called to Be Saints* (Rossetti), 153; *Lives of the English Saints* (Newman), 111n15; in *Romola* (Eliot), 183, 185, 187 *See also* hagiography
Sand, George, 147
Sandeman, Robert, 40
Scott, Benjamin, 15, 16
secularism, 1; anxieties about, 3–5, 7–8, 29–30, 92, 189, 206; Catholicism as antidote to, 23–24; and confession, 69n1; 70, 83; of domestic sphere, 11, 15–16, 100, 105; and fiction, 93; at fin de siècle, 190; in *Goblin Market* (Rossetti), 158; influence on popular constructions of marriage/domesticity, 35, 40–43, 66, 124; *Jane Eyre*'s (Brontë) response to, 53, 55; *Lady-Bird*'s (Fullerton) response to, 65; in *Romola* (Eliot), 171–72, 175–76, 184, 188; twenty-first century responses to, 209–10; Virgin Mary as emblem of, 161, 163–64, 168–170
Seek and Find (Christina Rossetti), 154
Sewell, Elizabeth Missing, 3, 15, 28, 30, 126–27, 208; E. Barrett Browning's description of, 114n17; biographical information, 108n12; compared to G. Eliot, 172n2; *Experience of Life*, 96, 109, 115–16, 118, 120, 123–25; *Ivors*, 112–14; literary reputation of, 26, 108n11, 110n14; *Margaret Percival*, 24, 154–55; response to *Lives of the English Saints* (Newman), 111n15; as "sick-souled" personality, 74–75
Sewell, William, 108n12
Seymour, Hobart M., 99
Sherwood, Mary Martha, 3–4, 15; biographical information, 98n8; encounter with "idolatry," 16; *The Nun*, 29; 99, 100n5, 102–4
Shirley (Charlotte Brontë), 51, 106
Sinclair, Catherine, 96; *Beatrice*, 17, 72, 98, 100–102, 103n6; letter to J. G. Lockhart, 6–7; *Popish Legends and Bible Truths*, 6n4
sisterhoods, 12, 18, 28, 36n9, 98n3, 100, 103n7, 110, 112, *See also* convents, nuns
Smith, Charles Bird, 132, 166
Spencer, John Ward, 133, 169
spinsters, 4, 26, 28–29, 96, 105n9, 106n10, 107–9, 112, 114, 118, 121, 123–24, 126, 194
St. Mary's Convent (Jeanie Selina Dammast), 98n2, 101–2
Swedenborg, Emmanuel, 135
Swedenborgianism, 134n8, 135–36

Tatam, W. K., 130, 133
Taylor, Fanny Margaret, 36n3, 108n11
Teodor, John, 126

Thirty-Nine Articles, 129, 151
Time Flies (Christina Rossetti), 153
Tonna, Charlotte Elizabeth, 100n5; as anti-Catholic activist, 1–5, 6n3, 14; attends profession ceremony, 103; condemnation of idolatry, 37; desire for martyrdom, 111n16; encounter with Irish nun, 97–98; habit of confession, 73, 75
Tormey, Michael, 167
Tractarianism: A. Besant's embrace of, 111; in Ellen Middleton, 78; emphasis on "good works," 106; J. H. Newman's role in, 25; E. Sewell's association with, 123; and term "Anglo-Catholic," 9n7; in Victorian fiction, 13n13; and views of Eucharist, 128n1, 151–52
transubstantiation, 4, 18, 26, 127, 159, 160, 172; Anglo-Catholic rejection of, 152, 153n20, 158; in Aurora Leigh (Barrett Browning), 29, 133n7, 136; in Goblin Market (Rossetti), 128n1, 151, 155–56; Protestant condemnations of, 129, 130n5, 131n6, 133, 144, 150
Trent, Council of, 128, 129
Trusted, Alice, 206n19

Ullathorne, William Bernard, 104, 169–70, 181
Under Which Lord? (Eliza Lynn Lynton), 14
Ursula (Elizabeth Missing Sewell), 108n12

Varieties of Religious Experience (William James), 69, 151, 176
Veil Lifted, The (Eliza Smith Richardson), 15, 98n2, 101–2
Victoria, Queen of England, 7, 78n6
Villette (Charlotte Brontë), 28, 36, 44n7, 69n1, 70, 76, 85n1, 86nn10–11, 87n12, 88–89, 92–94, 106, 108, 116, 139n12, 148
Virgin Mary, 2, 4n2, 16, 23, 27, 30, 38; in Aurora Leigh (Barrett Browning), 138–39, 144, 148; in Called to Be Saints, 153n21, 159; M. Field's devotion to, 203–205; in Jane Eyre (Brontë), 53–54; Marian apparitions and doctrine of Immaculate Conception, 160–68; Our Lady of La Salette, 170–71; in Romola (Eliot), 178–79, 181–82, 184–85, 188; in the twenty-first century, 189; in Villette (Brontë), 91
vocation, 29, 61, 66, 93, 150; to art/literature, 5, 18, 127, 136, 141–42, 195; to celibacy, 15; to marriage, 10, 23, 38, 42, 52, 65, 105, 118, 120; to missionary field, 50, 53–55; to organized religious life, 56, 102, 104, 106n10; to spinsterhood, 28, 96, 107, 109, 114

Whore of Babylon, 45, 138–39, 167
Whym Chow, 26, 30, 192, 196n10, 197nn11–12, 198n13, 199-202, 204–5, 207–8
Wilberforce, Samuel, 20, 165, 167
Wilson, Carus W., 165
Wiseman, Nicholas, 128–29, 164; Fabiola, 109n13
Wordsworth, Christopher, 167
Wordsworth, William, 95, 167
Works and Days (Michael Field), 30, 191–92n3, 194, 197, 204–5

Yonge, Charlotte: anxieties about idolatry, 11, 37; compared to E. M. Sewell, 108n11, 110; representation of spinsterhood, 105–7, 124

Zouaves, Papal, 181n3

www.ingramcontent.com/pod-product-compliance
Lightning Source LLC
Chambersburg PA
CBHW030135240426
43672CB00005B/134